THE
PASSION
TRANSLATION

2020 edition

THE BOOK OF

PSALMS

poetry on fire

BroadStreet
P U B L I S H I N G

A NOTE TO READERS

It would be impossible to calculate how many lives have been changed forever by the power of the Bible, the living Word of God! My own life was transformed because I believed the message contained in Scripture about Jesus, the Savior.

To hold the Bible dear to your heart is the sacred obsession of every true follower of Jesus. Yet to go even further and truly understand the Bible is how we gain light and truth to live by. Did you catch the word *understand*? People everywhere say the same thing: "I want to understand God's Word, not just read it."

Thankfully, as English speakers, we have a plethora of Bible translations, commentaries, study guides, devotionals, churches, and Bible teachers to assist us. Our hearts crave to know God—to not just know about him, but to know him as intimately as we possibly can in this life. This is what makes Bible translations so valuable, because each one will hopefully lead us into new discoveries of God's character. I believe God is committed to giving us truth in a package we can understand and apply, so I thank God for every translation of God's Word that we have.

God's Word does not change, but over time languages definitely do, thus the need for updated and revised translations of the Bible. Translations give us the words God spoke through his servants, but words can be poor containers for revelation because they leak! Meaning is influenced by culture, background, and many other details. Just imagine how differently the Hebrew authors of the Old Testament saw the world three thousand years ago from the way we see it today!

Even within one language and culture, meanings of words change from one generation to the next. For example, many contemporary Bible readers would be quite surprised to find unicorns are mentioned nine times in the King James Version (KJV). Here's one instance in Isaiah 34:7: "And the unicorns shall come down with them, and the bullocks with the bulls; and their land shall be soaked with blood, and their dust made fat with fatness." This isn't a result of poor translation, but rather an example of how our culture, language, and understanding of the world has shifted over the past few centuries. So, it is important that we have a modern English text of the Bible that releases revelation and truth into our hearts. The Passion Translation (TPT) is committed to bringing forth the potency of God's Word in relevant, contemporary vocabulary that doesn't distract from its meaning or distort it in any way. So many people have told us that they are falling in love with the Bible again as they read TPT.

We often hear the statement, "I just want a word-for-word translation that doesn't mess it up or insert a bias." That's a noble desire. But a word-for-word translation would be nearly unreadable. It is simply impossible to translate one Hebrew word for one English word. Hebrew is built from triliteral consonant roots. Biblical Hebrew had no vowels or punctuation. And Koine Greek, although wonderfully articulate, cannot always be conveyed in English by a word-for-word translation. For example, a literal word-for-word translation of the Greek in Matthew 1:18 would be something like this: "Of the but Jesus Christ the birth thus was. Being betrothed the mother of him, Mary, to

Joseph, before or to come together them she was found in belly having from Spirit Holy."

Even the KJV, which many believe to be a very literal translation, renders this verse: "Now the birth of Jesus Christ was on this wise: When as his mother Mary was espoused to Joseph, before they came together, she was found with child of the Holy Ghost."

This comparison makes the KJV look like a paraphrase next to a strictly literal translation! To some degree, every Bible translator is forced to move words around in a sentence to convey with meaning the thought of the verse. There is no such thing as a truly literal translation of the Bible, for there is not an equivalent language that perfectly conveys the meaning of the biblical text. Is it really possible to have a highly accurate and highly readable English Bible? We certainly hope so! It is so important that God's Word is living in our hearts, ringing in our ears, and burning in our souls. Transferring God's revelation from Hebrew and Greek into English is an art, not merely a linguistic science. Thus, we need all the accurate translations we can find. If a verse or passage in one translation seems confusing, it is good to do a side-by-side comparison with another version.

It is difficult to say which translation is the "best." "Best" is often in the eyes of the reader and is determined by how important differing factors are to different people. However, the "best" translation, in my thinking, is the one that makes the Word of God clear and accurate, no matter how many words it takes to express it.

That's the aim of The Passion Translation: to bring God's eternal truth into a highly readable heart-level expression that causes truth and love to jump out of the text and lodge inside our hearts. A desire to remain accurate to the text and a desire to communicate God's heart of passion for his people are the two driving forces behind TPT. So for those new to Bible reading, we hope TPT will excite and illuminate. For scholars and Bible students, we hope TPT will bring the joys of new discoveries from the text and prompt deeper consideration of what God has spoken to his people. We all have so much more to learn and discover about God in his holy Word!

You will notice at times we've italicized certain words or phrases. These portions are not in the original Hebrew, Greek, or Aramaic manuscripts but are implied from the context. We've made these implications explicit for the sake of narrative clarity and to better convey the meaning of God's Word. This is a common practice by mainstream translations.

We've also chosen to translate certain names in their original Hebrew or Greek forms to better convey their cultural meaning and significance. For instance, some translations of the Bible have substituted James for Jacob and Jude for Judah. Both Greek and Aramaic manuscripts leave these Hebrew names in their original forms. Therefore, this translation uses those cultural names.

The purpose of The Passion Translation is to reintroduce the passion and fire of the Bible to the English reader. It doesn't merely convey the literal meaning of words. It expresses God's passion for people and his world by translating the original, life-changing message of God's Word for modern readers.

We pray this version of God's Word will kindle in you a burning desire to know the heart of God, while impacting the church for years to come.

Please visit **ThePassionTranslation.com** for more information.

Brian Simmons and the translation team

PSALMS

Introduction

AT A GLANCE

Author: Multiple authors, including David, Solomon, Asaph, the prophetic singers of Korah's clan, and Moses

Audience: Originally Israel, but the Psalms speak to humanity in general

Date: From the monarchy to the postexilic era

Type of Literature: Poems, which reflect several types: wisdom, lament, prayer, praise, blessings, liturgy, and prophetic oracles

Major Themes: Praise, prayer, wisdom, prophecy, and Jesus Christ

Outline: The book of Psalms is really five books in one. Moses gave us the five books of the Law called the Pentateuch; David gave us the five books of the Psalms. Each division ends with a doxology that includes the word "Amen!" The last division ends with Psalm 150 as the doxology, forming an appropriate conclusion to this "Pentateuch of David." These five divisions have been compared to the first five books of the Bible:

Psalms 1–41 (Genesis) — Psalms of man and creation

Psalms 42–72 (Exodus) — Psalms of suffering and redemption

Psalms 73–89 (Leviticus) — Psalms of worship and God's house

Psalms 90–106 (Numbers) — Psalms of our pilgrimage on earth

Psalms 107–150 (Deuteronomy) — Psalms of praise and the Word

ABOUT PSALMS

I have loved the Psalms for over forty years. They have been my comfort and joy, leading me to the place where worship flows. When discouraged or downcast, I have never failed to take new strength from reading the Psalms. They charge my batteries and fill my sails. In fact, they seem to grow even more powerful as I grow older. Their thunder stirs me; their sweet melodies move me into the sacred emotions of a heart on fire. The dark rain clouds of grief turn to bright rainbows of hope just from meditating on David's soul-subduing songs.

The Psalms find the words that express our deepest and strongest emotions, no matter what the circumstances. Every emotion of our hearts is reflected in the Psalms. Reading the Psalms will turn sighing into singing and trouble into triumph. The word *praise* is found 189 times in this book. There is simply nothing that touches my heart like the Psalms. Thousands of years ago my deepest feelings were put to music—this is what we all delightfully discover when reading the Psalms!

A contemporary name for the book of Psalms could be *Poetry on Fire*. These 150 poetic masterpieces give us an expression of faith and worship. They become a mirror to the heart of God's people in our quest to experience God's presence. Much of Christianity has become so intellectualized that our emotions and artistic creativity are often set aside as unimportant in the worship of God. The Psalms free us to become emotional, passionate, sincere worshipers. It is time to sing the Psalms!

PURPOSE
The Psalms are clearly poetic. They are praises placed inside of poetry. Everyone who reads the Psalms realizes how filled with emotion they are! You will never be bored in reading the poetry that spills out of a fiery, passionate heart. These verses contain both poetry and music that touch the heart deeply, enabling you to encounter the heart of God through your emotional and creative senses.

AUTHOR AND AUDIENCE
Most of these poetic masterpieces come to us from David, King of Israel. He wrote them during specific periods of his life: when he was on the run from Saul, grateful for the Lord's protection and provision, scared for his future, mournful over his sin, and praising God with uplifted hands. Other authors include David's son Solomon, Moses, Asaph, and the prophetic singers of Korah's clan.

While they were written during specific periods in the history of Israel—from the monarchy to the postexilic eras—they connect to our own time as much as they reflect their time. So in many ways these poems are written to you and me. The original audience was the children of Israel, but the Psalms reflect the hopes and dreams, fears and failures of humanity in general.

MAJOR THEMES
Poetry of Praise. The Psalms are pure praise, inspired by the breath of God. Praise is a matter of life and breath. As long as we have breath we are told to praise the Lord. The Psalms release a flood of God-inspired insights that will lift heaviness off the human heart. The Psalms are meant to do for you what they did for David: they will bring you from your cave of despair into the glad presence of the King who likes and enjoys you.

Poetry of Prayer. Mixed with intercession, the Psalms become the fuel for our devotional life. Each psalm is a prayer. The early church recited and sang the Psalms regularly. Many contemporary worship songs have been inspired by this book of prayer-poetry!

Poetry of Wisdom. The Psalms unlock mysteries and parables, for within the purest praise is the cryptic language of a wise messenger. The wisdom of God is contained in these 150 keys; you have a key chain with master keys to unlock God's storehouse of wisdom and revelation. It is the "harp" (anointed worship) that releases divine secrets. Read carefully Psalm 49:4: "I will break open mysteries with my music, and my song will release riddles solved."

Poetry of Prophecy. Prophetic insights rest upon the Psalms. David's harp brings revelation and understanding to the people. Singers who tap into the insights of the Psalms will bring forth truths in their songs, which will break the hearts of people and release divine understanding to the church. Prophets must become musicians and musicians must become prophets for the key of David to be given to the church.

Poetry of Jesus Christ. As with every part of the Old Testament, we are called to read the Psalms in two ways: (1) as the original audience heard them in their ancient Hebrew world; and (2) as the fulfillment of messianic prophesies, submitting by faith that these poems point to Jesus Christ. Therefore, at one level, these poems are all about him. There are 150 Psalms, and each of them reveals a special and unique aspect of the God-man, Christ Jesus. We could say every Psalm is messianic in that each finds its fulfillment in Christ. Looking backward in light of Christ's revelation, we see they all point to our Lord Jesus, whom God has chosen as King over all.

Since these songs are all about Jesus, one of the keys to understanding the Psalms is to look for Jesus within its pages. Luke 24:44 says: "I told you that everything written about me would be fulfilled, including all the prophecies from the law of Moses through the Psalms and the writings of the prophets—that they would all find their fulfillment." There are many secrets about Jesus waiting to be discovered here!

PSALMS

Poetry on Fire

BOOK 1
THE GENESIS PSALMS
Psalms of man and creation

1 *a* THE TREE OF LIFE

¹What delight comes to the one who follows God's ways!*ᵇ*
  He won't walk in step with the wicked,
  nor share the sinner's way,
  nor be found sitting in the scorner's seat.
²His passion is to remain true to the Word of "I AM,"
  meditating day and night*ᶜ* on the true revelation of
  light.*ᵈ*

---

a 1 Although we cannot be sure, it is possible that Ezra compiled the
Psalms and wrote Ps. 1 as an "introduction" to the Psalter. Others
believe Ps. 1 was written by David or Jeremiah.

b 1:1 Psalm 1 is the contrast of those who follow God's ways with
those who choose their own path. Read through this psalm with the
purpose of learning how to live with God in the first place.

c 1:2 To meditate on the revelation of light day and night means to
meditate 24/7 on what is good and delightful. However, *day* signifies a period of enlightenment (Eph. 1:18) and *night* signifies a
period of obscurity. Both when we have the light of insight and
when we seem to be in the dark, meditation is the key to unlock the
revelation of God.

d 1:2 Or "Torah." From Ps. 1 we learn that the righteous and the
wicked are distinguished by what they delight in.

³He will be standing firm like a flourishing tree
  planted^a by God's design,
  deeply rooted by the brooks of bliss,
  bearing fruit in every season of life.
  He is never dry, never fainting,
  ever blessed, ever prosperous.^b
⁴But how different are the wicked.
  They are like chaff^c blown away by the wind.
⁵The wicked will not endure the day of judgment,
  for God will not defend them.
  Nothing they do will succeed or endure for long,
  for they have no part with those who walk in truth.
⁶But how different it is for the righteous!
  The Lord embraces their paths as they move forward
  while the way of the wicked leads only to doom.

2 THE CORONATION OF THE KING

Act I – The Nations Speak
¹How dare the nations plan a rebellion.
  Their foolish plots are futile!^d
²Look at how the power brokers of the world
  rise up to hold their summit
  as the rulers scheme and confer together
  against Yahweh and his Anointed King, saying:

---

a 1:3 Or "transplanted." That is, God planted our lives from where we were into a place of blessing. See Ps. 92:13–14.

b 1:3 The metaphors found in this verse can be paraphrased as "No matter what he sets out to do, he brings it to a successful conclusion."

c 1:4 Chaff is lifeless, only a shell without the kernel. Chaff depicts a life without the truth of Christ. See Ps. 35:5–6.

d 2:1 Or "Why are they devising emptiness?" Some Jewish scholars believe that Ps. 1 and Ps. 2 form one psalm, for the theme of both is the way of the godly versus the way of the ungodly.

³"Let's come together and break away from the Creator.
Once and for all let's cast off these controlling chains
of God and his Christ!"*a*

Act II – God Speaks
⁴God-Enthroned*b* merely laughs at them;
the Sovereign One mocks their madness!
⁵Then with the fierceness of his fiery anger,
he settles the issue*c* and terrifies them to death*d* with
these words:
⁶"I myself have poured out*e* my King on Zion,*f* my holy
mountain."*g*

Act III – The Son Speaks
⁷"I will reveal the eternal purpose of God.
For he has decreed over me, 'You are my favored Son.
And as your Father I have crowned you as my King
Eternal.
Today I became your Father.
⁸Ask me to give you the nations*h* and I will do it,
and they shall become your legacy.
Your domain will stretch to the ends of the earth.

a 2:3 The word found here for "Christ" is the Hebrew word for "Messiah" or "Anointed One."

b 2:4 The Aramaic is *Maryah*, the Aramaic form of YHWH or Lord Yahweh.

c 2:5 Or "In good time he drives them away."

d 2:5 Or "snorts with anger." The Hebrew word *'aph* ("fiery anger") has a homonym that means "nose."

e 2:6 The Hebrew word (*nacak*) is frequently used for pouring out a drink offering to God. See Num. 28:7. Jesus was "poured out" as a consecrated offering.

f 2:6 The word *Zion* is found 157 times in the Bible and 38 times in the Psalms.

g 2:6 For the believer today, Zion is not only a place but also a realm where Christ is enthroned.

h 2:8 Or in the Masoretic Text "Ask wealth of me."

⁹And you will shepherd them*a* with unlimited authority,
    crushing their rebellion as an iron rod*b* smashes jars
        of clay!' "

Act IV – The Holy Spirit Speaks

¹⁰"Listen to me, all you rebel kings
    and all you upstart judges of the earth.
    Learn your lesson*c* *while there's still time.*
¹¹Serve and worship the awe-inspiring God.
    Recognize his greatness and bow before him,
    trembling with reverence in his presence.*d*
¹²Fall facedown before him and kiss the Son*e*
    before his anger is roused against you.
    Remember that his wrath can be quickly kindled!
    But many blessings are waiting for all
    who turn aside to hide themselves in him!"

3 COVERED BY THE GLORY
*King David's song when he was forced to flee from
Absalom, his own son*

The Humbling of a King

¹Lord, I have so many enemies, so many who are
    against me.
²Listen to how they whisper their slander against me,
    saying:

---

a 2:9 As translated from the Septuagint.
b 2:9 God's "iron rod" can be a metaphor for the power of spiritual
truth. See Pss. 23:4; 45:6.
c 2:10 Or "Do what is wise."
d 2:11 Or "rejoice with trembling." The Hebrew word for "rejoice"
means "to spin around with excited emotions" or "to twirl."
e 2:12 Or "be ruled by the Son." The Hebrew word for "kiss" is *nashaq*
and can also mean "to be ruled by" or "be in subjection to" the Son.
Yet another possible translation of this difficult verse is "be armed
with purity."

"Look! He's hopeless! Even God can't save him from
   this!"

Pause in his presence[a]

The Help of God
   [3]But *in the depths of my heart I truly know*
   that you, Yahweh, have become my Shield;
   You take me and surround me with yourself.[b]
   Your glory[c] covers me continually.
   You lift high my head.[d]
   [4]I have cried out to you,[e] Yahweh, from your holy
   presence.[f]
   You send me a Father's help.

Pause in his presence

---

a 3:2 This is the Hebrew word *Selah*, a puzzling word to translate.
Most scholars believe it is a musical term for pause or rest. It is
used seventy-one times in the Psalms as an instruction to the music
leader to pause and ponder in God's presence. An almost identical
word, *Sela*, means "a massive rock cliff." It is said that when *Selah*
is spoken, the words are carved in stone in the throne room of the
heavens.

b 3:3 Many translations render this "You are a shield around me."
The ancient Hebrew can be translated "You, O Lord, are my taker"
(Augustine). The implication is that God shields us by taking us into
himself. Jesus Christ is the taker of humanity, the one who was made
flesh. He not only took our nature, he also took our sins that he
might take us into glory.

c 3:3 Or "my glory."

d 3:3 In the time of David, to lift up the head signified acquittal when
judged, being freed from the prison of shame. See 2 Kings 25:27–
28; Jer. 52:31.

e 3:4 The Hebrew reads "I have cried out to you with my voice." How
else do we cry out to God—isn't it always with our voice? But the word
for "voice" has many different Hebrew meanings. It can also mean "the
bleating of a lamb." David was God's lamb bleating out to his Shepherd
for help.

f 3:4 Or "from your holy hill."

The Song of Safety

[5]So now I'll lie down and sleep like a baby—
then I'll awake in safety, for you surround me with
your glory.
[6]Even though ten thousand dark powers[a] prowl around
me,
I won't be afraid.

The Secret of Strength

[7]Rise up and help me, Yahweh! Come and save me, God!
For you will slap them in the face,
breaking the power of their words to harm me.[b]
[8]For the Lord alone is my Savior.[c]
What a feast of favor and bliss he gives his people!
Pause in his presence

4 AN EVENING PRAYER FOR HELP
For the Pure and Shining One[d]
For the end,[e] a melody by King David

[1]God, you are my righteousness, my Champion
Defender.
Answer me when I cry for help!

---

a 3:6 Or "military troops."

b 3:7 Or "You broke the teeth [lies] of the wicked."

c 3:8 The Hebrew word used sixty times in the Psalms for deliverance
is *Yeshuah*, a variant form of the name for Jesus. This is pointing us
to where our salvation is found.

d 4 The Hebrew word used here, found in the inscription of fifty-four
Psalms, is usually rendered as "choirmaster" or "chief director of
music." It is taken from the root word for "shining" or "brilliant" (i.e.,
purity, holiness). Another way to translate "choirmaster" is "the shining
one" or "the one who glitters from afar." Jesus Christ is the chief musician of all eternity who sings in the midst of his people (Heb. 2:12).

e 4 As translated from the Septuagint. The Hebrew is "stringed instruments" or "smiting."

Whenever I was in distress, you enlarged me.[a]
I'm being squeezed again—I need your kindness
    right away!
Grant me your grace, hear my prayer, and set me
    free!
²Listen to me, you elite among men:
    How long will you defame my honor[b]
    and drag it down into shame?
    Will you ever stop insulting me?
    How long will you set your heart on shadows,
    chasing your lies and delusions?

Pause in his presence

³May we never forget that Yahweh works wonders[c]
    for every one of his devoted lovers.
    And this is how I know that he will answer my every
        prayer.
⁴Tremble in awe before the Lord, and do not sin
    against him.
    Be still upon your bed and search your heart before
        him.[d]

Pause in his presence

⁵Bring to Yahweh the sacrifice of righteousness and put
    your trust in him.
⁶Lord, prove them wrong when they say, "God can't
    help you!"

---

a 4:1 Or "you created room for me."

b 4:2 Or "my glorious one."

c 4:3 There is considerable variation in possible translations from different manuscripts. Some manuscripts read "Yahweh sets apart a faithful one for himself." Another possible translation is "Yahweh has revealed to me his marvelous love."

d 4:4 Or "Meditate on your bed and repent [lament]." It is always wise at the end of every day to cleanse our hearts in God's grace and mercy.

Let the light of your radiant face
break through and shine upon us!
⁷The intense pleasure you give me
surpasses the gladness of harvest time,
even more than when the harvesters
gaze upon their ripened grain
and when their new wine overflows.
⁸Now, because of you, Lord, I will lie down in peace
and sleep comes at once,
for no matter what happens, I will live unafraid!

5 SONG OF THE CLOUDED DAWN

For the Pure and Shining One
For her who receives the inheritance,ᵃ by King David

Morning Watch
¹Listen, Yahweh, to my passionate prayer!ᵇ
Can't you hear my groaning?
²Don't you hear how I'm crying out to you?
My King and my God, consider my every word,
for I am calling out to you.
³At each and every sunrise you will hear my voice
as I prepareᶜ my *sacrifice of* prayer to you.

---

a 5 The Hebrew word used here is *neliloth* or "flutes." It can also be translated "inheritances." The early church father Augustine translated this as "For her who receives the inheritance," meaning the church of Jesus Christ. The Father told the Son in Ps. 2 to ask for his inheritance; here we see it is the church that receives what Jesus asks for. We receive our inheritance of eternal life through the death and resurrection of the Son of God. The Septuagint reads "For the end," also found in numerous inscriptions of the Psalms.
b 5:1 Or "My words—give them a hearing, Lord!"
c 5:3 The Hebrew word for "prepare" is *'arak*, a priestly term for lighting the altar fire, preparing a sacrifice, and laying it out in order upon the altar to be consumed.

Every morning I lay out the pieces of my life on the
altar
and wait *for your fire to fall upon my heart.*[a]

Making It Right
[4]I know that you, God, are never pleased with
lawlessness,
and evil ones will never be invited into your house.
[5]Boasters collapse, unable to survive your scrutiny,
for your hatred of evildoers is clear.
[6]You will make an end of all those who lie.
How you hate their hypocrisy and despise all who
love violence!

Multitude of Mercy
[7]But I know that you will welcome me into your
house,
for I am covered by your covenant of mercy and
love.
So I come to your sanctuary[b] with deepest awe
to bow in worship and adore you.
[8]Yahweh, lead me in the pathways of your pleasure
just like you promised me you would,
or else my enemies will conquer me.
Smooth out your road in front of me,
straight and level, so that I will know where to walk.

---

a 5:3 Implied in the concept of preparing the morning sacrifice. The
Aramaic text states, "At dawn I shall be ready and shall appear before
you." The Hebrew can also be translated "I'll be on the watchtower
[for the answer to come]." See Pss. 59:16; 88:13; Hab. 2:1.
b 5:7 Or "I come to the temple of your holiness."

Multitude of Sins

⁹Their words are unreliable.
  Destruction is in their hearts,
  drawing people into their darkness with their
    speeches.*

  They are smooth-tongued deceivers, flattering with
    their words.
¹⁰Declare them guilty, O God!
  Let their own schemes be their downfall!
  Let the guilt of their sins collapse on top of them,
  for they rebel against you.

Multitude of Blessings

¹¹But let them all be glad,
  those who turn aside to hide themselves in you.
  May they keep shouting for joy forever!
  Overshadow them in your presence as they sing and
    rejoice.
  Then every lover of your name will burst forth with
    endless joy.
¹²Lord, how wonderfully you bless the righteous.
  Your favor wraps around each one and covers
    them
  under your canopy of kindness and joy.

---

a 5:9 Or "their throat is an open grave."

6 ᵃ A Cry for Healing

For the Pure and Shining One
A song for stringed instruments, for the new day[b] *by*
King David

How Long?

¹Yahweh, don't condemn me.
    Don't punish me in your fiery anger.[c]
²*Please deal gently with me,* Yahweh;
    show me mercy, for I'm sick and frail and weak.
    Heal me, Yahweh, for I'm falling apart.[d]
³My soul is so troubled; but you,
    Yahweh—how long?[e]

Return to Me

⁴Yahweh, turn to me and rescue my life
    because I know your faithful love will never fail me.

---

a 6 Psalm 6 is a part of the daily prayer ritual of religious Jews.

b 6 This is the Hebrew word *sheminith*. Although we cannot be certain, many scholars believe it to mean "eighth." It could represent a harp with eight strings, an octave, the eighth division of singers, the eighth day, or the eighth month. Eight is the biblical number of a new beginning, a new day. Jewish rabbis have taught that the number eight is the number of the future messianic age when Messiah comes and makes all things new.

c 6:1 David implied that he had sinned and needed forgiveness. This is the first of seven penitential psalms (32; 38; 51; 102; 130; 143).

d 6:2 Or "my bones are shaking." Bones are often used metaphorically for our inner being.

e 6:3 The Hebrew ends abruptly, with sudden silence and broken syntax. Words failed David, too broken to finish his sentence. This sudden silence is a figure of speech called aposiopesis.

⁵In the darkness of death who remembers *your name
in worship*?
How could I bring you praise if I'm buried in a
tomb?*ᵃ*

Extreme Anguish
⁶I'm worn out with my weeping and groaning.
Night after night I soak my pillow with tears,*ᵇ*
and flood my bed with weeping.
⁷My eyes *of faithᶜ* won't focus anymore, for sorrow fills
my heart.
There are so many enemies who come against me!

He Heard My Cry
⁸Turn from me, all you troublemakers!*ᵈ*
For Yahweh has turned to hear the sound of my
weeping.
⁹*Yes!* Yahweh *my healer* has heard all my pleading
and has taken hold of my prayers*ᵉ* and answered
them all.
¹⁰Now it's my enemies who have been shamed.
Terror-stricken, they will turn back again,*ᶠ*
knowing the bitterness of sudden disgrace!

---

a 6:5 Or "Sheol," the realm of the dead. This is the first psalm to mention
the grave (or Sheol). It is depicted in the poetic literature of the Hebrews
as a vast wasteland, a stronghold of darkness, and a beast of prey.

b 6:6 Or "I cause my bed to swim *with tears*." Our beds are frequently
the washing place where the sheep are sheared (Song. 4:2). The bed
was the place of David's sin; it became the place of his weeping. Even
as Adam sinned in a garden, Jesus wept in a garden over Adam's sin.

c 6:7 The Hebrew is singular, "My eye;" a likely metaphor for the eye
of his heart. David's faith was growing weak.

d 6:8 See Ps. 5:5; Matt. 7:23.

e 6:9 Or "accepted my prayers." The Hebrew word can mean "to
grasp," "to lay hold of," "to marry," or, figuratively, "to accept."

f 6:10 See Pss. 9:18; 31:8.

7 SONG FOR THE SLANDERED SOUL

David's passionate song[a] to Yahweh
To the tune of "Breaking the Curse of Cush, the
Benjamite"[b]

Rescue Me

[1]Yahweh, my God, I turn to hide my soul in you.
  Save me from all those who pursue and persecute
    me.
[2]There is none to deliver me *but you*!
  Don't let my foes fall upon me like fierce lions with
    teeth bared.
  Can't you see how they want to rip my soul to
    shreds?
[3]Yahweh, my God, if I have done evil like they say I
    have,
  and my hands are guilty,
[4]if I have wronged someone at peace with me,
  if I have betrayed a friend, repaying evil for good,
  or if I have unjustly harmed my enemy,
[5]*Then* let my enemy pursue and overtake me.
  Let them grind me into the ground.
  Let them take my life from me and drag my dignity
    through the dust!

Pause in his presence

---

a 7 The inscription reads "shiggaion," which means "a loud cry" and
  is taken from a Hebrew word that means "roar." It is a wild and passionate song. Have you ever been under such pressure that you felt
  like roaring? That is a "shiggaion." Some scholars believe the central
  thought of the word is that of wandering. It may also indicate the
  style of music to which the song was written.

b 7 The name Cush means "firelike," "burned," or "blackened." This
  person's identity is not definite, but some believe this is an oblique
  reference to Saul, whose heart was burned and blackened by his sin
  and whose character was "firelike." Saul was a Benjamite.

Vindicate Me

⁶Yahweh, arise in your anger against the anger*ᵃ* of my enemies.

Awaken your fury and stand up for me!

Execute the judgment*ᵇ* you have decreed against them.

⁷All the people gather around you.

Return to your place on high to preside over them.*ᶜ*

⁸You are Yahweh who judges the people.

Vindicate me *publicly*, Yahweh, and restore my honor and integrity.*ᵈ*

Declare me innocent.

⁹Once and for all, bring to an end the evil tactics of the wicked!

Establish the *cause of* the righteous,

for you are the righteous God, *the soul searcher*,

who tests every heart

to examine the thoughts and motives.*ᵉ*

¹⁰God, your wraparound presence is my shield.

You bring victory to all who are pure in heart.

¹¹God, your righteousness is revealed when you judge.

---

a 7:6 Or "outrages (plural)."

b 7:6 Or "Command justice!" It is in God's hands alone to bring true justice to the earth, for he is the Righteous Judge.

c 7:7 There is at least a hint here of the resurrection and ascension of Jesus, who had all authority to judge given to him and now rules from on high.

d 7:8 Augustine, an early church father, translates this word as "harmlessness." David saw himself as harmless to his enemies. This is what integrity is all about. We maintain our character even when misunderstood or persecuted. Are you like this?

e 7:9 Or "hearts and kidneys," which is a Hebraic way of saying all of human nature, including our thoughts, motives, and feelings.

Because of the strength of your forgiveness,
your anger does not break out every day.[a]

God's Lethal Weapons
[12-13]Yet if one does not repent,
you will not relent to sharpen[b] your *shining* sword.
You have an arsenal of lethal weapons
that you've prepared for them.
You have bent and strung your bow,
making your judgment-arrows shafts of burning fire.
[14]Look how the wicked conceive their evil schemes.
They go into labor with their lies and give birth to
trouble.
[15]They dig a pit *for others to fall into*,
not knowing that they will be the very ones
who will fall into it.
[16]Every pit-digger who works to trap and harm others
will be trapped by his own treachery.

Thankful Praise
[17]But I will give my thanks to you, Yahweh,
for you make everything right in the end.

---

a 7:11 As translated from the Septuagint. Although the Hebrew is
"God is angry during all the day," this verse has other possible translations. The Latin Vulgate: "God is a judge, righteous, strong, and
patient. Will he be angry every day?" The Septuagint: "not bringing
forth his anger every day." The Syriac: "he is not angry every day."
In other words, even though God judges righteously, his anger does
not break out every day. There are over ten words in Hebrew that
can be translated "anger." The word used in this verse is *za'am* and
comes from a word that means the "roar" or "groan" of a camel.

b 7:12–13 The Hebrew word for "sharpen" can also be translated
"brighten." God will make bright his sword of truth for the righteous
and to the ungodly. God's Word is a sword to bring light and judgment to the heart.

I will sing my highest praise to the God of the
  Highest Place!

8 GOD'S SPLENDOR
For the Pure and Shining One
Set to the melody of "For the Feast of Harvest"[a] by
King David

God's Majesty
[1]Yahweh, our Sovereign God,
  your glory streams from the heavens above,
  filling the earth with the majesty of your name!
  People everywhere see your splendor.
[2]You have built a stronghold by the songs of children.
  Strength rises up with the chorus of infants.
  This kind of praise has power to shut Satan's mouth.
  Childlike worship will silence[b]
  the madness of those who oppose you.

Human Dignity
[3]Look at the splendor of your skies,
  your creative genius glowing in the heavens.
  When I gaze at your moon and your stars,
  mounted like jewels in their settings,
  I know you are the fascinating artist who fashioned
    it all!

---

a 8 Or "For the director of music, according to gittith." *Gittith* could
  mean "winepress," or refer to a musical instrument common to the
  Gittites, making it a Philistine lute (2 Sam. 6:10–11; 15:18). The Mof-
  fat translation reads "Set to a vintage melody." This inscription in the
  Septuagint is "To the director over the wine vats."
b 8:2 Or "muzzle." There may be a vast difference between the glory
  of the heavens and the little mouths of children and babies, yet by
  both the majestic name of the Lord is revealed. It is amazing that
  perfected praises do not rise to God from the cherubim or seraphim,
  but from children and babies, the weakest of humanity.

But I have to ask this question:
⁴Why would you bother with puny, mortal man
or care about human beings?ᵃ
⁵Yet what honor you have given to men,
created only a little lower than Elohim,ᵇ
crownedᶜ with glory and magnificence.
⁶You have delegated to them
rulership over all you have made,
with everything under their authority,
placing earth itself under the feet *of your
image-bearers.*ᵈ
⁷⁻⁸All the created order and every living thing
of the earth, sky, and sea—
the wildest beasts and all that move in the paths of
the seaᵉ—
everythingᶠ is in submission *to Adam's sons.*
⁹Yahweh, our Sovereign God,
your glory streams from the heavens above,
filling the earth with the majesty of your name!
People everywhere see your splendor!

---

a 8:4 See Job 7:17–21; 25:2–6; Ps. 144:3.

b 8:5 This is the same Hebrew word used for the Creator-God in Gen. 1:1.

c 8:5 Or "surrounded."

d 8:6 The Septuagint translation of Ps. 8:5–7 is quoted in Heb. 2:6–8. Today, all things are not yet under our feet. Even mosquitoes still come to defeat us. But there will be a time of restoration because of Christ's redemption, when everything will rest beneath our authority. See Isa. 11:6–9; 65:25; Matt. 19:28; Rev. 20:4–6.

e 8:7–8 The "paths of the sea" speaks of God's way of deliverance (Isa. 11:15–16), for Jesus was the One who walked on the water (Job 9:8; Ps. 77:19).

f 8:7–8 Or "sheep and oxen, beasts of the field, birds of the air, fish of the sea, and everything that moves in the paths of the sea."

9 TRIUMPHANT THANKS
For the Pure and Shining One
To the tune of "The Secrets of the Son"[a]
A Psalm of David

Delighting in God
[1]I will worship you, Yahweh, *with extended hands*
  as my whole heart erupts with praise![b]
  I will tell everyone everywhere about your
    wonderful works!
[2]I will be glad and shout in triumph.
  I will sing praise to your *exalted* name, O Most High.

Deliverance
[3]For when you appear, I worship
  you while my enemies run in retreat.
  They stumble and perish before your presence.
[4]For you have stood up for my cause
  and vindicated me *when I needed you the most*.
  From your righteous throne you have given me
    justice.

Divine Judgment
[5]With a blast of your rebuke, nations are destroyed.
  You obliterated their names forever and ever.

---

a 9 As translated by Augustine, an early church father. The Hebrew
is "to the death of the son." Because of David's sin with Bathsheba,
the son born to them had to die, not as a judgment upon the child,
but as a sacrifice to cleanse David of his sin. This was God's way
of restoring David. A sinless son bore the guilt. This is a picture of
Jesus!

b 9:1 The Hebrew word for "praise" is *yadah*, which can mean "to
shoot [an arrow]" or "to worship with extended hands." It implies an
ecstatic burst of praise that is thrown into the heavens like a shout.
It is the praise that breaks strongholds. A fresh determination arose
in David's spirit to praise his way into victory.

⁶*The Lord thundered* and our enemies have been cut
  off,
    vanished in everlasting ruins.
    All their cities have been destroyed—
    even the memory of them has been erased.
⁷But Yahweh, *our mighty God*, reigns forever!
    He sits enthroned as King ready to render his verdicts
    and judge all with righteousness.
⁸He will issue his decrees of judgment,
    deciding what is right for the entire world,
    dispensing justice to all.
⁹All who are oppressed may come to Yahweh as a high
    shelter in the time of trouble, a perfect hiding place.
¹⁰For everyone who knows your *wonderful* name
    keeps putting their trust in you.
    They can count on you for help no matter what.
    O Lord, you will never, no never, neglect those
    who come to you.
¹¹Listen, everyone! Sing out your praises to the God
    who rules in Zion!
    Tell the world about all the miracles he has done!
¹²He tracks down killers and avenges bloodshed,
    but he will never forget the ones forgotten by others,
    hearing every one of their cries for justice.

Daughter of Zion

¹³So now, O Lord, don't forget me.
    Have mercy on me.
    Take note of how I've been humiliated
    at the hands of those who hate me.
    You are the one who can snatch me away from the
      gates of death.
¹⁴Then I will sing your praises as I pass through the
    gates
    of the Daughter of Zion, rejoicing in your deliverance!

¹⁵For the nations get trapped
in the very snares they set for others.
The hidden trap they set for the weak
has snapped shut upon themselves!
¹⁶Yahweh is famous for his justice.
While the wicked are digging a pit for others,
they are actually setting the terms for their own
judgment.
They will fall into their own pit.

Consider the truth of this[a]
and pause in his presence

Destruction of the Wicked

¹⁷*Don't forget this*: all the wicked will one day
fall into the darkness of death's domain,[b]
including the nations that forget God and reject his
ways.
¹⁸He will not forget the needs of the poor.
One day the needy will be remembered,
and their hopes will not be forever dashed in
disappointment.
¹⁹Yahweh, it's time to arise and judge
the nations who defy you.
Don't let rebellious men triumph.
²⁰Make them tremble in fear before your presence.
Place a lawgiver over them.
Make them know that they are only puny, frail
humans
who must give account to you!

Pause in his presence

---

a 9:16 The Hebrew word *higgaion* means "to consider the truth of the matter."

b 9:17 This is the word *Sheol*, the underworld, which is frequently translated "hell."

10^a THE CRY OF THE OPPRESSED

The Lord is Concealed

¹Lord, why do you seem so far away when evil is
near?
Why have you hidden yourself when I need you the
most?^b
²The arrogant in their elitist pride persecute the poor
and helpless.
May you pour out upon them
the very evil they've dreamed up against others!
³How they brag and boast of their cravings, exalting
the greedy.
They congratulate themselves as they despise you—
⁴these arrogant ones, so smug and secure!
In their delusion the wicked boast, saying,
"God doesn't care about what we do.
There's nothing to worry about!"
⁵So successful are they in their schemes
and prosperous in all their plans!
Your laws are far from them;
they scoff at their enemies.
⁶They boast that neither God nor men will bring them
down.
They sneer at all their enemies, saying in their
hearts,
"We'll have success in all we do
and never have to face trouble."
⁷Their mouths spew out cursing, lies, and threats.
Only trouble and turmoil come from all their plans.

---

a 10 It is likely that Pss. 9 and 10 were originally one acrostic psalm.
Eight Hebrew manuscripts unite them as well as the Aramaic, Septuagint, and the Latin Vulgate.
b 10:1 Or "when trouble is near."

8-9Like beasts lurking in the shadows of the city,
    they crouch silently in ambush, waiting for the
        innocent to pass by.
    Pouncing on the poor, they catch them in their snare
    to murder their prey in secret
    as they plunder their helpless victims.
10They crush the lowly as they fall beneath their brutal
    blows,
    watching their victims collapse in defeat!
11Then they say to themselves,
    "The Lofty One*a* is not watching while we do this.
    He doesn't even care! We can get away with it!"

The Lord is Concerned
12Now arise, Yahweh-God! Crush them once and for all!
    Don't forget the helpless and oppressed.
13How dare the wicked think they'll reject God and
    escape judgment.
    They say to themselves,
    "God won't hold me accountable."
14Lord, I know you see all that they're doing,
    noting their each and every deed.
    You know the trouble and turmoil they've caused.
    Now punish them thoroughly for all that they've
        done!
    The poor and helpless ones trust in you, Lord,
    for you are famous for being the helper of the
        fatherless.
    I know you won't let them down.
15Break the power of the wicked and all their strong-
    arm tactics.
    Search them out and destroy them
    for the evil things they've done.

---

a 10:11 This is the Hebrew name for God *El*, the "Lofty [Exalted] God."

¹⁶You, Yahweh, are King forever and ever!
All the nations will perish from your land.
¹⁷Yahweh, you have heard the desires of the humble
and seen their hopes.[a]
You will hear their cries and encourage their hearts.
¹⁸The orphans and the oppressed will be terrified no longer,
for you will bring them justice, and no earth-dweller
will trouble them again.

11 SONG OF THE STEADFAST
For the Pure and Shining One by King David

The Advice to Flee
¹My faith shelters my soul continually in Yahweh.
Why would you say to me:
"*Run away while you can!*
Fly away like a bird to hide in the mountains *for safety.*
²For your enemies have prepared a trap for you!
Can't you see them hiding
in their place of darkness and shadows?
They're set against all those who live upright lives.
³What can the righteous accomplish
when truth's pillars are destroyed and law and order
collapse?"

The Answer of Faith
⁴*Yet* Yahweh *is never shaken*[b]—
he is still found in his temple of holiness,

---

a 10:17 The tenderhearted, compassionate God is able to hear our unspoken desires. What moves our hearts moves his heart. How kind is Yahweh!

b 11:4 This is an implied contrast made explicit from the text. This psalm shows the contrast between what can be shaken and what is unshakable.

reigning as King Yahweh over all.
He closely watches and examines everything man
does.
With a glance, his eyes*a* examine every heart,
for his heavenly rule will prevail over all.
⁵Yahweh tests both the righteous *and the wicked.*
God's very soul detests lovers of violence.
⁶He will*b* rain down upon them judgment for their sins.
A scorching wind will be their lot in life.
⁷But remember this: Yahweh is the Righteous One who
loves
justice, and every godly one
will gaze upon his face!

12 SONG FOR THE NEW DAY
For the Pure and Shining One
A song of smiting, sung for the new day by King
*David*c

Intercession
¹Help, Lord! Save us! For godly ones are disappearing.
Where are the dependable, principled ones?
They're a vanishing breed!
²Everyone lies, everyone flatters, and everyone
deceives.
Nothing but empty talk, smooth talk, and
double-talk.

---

a 11:4 The actual Hebrew is "his eyelids." Some see the "eyelid" as the
lid of the ark of the covenant, which was the mercy seat.

b 11:6 Or "May he."

c 12 The events surrounding this psalm could be the killing of the
priests by Saul in 1 Sam. 22:17–19. Saul ordered the death of
"eighty-five men who wore the linen ephod." The killing rampage
continued until an entire community of priests had been slaughtered with their women and children. This great evil marked David
from that day forward. The inscription found in the Septuagint is
"The Eighth Psalm of David."

³⁻⁴You will destroy every proud liar who says, "We lie
all we want.
Our words are our weapons, and we won't be held
accountable.
Who can stop us?"
May Yahweh cut off their twisted tongues
and seal their lying lips.
May they all be silenced—those who boast and brag
with their
high-minded talk.

Intervention

⁵But the Lord says, "Now I will arise!
I will defend the poor,
those who were plundered, the oppressed,
and the needy who groan for help.
I will spring into action to rescue and protect them!"
⁶For every word Yahweh speaks is sure and reliable.
His truth is tested, found to be flawless, and ever
faithful.
It's as pure as silver refined seven times in a
crucible of clay.ᵃ

Inspiration

⁷⁻⁸Lord, you will keep us safe,
out of the reach of the wicked.
Even though they strut and prowl,
tolerating and celebrating what is worthless and
vile,
you will still lift up those who are yours!

---

a 12:6 The clay furnace ("crucible") is the heart of man. We are the
earthen vessels inside which God has placed his flawless words. His
words test us, they try us, and they refine us, seven times over, until
they are purified and assimilated into our spirits. The fire of testing
purifies us as vessels to carry the Word within our hearts.

13 Prayer Turns Depression into Delight[a]
For the Pure and Shining One
A Psalm of David

Depression
[1]*I'm hurting*, Lord—will you forget me forever?[b]
How much longer, Lord?
Will you look the other way when I'm in need?[c]
[2]How much longer must I cling to this constant grief?
I've endured this shaking of my soul.
So how much longer will my enemy have the upper
hand?

Intercession
[3]Take a good look at me, Yahweh, my God, and answer
me!
Breathe your life into my spirit.
Bring light to my eyes in this pitch-black darkness
or I will sleep the sleep of death.
[4]Don't let my enemy proclaim, "I've prevailed over
him."
For all my adversaries will celebrate when I fall.
[5]I have always trusted in your kindness, *so answer me.*
I will spin in a circle of joy

---

a 13 Some believe David composed this psalm shortly after being
anointed to be the king of Israel. David knew greatness was his destiny, but he struggled with the persecution and challenges that came
before his exaltation. In the wilderness David trusted and prayed his
way out.

b 13:1 This is the psalm that describes the journey from self to God,
from despair to delight, from feeling abandoned to feeling affirmed.
It begins with pain and ends with praise. Moaning gives way to
music. We each can take comfort in what David experienced.

c 13:1 David felt as though God was hiding his face from his cries.
David was left alone to wrestle with his doubts, feeling as though his
patience could hold on no longer. Have you ever been there?

when your salvation[a] lifts me up.
[6]I will sing my song of joy to you, Yahweh,
for in all of this you have strengthened my soul.
My enemies say that I have no Savior,
but I know that I have one in you!

14 GOD LOOKS DOWN FROM HEAVEN[b]
For the Pure and Shining One
A Psalm of David

No God
[1]Only the withering soul[c] would say to himself,
"There is no God."
Anyone who thinks like this is corrupt and callous,
devoid of what is good.
[2]Yahweh looks down *in love*,
looking over all of Adam's sons and daughters.
He's looking to see if there is anyone who acts wisely,
any who are searching for God and wanting to
please him.

None Who Are Good
[3]But everyone has wandered astray,
walking stubbornly toward evil.
Not one is good; he can't even find one.
[4]They live in luxury while exploiting my people!

---

a 13:5 The term for "salvation" is *yeshu'sh*, which is nearly identical to "Jesus, our Salvation." Our Savior plans blessings and hope for each of us as we trust in him.

b 14 With a few differences, Ps. 14 and Ps. 53 are nearly identical. Ps. 14 is practical; Ps. 53 is prophetic. Ps. 14 deals with the past, Ps. 53 with the future.

c 14:1 Or "fool." The word for "fool" comes from a Hebrew word meaning "withering." If we make no room for God, we have withered hearts, our moral sense of righteousness is put to sleep, and the noble aspirations of the heart shrivel up and die.

Won't these workers of wickedness ever learn?
They don't ever think of praying to God.

Overwhelmed with Dread
⁵But look at them now, in panic, trembling with terror.
For God is on the side of his godly *lovers.*
⁶Yahweh is always the safest place for the poor
when the workers of wickedness oppress them.

Overcome with Joy
⁷How I wish that Israel's rescue
would arise from the midst of Zion!
When Yahweh restores his people,
Jacob's joy will break forth
and Israel will be glad!

15 LIVING IN THE SHINING PLACE*ᵃ*
A poetic song by David

A Question Posed
¹Yahweh, who dares to dwell with you?
Who presumes the privilege of being close to you,
living next to you in your shining place*ᵇ* of glory?

---

a 15 The first line in Hebrew reads "Yahweh, who may abide [as a
guest] in your tent [tabernacle]?" Perhaps David's prophetic musicians sang this song of instruction as they laid the ark to rest in
David's tent. It is a song that reveals who will dwell in God's holy
presence and who will live with him in heaven's glory. It actually is
a description of Zion's perfect Man, Christ Jesus, and all those who
are transformed into his image (Rom. 8:29).

b 15:1 The Hebrew word for "sanctuary" is taken from a root word
for "shining place." This psalm gives us David's equivalent to Jesus'
Sermon on the Hillside. If we will dwell in the Holy Place, there must
first be a holy place in our spirits where God dwells. God's guests
must submit to the holiness that lives there. There is etiquette for
God's house revealed in this psalm.

The Answer Provided

[2]They are passionate and wholehearted,
always sincere and always speaking the truth—
for their hearts are trustworthy.
[3]They refuse to slander[a] or insult others;
they'll never listen to gossip or rumors,
nor would they ever harm a friend with their words.
[4]They will despise evil and evil workers
while commending the faithful ones who follow
after the truth.
They make firm commitments and follow through,
even at great cost.
[5]They never crush others with exploitation
and they would never be bought with a bribe
against the innocent.
Those who do these things will never be shaken;
they will stand firm forever.

16 THE GOLDEN SECRET

A precious song, engraved in gold,[b] by David

My Protection

[1]Keep me safe, O mighty God.
I run to you, my safe place.

---

a 15:3 The Hebrew word for "slander," *ragal*, means to spy on someone and look for evil to use against that person.

b 16 The Hebrew word used in the inscription is *michtam*. There are
many variations of translation for this word. Here are the major ones:
"golden," "graven," "a permanent writing," "precious," "hidden," "a
spiritual secret," or "jewel." The Septuagint renders this "a sculptured
writing of gold"; other translations call it a "golden poem." Perhaps
the most accepted translation of *michtam* is "engraved in gold." This
speaks of the divine nature engraved into our hearts by the Word. A
new humanity is now stamped with God-life, engraved in his golden
glory.

²I said to Yahweh,
  "You are my Maker and my Master.
  Any good thing you find in me has come from you."
³*And he said to me*, "My holy lovers
  in the land are my glorious ones,
  who fulfill all my desires."
⁴Yet there are those who yield to their weakness,ᵃ
  and they will have troubles unending.
  I never gather with such ones,ᵇ
  nor give them honor in any way.

My Portion

⁵Yahweh, you alone are my inheritance.
  You are my prize, my pleasure, and my portion.
  You hold my destiny *and its timing* in your hands.
⁶Your pleasant pathᶜ leads me to pleasant places.
  I'm overwhelmed by the privileges
  that come with following you!

My Praise

⁷The way you counsel me makes me praise you more,
  for your whispers in the night give me wisdom,
  showing me what to do next.
⁸Because I setᵈ you, Yahweh, always close to me,

---

a 16:4 As translated from the Septuagint.
b 16:4 As translated from the Septuagint.
c 16:6 Or "boundary lines."
d 16:8 The Hebrew word *shava* carries the sense of being equal or similar. David was not saying he was equal to Yahweh, but that he thought the way God thought. David had made his heart and mind to be identical with the heart and mind of God. Always before himself, before anything, were the desires of God. It was the heart and mind of God that had first place in David's heart and thoughts.

my confidence will never be weakened,[a]
for I experience your wraparound presence every
    moment.[b]
⁹My heart and soul explode with joy—full of glory!
Even my body will rest confident and secure.
¹⁰For you will not abandon me to the realm of death,
nor will you allow your Faithful One to experience
    corruption.[c]
¹¹Because of you, I know the path of life,
as I taste the fullness of joy in your presence.
At your right side[d] I experience *divine* pleasures
    forevermore!

17 A CRY FOR JUSTICE
A priestly prayer[e] of David

Hear Me!
¹Listen to me, Lord.
Hear the passionate prayer of this honest man.
My cause is just and my need is real.
I've done what's right and my lips speak truth.
²Examine and exonerate me.
Vindicate me and show the world I'm innocent.

---

a 16:8 It is possible to translate this section as "I have determined in my heart to be identical with the mind and heart of God, and I will not let my resolve be weakened."

b 16:8 Or "because he is at my right hand."

c 16:10 Or "the pit." This is likely a metaphor for Sheol.

d 16:11 Jesus was pierced in his side with the spear of man's hatred. Eternal pleasures are found hidden in the wounds of Christ, where Jesus responded to the world's hatred with sacred blood and water flowing from his side. Forgiveness and grace splashed on the dirt. We are now seated with Christ at his right side.

e 17 This is the Hebrew word *tephillah*, and it is found in the titles of five Psalms (17; 86; 90; 102; 142).

³For in a visitation of the night
    you inspected my heart and refined my soul in fire
    until nothing vile was found in me.
    I will not sin with my words.
⁴Following your word has kept me from wrong.
    Your ways have molded my footsteps, keeping me
    from going down the paths of the violent.
⁵My steps follow in the tracks of your chariot wheels,
    always staying in their path,
    never straying from your way.
⁶You will answer me, God; I know you always will.
    Hear my words like you always do as you listen to
        my every prayer.

Hide Me!

    ⁷Magnify the marvels of your mercy to all who seek
        you.*ᵃ*
    You are the *loving* Savior of all who turn aside
    to hide themselves in you.
⁸Protect me from harm;
    keep an eye on me as you would a child*ᵇ*
    who is reflected in the twinkling of your eye.
    Yes, hide me within the shelter of your embrace,
    under your outstretched wings.*ᶜ*
⁹Protect me there from all my foes.
    For there are many who surround my soul
    to completely destroy me.

---

a 17:7 As translated from the Septuagint.
b 17:8 Or "daughter."
c 17:8 This could also be a reference to the mercy seat, where sacred blood was sprinkled in the Holy of Holies. There the golden cherubim overshadowed all who entered the divine chamber (Ex. 25:18–20).

¹⁰They are pitiless, heartless—hard as nails,
   swollen with pride and filled with arrogance!
¹¹See how they close in on me,
   waiting for the chance to throw me to the ground.[a]
¹²They're like lions eager to tear me apart,
   like young and fearless lions lurking in secret,
   so ferocious and cruel—ready to rip me to shreds.

Help Me!

¹³Arise, God, and confront them!
   Challenge them with your might![b]
   Free me from their clutches and rescue me from
      their rage.
¹⁴Throw them down to the ground,
   those who live for only this life on earth.
   Thrust them out of their prosperity
   and into their portion in eternity,
   leaving their wealth and wickedness behind!
¹⁵As for me, because I am innocent, I will see[c] your
   face
   until I see you for who you really are.
   I will be satisfied in an awakening of your likeness
      in me!

---

a 17:11 This is also what the soldiers did to Jesus. They threw him to
   the ground and nailed him to the cross.
b 17:13 The word used here is "sword." An alternative translation
   would be "Rescue my soul from the wicked one, who is your sword."
   The wicked are sometimes God's tools to execute his judgments (Isa.
   10:5; Jer. 51:20).
c 17:15 The Hebrew word for "see," *chaza*, means "to see a vision."

18 *a* I LOVE YOU, LORD

A song[b] *to the Pure and Shining One by King David, his servant, composed when the Lord rescued David from all his many enemies, including from the brutality of Saul.*[c] *He said:*

¹I love you, Yahweh, and I'm bonded to you,[d]
   my strength!
²Yahweh, you're the bedrock beneath my feet,
   my faith-fortress, my *wonderful* deliverer,
   my God, my rock of rescue *where none can reach me.*
   You're the shield around me,
   the mighty power[e] that saves me,
   and my high place.
³All I need to do is to call on you,
   Yahweh, the praiseworthy God.
   When I do, I'm safe and sound in you—
   delivered from my foes!
⁴⁻⁵For when the cords of death wrapped around me
   and torrents of destruction overwhelmed me,[f]
   taking me to death's door,

---

a 18 This magnificent poem is so important to the Holy Spirit that it appears twice in the Bible. You will also find it in 2 Sam. 22.

b 18 There are fifty psalms that are described as "a song" in the inscription, and each one is a power song of victory and breakthrough.

c 18 Or "the paw of Saul." Saul was like a beast that chased David until his death.

d 18:1 David didn't employ the common Hebrew word for "love," *'ahav,* but instead used the Hebrew word for "pity" or "mercy." How could David have mercy for God? The word he used, *racham,* is the word for a mother who loves and pities her child so much it manifests with a deep love and emotional bond. This concept, although difficult to convey in English, carries the thought of embrace and touch. It could actually be translated "Lord, I want to hug you." Haven't you ever felt like that?

e 18:2 Or "horn" (i.e., horn of my salvation), which comes from a root word meaning "ray of brightness."

f 18:4–5 Or "waves of Sheol [death] engulfed me." See 2 Sam. 22:5.

⁶in my distress I cried out to you, the delivering God,
  and from your temple-throne you heard my troubled
    cry,
  and my sobs went right into your heart.*ᵃ*
⁷The earth itself shivered and shook.
  It reeled and rocked before him.
  As the mountains trembled, they melted away,
  for his anger was kindled on my behalf!
⁸Fierce flames leapt from his mouth,*ᵇ*
  erupting with blazing, burning coals as smoke
  and fire encircled him.
⁹⁻¹⁰He stretched heaven's curtain open and came to my
  defense.
  Swiftly he rode to earth as the stormy sky was
    lowered.
  He rode a chariot of thunderclouds amidst thick
    darkness;
  his steed was a cherub,
  soaring on outstretched wings of Spirit-Wind.
¹¹Wrapped in the thick-cloud darkness,
  his thunder-tabernacle surrounded him.
  He hid himself in mystery-darkness;
  the dense rain clouds were his garments.
¹²Suddenly the brilliance of his presence broke
  through
  with lightning bolts and hail—
  a tempest dropping coals of fire.
¹³The Lord thundered; the great God above every god
  spoke with his thunder-voice from the sky.
  The Most High uttered his voice!

---

a 18:6 This scene is not only a poetic portrayal of how God answered
  David's prayer, but also a picture of the sufferings of a greater Son
  of David, Jesus, who hung on the cross with cries of agony. God
  heard him and shook the planet as thick clouds covered the sun.
b 18:8 Or "nostrils."

¹⁴He released his lightning-arrows, and routed my foes.
See how they ran and scattered in fear!
¹⁵Then with his mighty roar he laid bare the
foundations of the earth,
uncovering the secret source of the sea.
The hidden depths of land and sea were exposed
by the blast of his hot breath.
¹⁶He rescued me from the mighty waters
and drew me to himself!
¹⁷Even though I was helpless in the hands
of my hateful, strong enemy,ᵃ
you were good to deliver me.
¹⁸When I was at my weakest,ᵇ my enemies attacked—
but the Lord held on to me.
¹⁹His love broke open the way,
and he brought me into a beautiful, broad place.ᶜ
He rescued me—because his delight is in me!ᵈ
²⁰He rewarded me for doing what's right and staying
pure.
²¹I will follow his commands and
I'll not sin by ceasing to follow him, no matter what.
²²For I've kept my eyes focused on his righteous words,
and I've obeyed everything that he's told me to do.
²³I've been blameless before him and followed all his
ways,
keeping my heart pure.

---

a 18:17 Death is our strong enemy. Only through Christ are we delivered from its grip.
b 18:18 Or "In the day of my calamity."
c 18:19 This could be the throne room of heaven.
d 18:19 Here in verses 16–19 you can see the glorious resurrection of
Christ as the Father reached down and kissed the Son with life and
love. Read it again and think of Christ in the tomb being raised by
the Father.

[24]And so Yahweh has rewarded me according to my
righteousness,
because I kept my heart clean before his eyes.
[25]*Good people will taste your goodness.*
And to those who are loyal to you,
you love to prove that you are loyal and true.
[26]And for those who are purified, they find you always
pure.
But you'll outwit the crooked and cunning with your
craftiness.
[27]To the humble you bring heaven's deliverance,
but the proud and haughty you disregard.
[28]God, all at once you turned on a floodlight for me!
You are the revelation-light in my darkness,
and in your brightness I can see the path ahead.
[29]With you as my strength I can crush an enemy horde,
advancing through every stronghold that stands in
front of me.[a]
[30]Yahweh, what a perfect God you are!
All Yahweh's promises have proven true.
What a secure shelter for all those
who turn to hide themselves in you,
the wraparound God.[b]
[31]Could there be any other god like Yahweh?
For there is not a more secure foundation[c] than you.
[32]God, you have wrapped me in power
and made my way perfect.
[33]Through you I ascend to the highest peaks
to stand strong and secure in you.[d]

---

a 18:29 Or "by my God I can jump over a wall."
b 18:30 The Hebrew word used here (often translated "shield") means
"to wrap around in protection." God himself is our shield of grace.
c 18:31 Or "rocky cliff."
d 18:33 Or "You make my legs like a deer to stand firm on the heights."

³⁴You've trained me with the weapons of warfare-worship;
   my arms can bend a bow of bronze.
³⁵You empower me for victory with your wraparound
   presence.
   Your power within makes me strong to subdue.
   By stooping down in gentleness,
   you made me great!
³⁶You've set me free, and now I'm standing complete,
   ready to fight some more!
³⁷I caught up with my enemies and conquered them
   and didn't turn back until the war was won!
³⁸I smashed them to pieces and
   I finished them once and for all; they're as good as
      dead.
³⁹You've placed your armor upon me
   and made my enemies bow low at my feet.
⁴⁰You've made them all turn tail and run,
   for through you I've destroyed them all!
⁴¹They shouted for help, but no one dared to rescue
   them.
   They cried out to Yahweh, but he refused to answer
      them.
⁴²So I pulverized them to powder and cast them to the
   wind.
   I swept them away like dirt on the floor.
⁴³You gave me victory on every side,
   for you make me a leader of nations.
   Even those I've never heard of come and bow at my
      feet.
⁴⁴As soon as they heard of me they submitted to me.
   Even the rebel foreigners obey my every word.
⁴⁵Their rebellion fades away as they come near;
   trembling in their strongholds,
   they come crawling out of their hideouts,
   cringing in fear before me.

⁴⁶Yahweh lives!
  Praise is lifted high to the unshakable God!
  Towering over all, my Savior-God is worthy to be
      praised!
⁴⁷Look how he pays back harm to all who harm me,
  subduing all who come against me.
⁴⁸He rescues me from my enemies;
  he lifts me up high and keeps me out of reach,
  far from the grasp of my violent foe.
⁴⁹So I thank you, Yahweh, with my praises!
  I will sing my song to the highest God,
  so all among the nations will hear me.ᵃ
⁵⁰You have given me, your king, great victories.
  You've always been tender and kind to me, your
      anointed one,
  your loving servant, David, and to all my descendants!

19 GOD'S WITNESSES
For the Pure and Shining One
A poem of praise by King David, his loving servant

God's Story in the Skies
¹God's splendor is a tale that is told,
  written in the stars.ᵇ
  Space itself speaks his story
  through the marvels of the heavens.
  His truth is on tour in the starry vault of the sky,
  showing his skill in creation's craftsmanship.
²Each day gushes out its messageᶜ to the next,
  night by night whispering its knowledge to all—

---

a 18:49 Paul quoted this verse as one of four prophecies to show that
  Christ came for all people, not just the Jews. See Rom. 15:9.
b 19:1 Or "The heavens are continually rehearsing the glory of God."
c 19:2 Or "speaks its prophecy."

³without a sound, without a word, without a voice
  being heard,
⁴yet all the world can hear its echo.
    Everywhere its message goes out.
    What a heavenly home God has set for the sun,
    shining in the superdome of the sky!
⁵See how he leaves his celestial chamber each
  morning,
    radiant as a bridegroom ready for his wedding,
    like a day-breaking champion eager to run his
        course.
⁶He rises on one horizon, completing his circuit on the
  other,
    warming lives and lands with his heat.

God's Story in the Scriptures
⁷Yahweh's Word*ᵃ* is perfect in every way;
    how it revives our souls!
    Yahweh's laws lead us to truth,
    and his ways change the simple into wise.
⁸Yahweh's teachings are right and make us joyful;
    his precepts are so pure!
    Yahweh's commands challenge us to keep close to
        his heart!
    The revelation-light of his Word makes my spirit
        shine radiant.
⁹Yahweh's decrees are trustworthy.
    The fear of Yahweh is pure, enduring forever.
¹⁰The rarest treasures of life are found in his truth.
    That's why God's Word is prized like others prize the
        finest gold.
    Sweeter also than honey are his living words—
    sweet words dripping from the honeycomb!

---

a 19:7 Or "The Torah."

¹¹For they warn us, your servants,
and keep us from following the wicked way,
giving a lifetime guarantee:
great success to every obedient soul!
¹²How would I discern the waywardness^a of my heart?
Lord, forgive my hidden flaws whenever you find
them.
¹³Keep cleansing me, God,
and keep me from my secret, selfish sins;
may they never rule over me!
For only then will I be free from fault
and remain innocent of rebellion.
¹⁴So may the words of my mouth, my
meditation-thoughts,
and every movement of my heart be always pure
and pleasing,
acceptable before your eyes, Yahweh,
my only Redeemer, my Protector.^b

20 A Victory Decree

For the Pure and Shining One
For the end times, by David^c

May God Hear You
¹In your day of danger may Yahweh answer and
deliver you.
May the name of the God of Jacob^d set you safely on
high!

---

a 19:12 The word *waywardness* is taken from the Hebrew word for
"errors."
b 19:14 Or "my rock [of protection]."
c 20 The inscription for Pss. 20–22 is "For the end times," as translated from the Septuagint.
d 20:1 Jacob was one transformed by God's grace, changed from a
schemer who took from others into Israel, God's prince.

²May supernatural help be sent from his sanctuary.
   May he support you from Zion's fortress!
³May he remember every gift you have given him
   and celebrate every sacrifice of love you have shown
      him.ᵃ

Pause in his presence

⁴May Yahweh give you every desire of your heart
   and carry out your every plan *as you go to battle.*
⁵When you succeed, we will celebrate and shout for
   joy.
   Flags will fly when victory is yours!
   Yes, God will answer your prayers, and we will
      praise him!
⁶I know Yahweh gives me all that I ask for
   and brings victory to his anointed king.
   My deliverance cry will be heard in his holy heaven.
   By his mighty hand miracles will manifest
   through his saving strength.
⁷Some find their strength in their weapons and
   wisdom,
   but my miracle-deliverance can never be won by
      men.
   Our boast is in Yahweh our God,
   who makes us strong and gives us victory!
⁸Our enemies will not prevail; they will only collapse
   and
   perish in defeat while we will rise up, full of
      courage.
⁹Give victory to our king, O Yahweh!
   The day we call on you, give us your answer!

---

a 20:3 Or "May he consider your burnt offerings generous."

21 THROUGH YOUR STRENGTH

For the end times, to the Pure and Shining One
David's poem of praise[a]

Looking Back

¹Yahweh, because of your strength the king is strong.
  Look how he rejoices in you!
  He bursts out with a joyful song because of your
    victory!
²For you have given him his heart's desire,
  anything and everything he asks for.
  You haven't withheld a thing from the king.
                              Pause in his presence

³Rich blessings overflow with every encounter with
  you,
  and you placed a royal crown of gold upon his
    head.
⁴He wanted life[b]—you have given it to him and more!
  The days of his blessing stretch on one after
    another, forever!
⁵You have honored him and made him famous.
  Glory-garments are upon him,
  and you surround him with splendor and majesty.
⁶Your victory heaps blessing after blessing upon him.
  What joy and bliss he tastes, rejoicing before your
    face![c]
⁷For the king trusts in Yahweh,
  and he will never stumble, never fall.
  The forever-love of the Most High holds him firm.

---

a 21 Think of this song as a praise song to Jesus, our true King.
b 21:4 This can be viewed as a prophecy of our Lord Jesus asking for
  resurrection-life. Every verse of this psalm is prophetic, pointing us
  to Jesus.
c 21:6 Or "You make him joyful in joy with your face!"

Looking Forward

[8]Your almighty hands have captured your foes.
  You uncovered all who hate you and you seized
    them.
[9-10]When you appear before them,
  unveiling the radiance of your face,
  they will be consumed by the fierce fire of your
    presence.
  Yahweh's flames will swallow them up.
  They and their descendants
  will be destroyed by an unrelenting fire.
[11]We will watch them fail,
  for these are the ones who plan their evil schemes
    against the Lord.
[12]They will turn and run at the sight of your
  judgment-arrows
  aimed straight at their hearts.

Looking Up

[13]Rise up and put your might on display!
  By your strength we will sing and praise your
    glorious power!

22 A PROPHETIC PORTRAIT OF THE CROSS[a]
For the Pure and Shining One
David's song of anguish
To the tune of "The Deer at the Dawning of the Day"[b]

The Cross

[1]God, my God!

---

a 22 Thirty-three prophecies from this psalm were fulfilled when Jesus
  was on the cross.
b 22 This could be an amazing picture of Christ giving birth at the
  cross to a generation of his seed. They are like children of God born
  in the dawning of that resurrection morning.

Why would you abandon me now?[a]
²Why do you remain distant,
    refusing to answer[b] my tearful cries in the day
    and my desperate cries for your help in the night?
    I can't stop sobbing.
    Where are you, my God?
³Yet I know that you are most holy.
    You are God-Enthroned, the praise of Israel.
⁴Our fathers' faith was in you—
    through the generations they trusted in you
    and you came through.
⁵Every time they cried out to you in their despair,
    you were faithful to deliver them;
    you didn't disappoint them.
⁶But I am like a worm,
    crushed and bleeding crimson,[c]
    treated as less than human.
    I've been despised and scorned by everyone!
⁷Mocked by their jeers, despised with their sneers,
    as all the people poke fun at me, spitting their
        insults,
⁸saying, "Is this the one who trusted in God?
    Now let's see if Yahweh will come to your rescue!
    Let's see how much he delights in him!"

---

a 22:1 When Jesus quoted these words while dying on the cross, he was identifying himself as the one David wrote about in this psalm. It is a breathtaking portrayal of what Jesus endured through his suffering for us. The psalm ends with another quotation of Jesus on the cross: "It is finished!"

b 22:2 David used poetic nuance here, for the word "answer" ('anah) is also a Hebrew homonym for "affliction."

c 22:6 The Hebrew word for "worm" is tola, which is also the word for "crimson" or "scarlet." Tola was a certain worm in the ancient Near East that, when crushed, bled a crimson color so strong it was used as a dye for garments. Jesus was not saying he was a despised worm, but that he will bleed as he is crushed for our sins.

⁹Lord, you delivered me safely from my mother's
   womb.
   You are the one who cared for me ever since I was a
      baby.
¹⁰Since the day I was born, I've been placed in your
   custody.
   You've cradled me throughout my days,
   and you've always been my God.
¹¹So don't leave me now, for trouble is all around me,
   and there's no one to help me.
¹²I'm surrounded by many violent foes like bulls;
   forces of evil encircle me like the strong bulls of
      Bashan.*a*
¹³Like ravenous, roaring lions tearing their prey,
   they pour curses from their mouths.
¹⁴Now I'm completely exhausted.*b*
   Every joint of my body has been pulled apart.
   My courage has melted away.
¹⁵I'm so thirsty and parched.
   My tongue sticks to the roof of my mouth.
   And now you lay me in the dust of death.
¹⁶They have pierced my hands and my feet.*c*
   Like a pack of wild dogs they tear at me,
   swirling around me with their hatred.
   A band of evil men surrounds me.
¹⁷I can count all my bones.
   Look at how they gloat over me and stare!

---

a 22:12 The root word for "bull" means "to break or destroy." The word
   Bashan, although known as a fertile land northeast of Lake Galilee,
   is also a word for "serpent." These represent the many demonic spirits who came against the Son of God as he was being crucified.
b 22:14 Or "I'm poured out like water."
c 22:16 As translated from some Hebrew manuscripts, Septuagint and
   Syriac; other Hebrew manuscripts read "Like the lion my hands and
   my feet." This is a powerful prophecy of crucifixion, given by David
   many centuries before crucifixion was invented by the Romans.

¹⁸With a toss of the dice they divide my clothes among
   themselves,
   gambling for my garments!
¹⁹Yahweh, please don't stay far away.
   My strength, come quickly to my rescue.
²⁰Give me back my life.
   Save me from this violent death.
   Save my precious one and only*a*
   from the power of these dogs!*b*
²¹Save me from all the power of the enemy,
   from this roaring lion raging against me
   and the power of his dark horde.

The Resurrection
²²I will declare your name before all my brothers
   and praise you in the midst of the congregation.*c*
²³Those who fear Yahweh, praise him!
   Let all the seed of Jacob glorify him with your
      praises.
   Stand in awe of him, all you offspring of Israel!
²⁴For he has not despised my cries of deep despair.
   He's my first responder to my sufferings,
   and when I was in pain,

---

a 22:20 Or "unique" or "darling." Each of us is that "one and only"
child or "unique darling" mentioned here in this psalm. See Song.
6:9. On the cross, Jesus—like a deer giving birth at the dawning
light (see inscription of Ps. 22)—cared less that his body was being
torn apart and more about our protection and salvation. He prayed
for us as he faced death on the cross.

b 22:20 The "dogs" are metaphors for evil spirits who were bent on
destroying Jesus on the cross. The Hebrew word for "dog" is taken
from a root word meaning "to attack."

c 22:22 Between v. 21 and v. 22 the glorious resurrection of Jesus
takes place. The music is elevated to a higher key as victory is
sounded forth. "My people gather" is a reference to the church that
was birthed through his resurrection glory. (See also v. 25.)

he was there all the time and heard the cries of the
afflicted.

²⁵You're the reason for my praise; it comes from you
and goes to you.

I will keep my promise to praise you before all who
fear you

among the congregation of your people.

²⁶Let all the poor and broken eat until satisfied.

Bring Yahweh praise and you will find him.

May your hearts overflow with life forever!

²⁷From the four corners of the earth,

the peoples of the world will remember and return
to Yahweh.

Every nation will come and worship him.

²⁸For Yahweh is King of all, who takes charge of all the
nations.

²⁹The wealthy of this world will feast in fellowship with
him

right alongside the humble of heart,

bowing down to the dust, forsaking their own souls.

They will all come and worship this worthy King!

³⁰His *spiritual* seed*ᵃ* shall serve him.

Future generations will hear from us

about the wonders of the Victorious Lord.

³¹His generation yet to be born will glorify him.

And they will all declare, "It is finished!"*ᵇ*

---

a 22:30 Jesus, our crucified Savior, had no natural offspring. These are
the sons and daughters who were birthed by the work of the cross.

b 22:31 Or "He has done it!" See John 19:30.

23 THE GOOD SHEPHERD
David's poetic praise to God

¹Yahweh is my best friend and my shepherd.ᵃ
  I always have more than enough.ᵇ
²He offers a resting place for me in his luxurious love.ᶜ
  His tracks take me to an oasis of peace near *the
    quiet brook of bliss.*ᵈ
³That's where he restores and revives my life.ᵉ
  He opens before me the right path

---

a 23:1 The word most commonly used for "shepherd" is taken from the root word *ra'ah*, which is also the Hebrew word for "best friend." This translation includes both meanings. The unique term for shepherd is *ro'eh tzon*—"lover of the flock." This teaches us that a shepherd was not just a responsible overseer, but a caring father figure, tending to his flock out of a deep sense of love. Shepherds were also fierce protectors of their flocks. Jesus is the Fierce Protector of his people.

b 23:1 Or "I lack nothing." What a wonderful declaration over your life! To never be in lack, always possessing more than enough. Our God meets our emotional, physical, and spiritual needs.

c 23:2 Or "in spring [green] meadows." A good shepherd knows where to pasture his flock. These green meadows would be a resting place, free from all fear. The Greek verb "to love" is *agapao*, which is a merging of two words and two concepts. *Ago* means "to lead like a shepherd," and *pao* is a verb that means "to rest." Love is our Shepherd leading us to the place of true rest in his heart.

d 23:2 The Hebrew word *menuhâ* means "the waters of a resting place." See Isa. 11:10.

e 23:3 Or "he causes my life [or "soul," Hb. *nephesh*] to return." So often life drains out of us through our many activities, but, as David found, God restores our well-being when we pursue what pleases God and when we rest in him.

and leads me along in his footsteps of righteousness[a]
so that I can bring honor to his name.
[4]Even when your path takes me through
the valley of deepest darkness,
fear will never conquer me, for you already have!
Your authority is my strength and my peace.[b]
The comfort of your love takes away my fear.
I'll never be lonely, for you are near.
[5]You become my delicious feast
even when my enemies dare to fight.
You anoint me with the fragrance of your Holy
Spirit;[c]
you give me all I can drink of you until my cup
overflows.[d]

[6]*So why would I fear the future?*
Only goodness and tender love pursue me all the
days of my life.

---

a 23:3 Or "circular paths of righteousness." It is a common trait for sheep
on the hillsides of Israel to circle their way up higher. They eventually
form a path that keeps leading them higher. This is what the psalm is
referring to here. Each step we take following our Shepherd will lead
us higher, even though it may seem we are going in circles.

b 23:4 Or "Your rod and your staff, they comfort me."

c 23:5 Or "You anoint my head with oil." "Oil" or "fragrance" becomes
a symbol of the Holy Spirit.

d 23:5 Or "your cup cheers me like the best wine (LXX)," or "my chalice
that inebriates me, how goodly it is (Vulgate)."

Then afterward, when my life is through,
I'll return to your glorious presence[a] to be forever
  with you!

24 THE KING OF GLORY
David's poetic praise to God[b]

Creation's King
[1]Yahweh claims the world as his.
  Everything and everyone belong to him!
[2]He's the one who pushed back oceans[c]
  to let the dry ground appear,
  planting firm foundations for the earth.

Who Comes before the King?
[3]Who, then, is allowed to ascend the mountain of
  Yahweh?
  And who has the privilege of entering into God's
    Holy Place?
[4]Those who are clean—whose works and ways are
  pure,
  whose hearts are true and sealed by the truth,
  those who never deceive, whose words are sure.
[5]They will receive Yahweh's blessing
  and righteousness given by the Savior-God.

---

a 23:6 Or "return to Yahweh's palace."

b 24 The Septuagint adds "for the Sabbath." Ps. 24 celebrates God
as the Warrior-King, ruling over a kingdom of purity and holiness.
Pss. 22–24 form a trilogy. Ps. 22 speaks of the Savior's cross, Ps. 23
speaks of the Shepherd's staff, and Ps. 24 speaks of the Sovereign
King. We see three viewpoints of Jesus' love for us: Ps. 22—the Good
Shepherd (John 10:11), Ps. 23—the Great Shepherd (Heb. 13:20),
and Ps. 24—the Chief Shepherd (1 Peter 5:4).

c 24:2 Or "who established it upon the ocean currents."

⁶They will stand before God,
for they seek the pleasure of God's face,ᵃ the God of
Jacob.

Pause in his presence

The King is Coming!
⁷So wake up, you living gateways!
Lift up your heads, you doorways of eternity!ᵇ
Welcome the King of Glory,
for he is about to come through you.
⁸You ask, "Who is this King of Glory?"
Yahweh, armed and ready for battle,
Yahweh, invincible in every way!
⁹So wake up, you living gateways, and rejoice!
Fling wide, you eternal doors!
Here he comes; the King of Glory is ready to come
in.
¹⁰You ask, "Who is this King of Glory?"
He is Yahweh, armed and ready for battle,
the Mighty One, the invincible commander of
heaven's hosts!ᶜ
Yes, he is the King of Glory!

Pause in his presence

---

a 24:6 The Hebrew is plural ("faces").

b 24:7 God's people are identified as living gates and doorways. When God opens the doors of eternity within us, no one is able to shut them. To "lift up" our heads is a figure of speech for a bold confidence that brings rejoicing and hope.

c 24:10 Or "Yahweh Tseva'ot." The word *tseva'ot* is the plural of the word *tsava*, a feminine noun meaning "force." When these two Hebrew nouns are placed together, they would be translated as "Yahweh of the forces."

25 Don't Fail Me, God!
King David's poetic praise to God

¹*Always* I will lift up my soul into your presence, Yahweh.
²*Be there for me*, my God, for I keep trusting in you.
Don't allow my foes to gloat over me or
the shame of defeat to overtake me.
³Could anyone be disgraced
when he has entwined his heart with yours?
But my foes will all be defeated and ashamed
when they harm the innocent.
⁴Direct me, Yahweh, throughout my journey
so I can experience your plans for my life.
Reveal the life-paths *that are pleasing to you.*
⁵Escort me into your truth; *take me by the hand* and
teach me.*ᵇ*
For you are the God of my salvation;
I have wrapped my heart into yours all day long!*ᶜ*
⁶⁻⁷Forgive my failures as a young man,
and overlook the sins of my immaturity.
Give me grace, Yahweh! Always look at me
through your eyes of love—
your forgiving eyes of mercy and compassion.
When you think of me, see me as one you love and
care for.

---

a 25 Psalms 25–39 are fifteen poetic songs about bringing pure worship before God. Pss. 25–29 speak of our confidence to worship God. Pss. 30–34 point us to receiving life eternal from our Hero-God. The last five, Pss. 35–39, bring us to the importance of personal purity and holiness before God as we worship him in truth.

b 25:5 Or "Reveal your truth to me as I move forward."

c 25:5 The Hebrew word most commonly translated as "wait" (wait upon the Lord) is *qavah*, which also means "to tie together by twisting" or "to entwine" or "to wrap tightly." This is a beautiful concept of waiting upon God, not passively, but entwining our hearts with him and his purposes.

⁸How good you are to me!
  When people turn to you, Yahweh,
  they discover how easy you are to please—so
    faithful and true!
  Joyfully you teach them the proper path,
  even when they go astray.
⁹Keep showing the humble your path,
  and lead them into the best decision.
  Bring revelation-light that trains them in the truth.
¹⁰Loving are all the ways of Yahweh, loving and
  faithful for those who keep his covenant.
¹¹For the honor of your name, Yahweh,
  never count my many sins, and forgive them all—
  lift their burden off of my life!ᵃ
¹²Who are they that live in the holy fear of Yahweh?
  You will show them the right path to take.
¹³Then prosperity and favor will be their portion,
  and their descendants will inherit the earth.
¹⁴There's a private place reserved for the devoted
  lovers of Yahweh,
  where they sit near him and receive
  the revelation-secrets of his promises.ᵇ
¹⁵Rescue me, Yahweh, for you free my feet from every
  trap.
¹⁶Sorrows fill my heart as I feel helpless, mistreated—
  I'm all alone and in misery!
  Come closer to me now, for I need your mercy.
¹⁷Turn to me, for my problems seem to be going from
  bad to worse.
  Only you can free me from all these troubles!

---

a 25:11 The Hebrew word used here for "forgive" or "pardon" is a rare word used only twice in the Old Testament and comes from a root word meaning "to lift off a burden."
b 25:14 Or "covenant."

¹⁸Until you lift this burden, the burden of all my sins,
  my troubles and trials will be more than I can handle.
  Can't you feel my pain?
¹⁹Vicious, violent[a] enemies hate me.
  There are so many, Lord. Can't you see?
²⁰Will you protect me from their power against me? I
  have taken shelter in you.
  Let it never be said that when I trusted you,
  you didn't come to my rescue.
²¹Your perfection and faithfulness are my bodyguards,
  for you are my hope and I trust in you as my only
    protection.
²²Zealously, God, we ask you
  to come save Israel from all her troubles,
  for you provide the ransom price for your people![b]

26 DECLARE ME INNOCENT
King David's poetic praise to God

David's Trust and Transparency
¹Yahweh, be my judge and declare me innocent!
  Clear my name, for I walk in integrity
  and trust you without wavering.
²Yahweh, you can scrutinize me.
  Refine my heart and probe my every thought.
  Put me to the test and you'll find me true.
³I will never lose sight of your steadfast love for me.
  Your faithfulness has steadied my steps.

---

a 25:19 This is the Hebrew word *hamas*.

b 25:22 Psalm 25 is an acrostic psalm; that is, in the Hebrew text
  every verse begins with a progressive letter of the alphabet. It is
  considered a poetic device of Hebrew literature. Go back through
  the psalm and notice how many verses begin with the next letter of
  our English alphabet. See if you can find them.

David's Truthfulness

⁴I won't keep company with tricky, two-faced men,
    nor will I go the way of those with hidden motives.
⁵I despise the sinner's hangouts.
    You won't find me walking with the wicked.
⁶⁻⁷When I come to your altar, Yahweh,
    I'll be clean before you,[a]
    approaching with songs of thanksgiving,
    singing songs of your mighty miracles.

David's Testimony

⁸Yahweh, I love to live in your house, this dwelling
    place of dazzling glory!
⁹Don't treat me as one of these scheming sinners
    who plot violence against the innocent.
¹⁰Look how they devise their wicked plans;
    their hands are always ready to receive a bribe.
¹¹*I'm not like them, Lord—not at all.*
    Save me, redeem me with your mercy,
    for I have chosen to walk only in what is right.
¹²Among the worshipers I will praise Yahweh,
    for I am safe and secure because of you!

27 FEARLESS FAITH

David's poetic praise to God before he was anointed king[b]

¹Yahweh is my revelation-light[c]
    and the source of my salvation.
    I fear no one!

---

a 26:6–7 Or "I wash my hands in innocence."
b 27 Inscription from the Septuagint. Most Bible scholars agree this psalm was written during the time of a devastating war where David witnessed the cruelty, savagery, and horrors of war.
c 27:1 See John 1:5, 9; 1 John 1:5.

I'll never turn back and run, for you, Yahweh,
surround and protect me.
²When evil ones come to destroy me,
they will be the ones who turn back.
³My heart will not fear even if an army rises to attack.
I will not be shaken, even if war is imminent.
⁴Here's the one thing I crave from Yahweh,
the one thing I seek above all else:
I want to live with him every moment in his house,ᵃ
beholding the marvelous beautyᵇ of Yahweh,
filled with awe, delighting in his glory and grace.
I want to contemplateᶜ in his temple.
⁵⁻⁶In the day of trouble, he will treasureᵈ me in his
shelter,
under the cover of his tent.
He will lift me high upon a rock,
out of reach from all my enemies who surround me.
Triumphant now, I'll bring him my offerings of praise,
singing and shouting with ecstatic joy!
Yes, I will sing praises to Yahweh!

---

a 27:4 A temple had not yet been built when David wrote this psalm. He was saying that he longs to be surrounded with God's presence, enclosed and encircled with holiness.

b 27:4 The meaning of the Hebrew word for "beauty" (*no'am*) is not easily conveyed by one English word. It can also be translated "sweetness," "pleasantness," "friendliness," "graciousness," "goodness," "loveliness," "splendor," or "delightfulness." Take each of these terms and read the verse again, inserting the possible alternatives. We must be captured by the awesomeness of God each time we come before him and rejoice in his friendship.

c 27:4 The Hebrew verb *baqar* can also mean "inquire," "meditate," "take pleasure in," and, in a general sense, "worship," "pray," or "seek [guidance]." However, *baqar* comes from a root word that means "to arise at dawn." Perhaps David was saying that he would arise every dawn to take pleasure in God.

d 27:5–6 Or "hide," "save," "store," "esteem."

⁷Hear my cry. Show me mercy, and send the help I
    need!
⁸I heard *your voice* in my heart say, "Come, seek my
    face;"
    my inner being responded,
    "Yahweh, I'm seeking your face with all my heart."
⁹So don't turn your face away from me.*ᵃ*
    You're the God of my salvation;
    how can you reject your servant in anger?
    You've been my only hope,
    so don't forsake me now when I need you!
¹⁰My father and mother abandoned me.
    But you, Yahweh, took me in and made me yours.*ᵇ*
¹¹Now teach me, Yahweh, all about your ways and tell
    me what to do.
    Make it clear for me to understand,
    for I am surrounded by *waiting* enemies.
¹²Don't let them defeat me, Lord.
    You can't let me fall into their clutches!
    They keep accusing me of things I've never done,
    breathing out violence against me.
¹³Yet I believe with all my heart
    that I will see again your goodness, Yahweh, in the
        land of life eternal!
¹⁴Here's what I've learned through it all:
    Don't give up; don't be impatient;
    be entwined as one with the Lord.*ᶜ*
    Be brave and courageous, and never lose hope.
    Yes, keep on waiting—*for he will never disappoint
        you*!

---

a 27:9 The Septuagint is "Don't overlook me."
b 27:10 Every child needs four things: acceptance, focused attention,
    guidance, and protection. All four of these emotional needs are met
    by God (vv. 7–14). See Isa. 40:11; Rom. 8:15–16.
c 27:14 Or "wait upon the Lord." See footnote on Ps. 25:5.

28 My Strength and Shield
David's poetic praise to God

My Defender
¹I'm pleading with you, Yahweh, help me!ᵃ
Don't close your ears to my cry, for you're my
defender.ᵇ
If you continue to remain aloof and refuse to
answer me,
I might as well give up and die.
²Hear my cry for help as I turn toward your mercy
seat,
as I lift my hands toward your sacred sanctuary.
³Don't allow me to be punished along with the
wicked—
these hypocrites who speak sweetly to their
neighbors' faces
while holding evil against them in their hearts.

My Vindication
⁴Go ahead and punish them as they deserve.
Let them be paid back for all their evil plans
in proportion to their wickedness.
⁵Since they don't care anything about you,
or understand the great things you've done,
take them down *like an old building being
demolished*,
never again to be rebuilt.
⁶But Yahweh, may your name be blessed *and built up*!
For you have answered my passionate cry for mercy.

ᵃ 28:1 This psalm was likely written when David was exiled because
of the rebellion of his son Absalom. He was not longing and looking
for his throne but for God's throne (see v. 2).
ᵇ 28:1 Or "my rocky summit."

My Strength

⁷Yahweh is my strength and my wraparound shield.
    When I fully trust in you, help is on the way.
    I jump for joy and burst forth with ecstatic,
        passionate praise!
    I will sing songs of what you mean to me!
⁸You will be the inner strength of all your people,
    Yahweh, the mighty protector of all,
    and the saving strength for all your anointed ones.
⁹Save your people whom you love, and bless your
    chosen ones.
    Be our shepherd leading us forward,
    forever carrying us in your arms!

29 THE GLORY-GOD THUNDERS

King David's poetic praise to God for the last days
The Feast of Tabernacles[a]

¹Proclaim his majesty, all you mighty sons of Yahweh,[b]
    giving all the glory and strength back to him!
²Be in awe before his majesty.
    Be in awe before such power and might!
    Come worship wonderful Yahweh, arrayed in all his
        splendor,
    bowing in worship as he appears in the beauty of
        holiness.

---

a 29 The additional words of the inscription are found in the Septuagint. Ps. 29 is one of the loveliest poems ever written. It is pure and
unrestrained praise. The name Yahweh is found eighteen times in
eleven verses. David was a prophetic seer, and this psalm can properly be interpreted to speak of God's majesty revealed in the last days.

b 29:1 *Mighty sons of Yahweh* in Hebrew is *beni 'elim. 'Elim* is from the
root word *elah*, which is the word for "God," "gods," "mighty warriors," "mighty men," "heroes," "angels," and "heavenly beings," and
could be used to describe anyone who shows any strength or power.

Give him the honor due his name.
Worship him wearing the glory-garments
of your holy, priestly calling!
³⁻⁴The voice of the Lord echoes through the skies and
seas.

The Glory-God reigns as he thunders in the clouds.
So powerful is his voice, so brilliant and bright—
how majestic as he thunders over the great waters!ᵃ
⁵His tympanic thunder topples the strongest of trees.ᵇ
His symphonic sound splinters the mighty forests.
⁶Now he moves Zion'sᶜ mountains by the might of his
voice,

shaking the snowy peaks with his earsplitting sound!
⁷The lightning-fire flashes, striking as he speaks.
⁸God reveals himself when he makes the fault lines quake,
shaking deserts, speaking his voice.
⁹God's mighty voice makes the deer to give birth.ᵈ
His thunderbolt-voice lays the forest bare.
In his temple all fall before him with each one
shouting,
"Glory, glory, the God of glory!"ᵉ
¹⁰Above the furious flood,ᶠ the Enthroned One reigns,
the King-God rules with eternity at his side.

---

a 29:3–4 The sea ("great waters") is a term often used in the Bible to
symbolize the sea of humanity. See Isa. 57:20; Rev. 17:15.

b 29:5 Trees in the Bible are symbols used for men. The strongest of
men are toppled and bowed down when the Glory-God speaks.

c 29:6 Or "Sirion" (Mount Hermon), an ancient term for Mount Zion.
See Ps. 133.

d 29:9 Or "God's mighty voice makes the oaks to whirl."

e 29:9 The Septuagint reads "Those who give him glory he carries to
his house."

f 29:10 The Hebrew word for "flood" is found thirteen times in the Bible
and is always used in connection to man's rebellion and turning away
from God. Thirteen is the biblical number signifying apostasy. Sitting
as King, he rules even over the dark flood of evil to make it end.

¹¹This is the one who gives his strength and might to
   his people.
   This is the Lord giving us his kiss of peace.ᵃ

30 HE HEALED ME
King David's poetic praise to God
A song for the Feast of Dedication of the dwelling
place

¹Lord, I will exalt you and lift you high,
   for you have lifted me up on high!
   Over all my boasting, gloating enemies,
   you made me to triumph.
²O Lord, my healing God,
   I cried out for a miracle and you healed me!
³You brought me back from the brink of death,
   from the depths below.
   Now here I am, alive and well, fully restored!
⁴O sing and make melody, you steadfast lovers of God.
   Give thanks to him every time you reflect on his
      holiness!
⁵I've learned that his anger lasts for a moment,
   but his loving favor lasts a lifetime!ᵇ
   We may weep through the night,
   but at daybreak it will turn into shouts of ecstatic
      joy.

---

a 29:11 In Jewish synagogues this psalm is read on the first day of the
Feast of Pentecost. The Christian church was born on Pentecost two
thousand years ago when the mighty "storm" of the Spirit came into
the upper room. See Acts 2. The last word of this psalm is "peace."
It begins with a storm, but God brings his people peace even in the
midst of storms.

b 30:5 The Septuagint reads "There is wrath in his anger but life in his
will [promise]."

⁶⁻⁷I remember boasting, "I've got it made!
   Nothing can stop me now!
   I'm God's favored one; he's made me steady as a
      mountain!"
   But then suddenly, you hid your face from me.
   I was panic-stricken and became depressed.
⁸Still I cried out to you, Lord God. I shouted out for
   mercy, saying,
⁹"What would you gain in my death,
   if I were to go down to the depths of darkness?
   Will a grave sing your song?
   How could death's dust declare your faithfulness?"
¹⁰So hear me now, Lord; show me your famous
   mercy.
   O God, be my Savior and rescue me!
¹¹Then he broke through and transformed all my
   wailing
   into a whirling dance of ecstatic praise!
   He has torn the veil and lifted from me
   the sad heaviness of mourning.
   He wrapped me in the glory-garments of gladness.
¹²How could I be silent when it's time to praise you?
   Now my heart sings out, bursting with joy—
   a bliss inside that keeps me singing,
   "I can never thank you enough!"

31 How Great Is Your Goodness
For the Pure and Shining One
A song of poetic praise by King David

¹I trust you, Lord, to be my hiding place.
   Don't let me down.
   Don't let my enemies bring me to shame.
   Come and rescue me, for you are the only God
   who always does what is right.

[2]Rescue me quickly when I cry out to you.
   At the sound of my prayer may your ear be turned
      to me.
   Be my strong shelter and hiding place on high.
   Pull me into victory and breakthrough.
[3–4]For you are my high fortress, where I'm kept safe.
   You are to me a stronghold of salvation.
   When you deliver me out of this peril,
   it will bring glory to your name.
   As you guide me forth I'll be kept safe
   from the hidden snares of the enemy—
   the secret traps that lie before me—
   for you have become my rock of strength.
[5]Into your hands I now entrust my spirit.[a]
   O Lord, the God of faithfulness,
   you have rescued and redeemed me.
[6]I despise these deceptive illusions,
   all this pretense and nonsense,
   for I worship only you.
[7]In mercy you have seen my troubles, and you have
      cared for me;
   even during this crisis in my soul I will be radiant
      with joy,
   filled with praise for your love and mercy.
[8]You have kept me from being conquered by my
      enemy;
   you broke open the way to bring me to freedom,[b]
   into a beautiful, broad place.[c]

---

[a] 31:5 This was quoted by Jesus as he was dying on the cross. See Matt. 27:50.

[b] 31:8 This is a picture of the stone rolled away from the tomb of Jesus.

[c] 31:8 This could be the throne room where Jesus ascended after his death.

⁹O Lord, help me again! Keep showing me such mercy.
For I am in anguish, always in tears,
and I'm worn out with weeping.
I'm becoming old because of grief; my health is
broken.
¹⁰I'm exhausted! My life is spent with sorrow,
my years with sighing and sadness.
Because of all these troubles, I have no more strength.
My inner being*a* is so weak and frail.
¹¹My enemies say, "You are nothing!"
Even my friends and neighbors hold me in contempt!
They dread seeing me,
and they look the other way when I pass by.
¹²I am totally forgotten, buried away like a dead man,
discarded like a broken dish thrown in the trash.
¹³I overheard their whispered threats, the slander of
my enemies.
I'm terrified as they plot and scheme to take my life.
¹⁴I'm desperate, Lord! I throw myself upon you,
for you alone are my God!
¹⁵My life, my every moment, my destiny—it's all in
your hands.
So I know you can deliver me
from those who persecute me relentlessly.
¹⁶Smile*b* on me, your servant.
Let your undying love and glorious grace
save me from all this gloom.
¹⁷As I call upon you, let my shame and disgrace
be replaced by your favor once again.
But let shame and disgrace fall instead upon the
wicked—

---

a 31:10 The Hebrew text reads "My bones grow weak." Bones in the
Bible are symbols of our inner being.
b 31:16 Or "Cause your face to shine."

those going to their own doom,
drifting down in silence to the dust of death.
[18]At last their lying lips will be muted in their graves.
For they are arrogant, filled with contempt and
conceit
as they speak against the godly.
[19]Lord, how wonderful you are!
You have stored up so many good things for us,
like a treasure chest heaped up and spilling over
with blessings—
all for those who honor and worship you!
Everybody knows what you can do
for those who turn and hide themselves in you.
[20]So hide all your beloved ones
in the sheltered, secret place before your face.
Overshadow them with your glory-presence.
Keep them from these accusations, the brutal insults
of evil men.
Tuck them safely away in the tabernacle where you
dwell.
[21]The name of the Lord is blessed and lifted high!
For his marvelous miracle of mercy protected me
when I was overwhelmed by my enemies.
[22]I spoke hastily when I said, "The Lord has deserted me."
For in truth, you did hear my prayer and came to
rescue me.
[23]Listen to me, all you godly ones: Love the Lord with
passion!
The Lord protects and preserves all those who are
loyal to him.
But he pays back in full all those who reject him in
their pride.
[24]So cheer up! Take courage, all you who love him.
Wait for him to break through for you, all who trust
in him!

32 FORGIVEN

A poem of insight and instruction by King David[a]

¹What bliss belongs to the one
  whose rebellion has been forgiven,[b]
  those whose sins are covered *by blood*.
²What bliss belongs to those
  who have confessed their corruption[c] to God!
  For he wipes their slates clean
  and removes hypocrisy from their hearts.
³Before I confessed my sins, I kept it all inside;
  my dishonesty devastated my inner life,
  causing my life to be filled with frustration,
  irrepressible anguish, and misery.
⁴The pain never let up, for your hand of conviction
  was heavy on my heart.
  My strength was sapped, my inner life dried up
  like a spiritual drought within my soul.

                                    Pause in his presence

⁵Then I finally admitted to you all my sins,
  refusing to hide them any longer.

---

a 32 David wrote this psalm after he seduced the wife of his most loyal
  soldier, then had him killed to try to keep her pregnancy a secret.
  This sin with Bathsheba brought great disgrace to David, yet he
  found complete forgiveness in God's mercy. The apostle Paul chose
  the first two verses of Ps. 32 to support the important doctrine of salvation by grace through faith. See Rom. 4:5–8. This was Augustine's
  favorite psalm. He had it written on the wall near his bed before he
  died so he could meditate on it.

b 32:1 The Hebrew word for "forgiven" means "lifted off." Sin's guilt
  is a burden that must be lifted off our souls. The Septuagint reads
  "because they have not hidden their sins."

c 32:2 David used three Hebrew words to describe sin in these first
  two verses: "rebellion," "sins" (failures, falling short), and "corruption" (crookedness, the twisting of right standards).

I said, "My life-giving God,
I will openly acknowledge my evil actions."
And you forgave me!
All at once the guilt of my sin washed away
and all my pain disappeared!

Pause in his presence

⁶This is what I've learned through it all:
All believers should confess their sins to God;
do it every time God has uncovered you
in the time of exposing.
For if you do this, when sudden storms of life
overwhelm,
you'll be kept safe.
⁷Lord, you are my secret hiding place,
protecting me from these troubles,
surrounding me with songs of gladness!
Your joyous shouts of rescue release my
breakthrough.

Pause in his presence

⁸⁻⁹I hear the Lord saying, "I will stay close to you,
instructing and guiding you along the pathway for
your life.
I will advise you along the way
and lead you forth with my eyes as your guide.
So don't make it difficult; don't be stubborn
when I take you where you've not been before.
Don't make me tug you and pull you along.
Just come with me!"
¹⁰So my conclusion is this:
Many are the sorrows and frustrations
of those who don't come clean with God.
But when you trust in the Lord for forgiveness,
his wraparound love will surround you.

¹¹So celebrate the goodness of God!
He shows this kindness to everyone who is his.
Go ahead—shout for joy,
all you upright ones who want to please him!

33 A SONG OF PRAISE
Poetic praise by King David^a

¹It's time to sing and shout for joy!
Go ahead, all you redeemed ones, do it!
Praise him with all you have,
for praise looks lovely on the lips of God's devoted
lovers.
²Play the guitar as you lift your praises loaded with
thanksgiving.
Sing and make joyous music with all you've got
inside.
³Compose new melodies^b that release new praises to
the Lord.
Play his praises on instruments
with the anointing and skill he gives you.
Sing and shout with passion; make a spectacular
sound of joy—
⁴For God's Word is something to sing about!
He is true to his promises, his word can be trusted,
and everything he does is reliable and right.
⁵The Lord loves seeing justice on the earth.
Anywhere and everywhere you can find his faithful,
unfailing love!

---

a 33 Most manuscripts have no inscription for this psalm. However, ancient Qumran evidence suggests this is the original inscription that was later omitted.

b 33:3 There are seven new songs mentioned in the Bible. Six are in the Psalms (33:3; 40:3; 96:1; 98:1; 144:9; 149:1) and one is in Isaiah (42:10).

⁶All he had to do was speak by his Spirit-Wind
  command,
    and God created the heavenlies.
    Filled with galaxies and stars,
    the vast cosmos he wonderfully made.
⁷His voice scooped out the seas.
    The ocean depths he poured into vast reservoirs.
⁸With breathtaking wonder,
    let everyone worship Yahweh, this awe-inspiring
      Creator.
⁹He breathed words and worlds were birthed.
    "Let there be," and there it was—
    springing forth the moment he spoke,
    no sooner said than done!
¹⁰With his breath he scatters the schemes of nations who
    oppose him;
    they will never succeed.
¹¹His destiny-plan for the earth stands sure.
    His forever-plan remains in place and will never fail.
¹²Blessed and prosperous is that nation who has God
    as their Lord!
    They will be the people he has chosen for his own.
¹³⁻¹⁵The Lord looks over us from where he rules in
    heaven.
    Gazing into every heart from his lofty dwelling
      place,
    he observes all the peoples of the earth.
    The Creator of our hearts considers and examines
      everything we do.
¹⁶Even if a king had the best-equipped army,
    it would never be enough to save him.
    Even if the best warrior went to battle,
    he could not be saved simply by his strength alone.
¹⁷Human strength and the weapons of man
    are false hopes for victory;

they may seem mighty, but they will always
   disappoint.
[18]The eyes of the Lord are upon
   even the weakest worshipers who love him—
   those who wait in hope and expectation
   for the strong, steady love of God.
[19]God will deliver them from death,
   even the certain death of famine, with no one to
      help.
[20]The Lord alone is our radiant hope
   and we trust in him with all our hearts.
   His wraparound presence will strengthen us.
[21]As we trust, we rejoice with an uncontained joy
   flowing from Yahweh!
[22]Let your love and steadfast kindness overshadow us
   continually,
   for we trust and we wait upon you!

34 GOD'S GOODNESS
*A song by King David composed after his escape
from the king when he pretended to be insane*

[1]Lord! I'm bursting with joy over what you've done for
   me!
   My lips are full of perpetual praise.
[2]I'm boasting of you and all your works,
   so let all who are discouraged take heart.
[3]Join me, everyone! Let's praise the Lord together.
   Let's make him famous!
   Let's make his name glorious to all.
[4]Listen to my testimony: I cried to God in my distress
   and he answered me. He freed me from all my fears!
[5]Gaze upon him, join your life with his, and joy will come.
   Your faces will glisten with glory.
   You'll never wear that shame-face again.

⁶When I had nothing, desperate and defeated,
  I cried out to the Lord and he heard me,
  bringing his miracle-deliverance when I needed it
    most.*ᵃ*
⁷The angel of Yahweh stooped down to listen as I
  prayed,
  encircling me, empowering me, and showing me
    how to escape.
  He will do this for everyone who fears God.
⁸Drink deeply*ᵇ* of the pleasures of this God.
  Experience for yourself the joyous mercies he gives
  to all who turn to hide themselves in him.
⁹Worship in awe and wonder, all you who've been
  made holy!
  For all who fear him will feast with plenty.
¹⁰Even the strong and the wealthy*ᶜ* grow weak and
  hungry,
  but those who passionately pursue the Lord
  will never lack any good thing.
¹¹Come, children of God, and listen to me.
  I'll share the lesson I've learned of fearing the Lord:
¹²⁻¹³Do you want to live a long, good life,
  enjoying the beauty that fills each day?
  Then never speak a lie or allow wicked words
  to come from your mouth.

---

a 34:6 David wrote this psalm at perhaps the lowest point in his life.
  He was alone. He had to part from Jonathan, his dearest friend. He
  was being chased by Saul and his paid assassins. He had run to
  hide in the cave of Adullam (meaning "their prey"). Yet the beautiful
  sounds of praise were heard echoing in his cavern. This is a lesson
  for all of us: we praise our way out of our difficulties into his light.
b 34:8 Many translations read "Taste and see." The Hebrew root word
  for "see" is taken from a word that means "to drink deeply."
c 34:10 Following the ancient versions (Septuagint, Syriac, and Vulgate), this phrase is translated "rich ones." Modern translations read
  "young lions."

[14]Keep turning your back on every sin,
and make "peace" your life motto.
Practice being at peace with everyone.[a]
[15]The Lord sees all we do;
he watches over his friends day and night.
His godly ones receive the answers they seek
whenever they cry out to him.
[16]But the Lord has made up his mind to oppose
evildoers
and to wipe out even the memory of them
from the face of the earth.[b]
[17]Yet when holy lovers of God cry out
to him with all their hearts,
the Lord will hear them and come to rescue them
from all their troubles.
[18]The Lord is close to all whose hearts are crushed by
pain,
and he is always ready to restore the repentant one.
[19]Even when bad things happen to the good and godly
ones,
the Lord will save them and not let them be
defeated
by what they face.
[20]God will be your bodyguard to protect you
when trouble is near.
Not one bone will be broken.

---

a 34:14 Twice in this verse David used the Hebrew word *shalom*. This word means much more than "peace." It means wholeness, wellness, well-being, safe, happy, friendly, favor, completeness, to make peace, peace offering, secure, to prosper, to be victorious, to be content, tranquil, quiet, and restful. So *shalom* is used to describe those of us who have been provided all that is needed to be whole and complete and break off all authority that would attempt to bind us to chaos.

b 34:16 See 1 Peter 3:10–12.

²¹Evil will cause the death of the wicked,
    for they hate and persecute the devoted lovers of
        God.
    Make no mistake about it:
    God will hold them guilty and punish them;
    they will pay the penalty!
²²But the Lord has paid for the freedom of his servants,
    and he will freely pardon those who love him.
    He will declare them free and innocent
    when they turn to hide themselves in him.

35 RESCUE ME
A poetic song by King David[a]

Part One – David, a Warrior
¹O Lord, fight for me! Harass the hecklers; accuse my
    accusers.
    Fight those who fight against me.
²⁻³Put on your armor, Lord; take up your shield and
    protect me.
    Rise up, mighty God! Grab your weapons of war
    and block the way of the wicked who come to fight
        me.
    Stand for me when they stand against me!
    Speak over my soul: "I am your strong Savior!"[b]

---

a 35 This is the first of seven Psalms in which David cried out for vengeance upon his enemies (see Pss. 52; 58; 59; 69; 109; 137).

b 35:2–3 The Aramaic word used here is found thirty-three times in
the Psalms and clearly means "Savior." Although a New Testament
concept, David had a deep understanding almost one thousand
years before the Savior was born that God would become his Savior.
The Hebrew word for "Savior," *Yasha*, is very similar to the name
Jesus, *Yeshua*.

⁴Humiliate those who seek my harm. Defeat them all!
  Frustrate their plans to defeat me and drive them
    back.
  Disgrace them all as they have devised their plans
    to disgrace me.
⁵Blow them away like dust in the wind,
  with the angel of Almighty God driving them back!
⁶Make the road in front of them nothing but slippery
  darkness,
  with the angel of Yahweh behind them, chasing
    them away!
⁷For though I did nothing wrong to them, they set a
  trap for me,
  wanting me to fail and fall.
⁸Surprise them with your ambush, Lord,
  and catch them in the very trap they set for me.
  Let them be the ones to fail and fall into destruction!
⁹Then my fears will dissolve into limitless joy;
  my whole being will overflow with gladness
  because of your mighty deliverance.
¹⁰Everything inside of me will shout it out:
  "There's no one like you, Lord!"
  For look at how you protect the weak and helpless
  from the strong and heartless who oppress them.

Part Two – David, a Witness
  ¹¹They are malicious men, hostile witnesses of wrong.
    They rise up against me, accusers appearing out of
      nowhere.
  ¹²When I show them mercy, they bring me misery.
    I'm forsaken and forlorn, like a motherless child.
  ¹³I even prayed over them when they were sick.
    I was burdened and bowed low with fasting
    and interceded for their healing,
    and I didn't stop praying.

[14]I grieved for them, heavyhearted,
   as though they were my dearest family members
   or my good friends who were sick,
   nearing death, needing prayer.
[15]But when I was the one who tripped up and stumbled,
   they came together to slander me,
   rejoicing in my time of trouble, tearing me to shreds
   with their lies and betrayal.
[16]These nameless ruffians,
   mocking me like godless fools at a feast—
   how they delight in throwing mud on my name.
[17]God, how long can you just stand there doing nothing?
   Now is the time to act.
   Rescue me from these brutal men,
   for I am being torn to shreds by these beasts
   who are out to get me.
   Save me from their rage, their cruel grasp.
[18]Then I will praise you wherever I go.
   And when everyone gathers for worship,
   I will lift up your praise with a shout
   in front of the largest crowd I can find!

Part Three – David, a Worshiper

[19]Don't let those who fight me for no reason be victorious.
   Don't let them succeed, these heartless haters
   who come against me with their gloating sneers.
[20]They are the ones who would never seek peace as
   friends,
   for they are ever devising deceit against the
      innocent ones
   who mind their own business.
[21]They open their mouths with ugly grins,
   gloating with glee over my every fault.
   "Look," they say, "we caught him red-handed!
   We saw him fall with our own eyes!"

²²Yahweh, my caring God, you have been there all
along.
You have seen their hypocrisy.
Yahweh, don't let them get away with this.
Don't walk away without doing something.
²³Now is the time to awake! Rise up, Lord!
Vindicate me, my Lord and my God!
²⁴You have every right to judge me, Lord,
according to your righteousness,
but don't let them rejoice over me when I stumble.
^{25–26}Let them all be ashamed of themselves,
humiliated when they rejoice over my every blunder.
Shame them, Lord, when they say, "We saw what he
did.
Now we have him right where we want him.
Let's get him while he's down!"
Make them look ridiculous when they exalt
themselves over me.
May they all be disgraced and dishonored!
²⁷But let all my true friends shout for joy,
all those who know and love what I do for you.
Let them all say, "The Lord is great,
and he delights in the prosperity of his servant."
²⁸Then I won't be able to hold it in—
everyone will hear my joyous praises all day long!
Your righteousness will be the theme of my glory-
song of praise!

36 THE BLESSING OF THE WISE
A poetic song by King David, the servant of the Lord

¹The rebellion of sin speaks as an oracle of God,
speaking deeply to the conscience of wicked men.^a

---

a 36:1 Or "The heart of the wicked is rebellious to the core."

Yet they are still eager to sin,
   for the fear of God is not before their eyes.
²See how they flatter themselves,
   unable to detect and detest their sins.
   They are crooked and conceited,
   convinced they can get away with anything.
³Their wicked words are nothing but lies.
   Wisdom is far from them.
   Goodness is both forgotten and forsaken.
⁴They lie awake at night to hatch their evil plots,
   always planning their schemes of darkness,
   and never once do they consider the evil of their ways.
⁵But you, O Lord, your mercy-seat love is limitless,
   reaching higher than the highest heavens.
   Your great faithfulness is infinite,
   stretching over the whole earth.
⁶Your righteousness is unmovable,
   just like the mighty mountains.
   Your judgments are as full of wisdom
   as the oceans are full of water.
   Your tender care and kindness leave no one forgotten,
   not a man or even a mouse.
⁷O God, how extravagant is your cherishing love!
   All mankind can find a hiding place
   under the shadow of your wings.
⁸All may drink of the anointing from the abundance*ᵃ* of
   your house.*ᵇ*
   All may drink their fill from the rivers of Eden.*ᶜ*

---

a 36:8 The Hebrew word translated "abundance" is literally "butterfat" or "oil." It is a symbol of the anointing of the Holy Spirit.
b 36:8 Or "They will be satisfied [or watered] in the abundance of your house."
c 36:8 Or "Eden's rivers of pleasure." The garden of Eden had flowing rivers of delight. Eden means "pleasure." The Hebrew word used here is the plural form of Eden.

⁹The fountain of life flows from you*a* *to satisfy me.*
 In your light *of holiness* we receive the light *of
 revelation.*
¹⁰Lord, keep pouring out your unfailing love
 on those who are near you.
 Release more of your blessings to those who are
 loyal to you.
¹¹Don't let these proud boasters trample me down;
 don't let them push me around
 by the sheer strength of their wickedness.
¹²There they lie in the dirt, these evil ones,
 thrown down to the ground, never to arise again!

37 A Song of Wisdom
*Poetic praise by King David*b

¹Don't follow after the wicked ones or be jealous of
 their wealth.
 Don't think for a moment they're better off than you.
²They *and their short-lived success*
 will soon shrivel up and quickly fade away,
 like grass clippings in the hot sun.
³Keep trusting in the Lord and do what is right in his
 eyes.
 Fix your heart on the promises of God, and you will
 dwell in the land,
 feasting on his faithfulness.
⁴Find your delight*c* and true pleasure in Yahweh,
 and he will give you what you desire the most.

---

a 36:9 See Prov. 10:11; 13:14; John 1:4.
b 37 Psalm 37 is an acrostic psalm, in which every other verse begins
 with a successive letter of the Hebrew alphabet.
c 37:4 The word *delight* means "to be soft or tender."

⁵Give*ᵃ* God the right to direct your life,
  and as you trust him along the way,
  you'll find he pulled it off perfectly!
⁶He will appear*ᵇ* as your righteousness,
  as sure as the dawning of a new day.
  He will manifest as your justice,
  as sure and strong as the noonday sun.
⁷Quiet your heart in his presence
  and wait*ᶜ* patiently for Yahweh.
  And don't think for a moment that the wicked, in
    their prosperity,
  are better off than you.
⁸Stay away from anger and revenge.
  Keep envy far from you, for it only leads you into
    lies.
⁹For one day the wicked will be destroyed,
  but those who trust in the Lord
  will inherit the land.
¹⁰Just a little while longer and the ungodly will vanish;
  you will look for them in vain.
¹¹But the humble of heart will inherit every promise*ᵈ*
  and enjoy abundant peace.
¹²Let the wicked keep plotting against the godly
  with all their sneers and arrogant jeers.
¹³God laughs at the wicked and their plans,
  for he knows their day is coming!

---

a 37:5 The Hebrew word used here can be translated "commit," which means "to roll over your burdens on the Lord."

b 37:6 The Hebrew verb found here is also used for giving birth. Perhaps this is a reference to the birth of Christ, our righteousness.

c 37:7 The root word of the word for "wait" can mean "to whirl" or "to be in labor [give birth]." What an unusual concept for waiting on God. We may feel like we're being *whirled* around by our circumstances, but in the end, our season of waiting *gives birth* to greater things.

d 37:11 See Matt. 5:5.

¹⁴Evil ones take aim at the poor and helpless;
  they are ready to slaughter those who do right.
¹⁵But the Lord will turn all their weapons of
  wickedness back on themselves,
    piercing their pride-filled hearts until they are
      helpless.
¹⁶It is much better to have little
  combined with much of God
  than to have the fabulous wealth of the wicked and
    nothing else.
¹⁷For the Lord takes care of all his forgiven ones
  while the strength of evil men will surely slip
    away.
¹⁸Day by day the Lord watches the good deeds of the
  godly,
  and he prepares for them his forever-reward.
¹⁹Even in a time of disaster he will watch over them,
  and they will always have more than enough
  no matter what happens.
²⁰All the enemies of God will perish.
  For the wicked have only a momentary value, a
    fading glory.
  Then one day they vanish! Here today, gone
    tomorrow.
²¹They break their promises, borrowing money
  but never paying it back.
  The good man returns what he owes with some
    extra besides.
²²Yahweh's blessed ones receive the land,
  but the cursed ones will be cut off
  with nothing to show for themselves.
²³When Yahweh delights in how you live your life,
  he establishes your every step.
²⁴If they stumble badly they will still survive,
  for the Lord lifts them up with his hands.

²⁵I was once inexperienced,^{*a*} but now I'm old.
Not once have I found a lover of God forsaken by
him,
nor have any of their children gone hungry.
²⁶Instead, I've found the godly ones
to be the generous ones who give freely to others.
Their children are blessed and become a blessing.
²⁷If you truly want to dwell forever in God's presence,
forsake evil and do what is right in his eyes.
²⁸The Lord loves it when he sees us walking in his
justice.
He will never desert his devoted lovers;
they will be kept forever in his faithful care,
but the descendants of the wicked will be banished.
²⁹The faithful lovers of God will inherit the earth
and enjoy every promise of God's care,
dwelling in peace forever.
³⁰God-lovers make the best counselors.
Their words possess wisdom and are right and
trustworthy.
³¹The ways of God are in their hearts
and they won't swerve from the paths of steadfast
righteousness.
³²Evil ones spy on the godly ones, stalking them
to find something they could use to accuse them.
They're out for the kill!
³³But God will foil all their plots.
The godly will not stand condemned when brought
to trial.
³⁴So don't be impatient for Yahweh to act;
keep moving forward steadily in his ways,

---

a 37:25 Or "immature." The Hebrew word *na'ar* has a homonym that
means "to be driven out," which may be a reference to David being
driven out of Jerusalem by Absalom.

and he will exalt you to possess the land.
You'll watch with your own eyes
and see the wicked lose everything.
35I've already seen this happen.
Once I saw a wicked and violent man
overpower all who were around him,
a domineering tyrant with his prideful and
oppressive ways.
36Then he died and was forgotten.
Now no one cares that he is gone forever.
37But you can tell who are the blameless and
spiritually mature.
What a different story with them!
The godly ones will have a peaceful, prosperous
future
with a happy ending.
38Every evil sinner will be destroyed, obliterated.
They'll be utter failures with no future!
39But the Lord will be the Savior of all who love him.
Even in their time of trouble, God will live in them
as strength.
40Because of their faith in him, their daily portion will
be
a Father's help and deliverance from evil.
This is true for all who turn to hide themselves in
him!

38 A GROAN BEFORE THE THRONE
A poetic lament to remember, by King David[a]

1O Lord, don't punish me angrily for what I've done.
Don't let my sin inflame your wrath against me.

---

a 38 The Septuagint has in the inscription "To be remembered on the
Sabbath."

²For the arrows of your conviction have pierced me
   deeply.
   Your blows have struck my soul and crushed me.
³Now my body is sick.
   My health is totally broken because of your anger,
   and it's all due to my sins!
⁴I'm overwhelmed, swamped, and submerged
   beneath the heavy burden of my guilt.
   It clings to me and won't let me go.
⁵My rotting wounds are a witness against me.
   They are severe and getting worse,
   reminding me of my failure and folly.
⁶I am completely broken because of what I've done.
   Gloom is all around me.
   My sins have bent me over to the ground.
⁷⁻⁸My inner being is shriveled up;
   my self-confidence crushed.
   Sick with fever, I'm left exhausted.
   Now I'm as cold as a corpse, and nothing is left
      inside me
   but great groaning filled with anguish.
⁹Lord, you know all my desires and deepest longings.
   My tears are liquid words, and you can read them all.
¹⁰⁻¹¹My heart beats wildly, my strength is sapped,
   and the light of my eyes is going out.
   My friends stay far away from me, avoiding me like
      the plague.
   Even my family wants nothing to do with me.
¹²Meanwhile my enemies are out to kill me,
   plotting my ruin, speaking of my doom
   as they spend every waking moment
   planning how to finish me off.
¹³⁻¹⁴I'm like a deaf man who no longer hears.
   I can't even speak up, and words fail me;
   I have no argument to counter their threats.

¹⁵Lord, the only thing I can do is wait and put my hope in you.
I wait for your help, my God.
¹⁶So hear my cry and put an end to their strutting in pride,
to those who gloat when I stumble in pain.
¹⁷I'm slipping away and on the verge of a breakdown,
with nothing but sorrow and sighing.ᵃ
¹⁸I confess all my sin to you; I can't hold it in any longer.
My agonizing thoughts punish me for my wrongdoing;
I feel condemned as I consider all I've done.
¹⁹My enemies are many.
They hate me and persecute me,
though I've done nothing against them to deserve it.
²⁰I show goodness to them and get paid evil in return.
And they hate me even more when I stand for what is right.
²¹So don't forsake me now, Lord!
Don't leave me in this condition.
²²God, hurry to help me. Run to my rescue!
For you're my Savior and my only hope!

39 A CRY FOR HELP
For the Pure and Shining One
*A song of praising by King David*ᵇ

¹⁻²Here's my life motto, the truth I live by:
I will guard my ways for all my days.

ᵃ 38:17 The Septuagint reads "I am prepared for all of their whips—prepared to suffer."
ᵇ 39 The Hebrew inscription includes the name Jeduthun, which can be translated "praising."

I will speak only what is right, guarding what I
    speak.
Like a watchman guards against an attack of the
    enemy,
I'll guard and muzzle my mouth
when the wicked are around me.
I will remain silent and will not grumble
or speak out of my disappointment.
But the longer I'm silent, the more my pain grows
    worse!
³⁻⁴My heart burned with a fire within me,
and my thoughts eventually boiled over
until they finally came rolling out of my mouth:
"Lord, help me to know how fleeting my time on
    earth is.
Help me to know how limited is my life
and that I'm only here but for a moment more.
⁵What a brief*ᵃ* time you've given me to live!
Compared to you my lifetime is nothing at all!
Nothing more than a puff of air—I'm gone so
    swiftly.
So too are the grandest of men;
they are nothing but a fleeting shadow!"

Pause in his presence

⁶We live our lives like those living in shadows.*ᵇ*
All our activities and energies are spent for things
    that pass away.
We gather, we hoard, we cling to our things,
only to leave them all behind for who knows who.

---

a 39:5 Interestingly, the Hebrew word for "brief" in this verse is "a
handbreadth," or the span of a man's hand. Our life's duration is
compared to a mere six-inch span!

b 39:6 Or "like phantoms going to and fro."

[7]And now, God,[a] I'm left with one conclusion:
   my only hope is to hope in you alone!
[8]Save me from being overpowered by my sin;
   don't make me a disgrace before the degenerate.
[9]Lord, I'm left speechless and I have no excuse,
   so I'll not complain any longer.
   Now I know you're the one who is behind it all.
[10]But I can't take it much longer.
   Spare me these blows from your discipline-rod.
   For if you are against me, I will waste away to
     nothing.
[11]No one endures when you rebuke and discipline us
   for our sins.
   Like a cobweb is swept away with a wave of the
     hand,
   you sweep away all that we once called dear.
   How fleeting and frail our lives!
   We're nothing more than a puff of air.

Pause in his presence

[12]Lord, listen to all my tender cries.
   Read my every tear, like liquid words that plead for
     your help.
   I feel all alone at times, like a stranger to you,
   passing through this life just like all those before
     me.
[13]Don't let me die without restoring
   joy and gladness to my soul.
   May your frown over my failure
   become a smile over my success.

---

a 39:7 The Aramaic is *Maryah*, the Aramaic form of YHWH or Lord
  Yahweh.

40 A JOYFUL SALVATION
For the Pure and Shining One
A song of poetic praise by King David

¹I waited and waited and waited some more,
   patiently, knowing God would come through for me.
   Then, at last, he bent down and listened to my cry.
²He stooped down to lift me out of danger
   from the desolate pit I was in,
   out of the muddy mess I had fallen into.
   Now he's lifted me up into a firm, secure place
   and steadied me while I walk along his ascending
      path.
³A new song for a new day rises up in me
   every time I think about how he breaks through for
      me!
   Ecstatic praise pours out of my mouth until
   everyone hears how God has set me free.
   Many will see his miracles;
   they'll stand in awe of God and fall in love with
      him!
⁴Blessing after blessing comes to those who love and
   trust the Lord.
   They will not fall away,
   for they refuse to listen to the lies of the proud.
⁵O Lord, our God, no one can compare with you.
   Such wonderful works and miracles are all found
      with you!
   And you think of us all the time
   with your countless expressions of love—
   far exceeding our expectations!
⁶It's not sacrifices that really move your heart.
   Burnt offerings, sin offerings—those aren't what
      bring you joy.
   But when you open my ears and speak to me,

I become your willing servant, your prisoner of love
for life.ᵃ
⁷So I said, "Here I am! I'm coming *to you as a sacrifice,*ᵇ
for in the prophetic scrolls of your book
you have written about me.
⁸I delight to fulfill your will, my God,
for your living words are written upon the pages of
my heart."
⁹I tell everyone everywhere the truth of your
righteousness.
And you know I haven't held back in telling the
message to all.
¹⁰I don't keep it a secret or hide the truth.
I preach of your faithfulness and kindness,
proclaiming your extravagant love to the largest
crowd I can find!
¹¹So Lord, don't hold back your love or withhold
your tender mercies from me.
Keep me in your truth and let your compassion
overflow to me
no matter what I face.
¹²Evil surrounds me; problems greater than I can solve
come one after another.
Without you, I know I can't make it.
My sins are so many!
I'm so ashamed to lift my face to you.
For my guilt grabs me and stings my soul
until I am weakened and spent.

---

a 40:6 The Septuagint is "a body you have prepared for me." The
Hebrew reads "You have pierced my ear." This is a Hebraic reference
to being a bond servant whose ear has been pierced by his master to
signify the servant's desire to serve for life. See Ex. 21:1–6; Isa. 50:5;
Heb. 10:5.

b 40:7 Implied in the context. See Heb. 10:5–7.

[13]Please, Lord! Come quickly and rescue me!
Take pleasure in showing me your favor and restore
me.
[14]Let all who seek my life be humiliated!
Let them be confused and ashamed, God.
Scatter those who wish me evil; they just want me
dead.
[15]Scoff at every scoffer and cause them all to be utter
failures.
Let them be ashamed and horrified by their
complete defeat.
[16]But let all who passionately seek you
erupt with excitement and joy over what you've
done!
Let all your devoted lovers rejoice continually in the
Savior,[a] saying,
"How great and glorious is our God!"
[17]Lord, in my place of weakness and need, I ask again:
Will you come and help me?
I know I'm always in your thoughts.
You are my true Savior and hero,
so don't delay to deliver me now, for you are my
God.

41 I NEED YOU, LORD
*King David's poetic song for the Pure and Shining
One*

[1]God always blesses those who are kind to the poor
and helpless.
They're the first ones God helps
when they find themselves in any trouble.

---

a 40:16 This verse contains the root word for Yeshua in Hebrew.

²The Lord will preserve and protect them.
They'll be honored and esteemed*a*
while their enemies are defeated.
³When they are sick, lying upon their bed of suffering,
God will restore them.
He will raise them up again and restore them back
to health.
⁴So *in my sickness* I say to you,
"Lord, be my kind healer.
Heal my body and soul; heal me, God!
For I have confessed my sins to you."*b*
⁵But those who hate me wish the worst for me, saying,
"When will he die and be forgotten?"
⁶And when these "friends" come to visit me
with their pious sympathy and their hollow words
and with hypocrisy hidden in their hearts,
I can see right through it all.
For they come merely to gather gossip about me,
using all they find to mock me with malicious hearts
of slander.
⁷They are wicked whisperers who imagine the worst
for me,
repeating their rumors, saying,
⁸"He got what he deserved; it's over for him!
The spirit of infirmity*c* is upon him,
and he'll never get over this illness."

---

a 41:2 Or "They will be blessed in the land."
b 41:4 Or "For I have sinned against you."
c 41:8 Or "A thing of Belial" or "An affliction from the abandoned one."

⁹Even my ally, my friend, has turned against me.
    He was one I totally trusted with my life,
    sharing supper with him,ᵃ
    and now he shows me nothing but betrayal and
        treachery.
    He has sold me as an enemy.ᵇ
¹⁰So Lord, please don't desert me when I need you!
    Give me grace and get me back on my feet
    so I can triumph over them all.
¹¹Then I'll know you're pleased with me
    when you allow me to taste victory over all my
        foes.
¹²Now stand up for me and don't let me fall,
    for I've walked with integrity.
    Keep me before your face forever.
¹³Everyone praise the Lord God of Israel, always and
    forever!
    For he is from eternity past
    and will remain for the eternity to come.
    That's the way it will be forever.
    Faithful is our King! Amen!ᶜ

---

a 41:9 In the ancient Near Eastern culture, sharing a meal together
    was a sign of covenant friendship.
b 41:9 The Hebrew literally reads "He lifted up his heel against me."
    This is a powerful figure of speech meaning he was sold as an
    enemy and was treated treacherously. This verse was quoted, in
    part, by Jesus at the Last Supper (see John 13:18 and footnote).
c 41:13 Some scholars believe this last verse was added as a "dox-
    ology of praise," marking the end of the first book of Psalms. The
    word amen could be translated as "Faithful is our King!"

BOOK 2
THE EXODUS PSALMS
Psalms of suffering and redemption

42 A CRY FOR REVIVAL[a]
For the Pure and Shining One
A contemplative poem for instruction by the
prophetic singers of Korah's clan[b]

¹I long to drink of you, O God,
  to drink deeply from the streams of pleasure
  flowing from your presence.
  My longings overwhelm me for more of you![c]
²My soul thirsts, pants, and longs for the living God.
  I want to come and see the face of God.
³Day and night my tears keep falling
  and my heart keeps crying for your help,
  while my enemies mock me over and over, saying,
  "Where is this God of yours? *Why doesn't he help*
    you?"
⁴So I speak over my heartbroken soul,
  "Take courage. Remember when you used to be
  right out front leading the procession of praise
  when the great crowd of worshipers
  gathered to go into the presence of the Lord?

---

a 42 Psalms 42 and 43 were originally composed as one psalm and
later made into two.

b 42 Korah was the great-grandson of Levi. The sons of Korah (translated here as the "prophetic singers of Korah's clan") were Levit-
ical singers. David chose them to preside over the music of the
tabernacle-tent on Mount Zion.

c 42:1 The literal Hebrew is "as the deer pants for the riverbank
[water's edge]." This translation takes the metaphor of a hunted deer
and puts it into terms that transfer the meaning into today's context.
David was describing the passion and longing he had that was yet
unfulfilled.

You shouted with joy as the sound of passionate
  celebration
filled the air and the joyous multitude of lovers
honored the feast of the Lord!"
⁵So then, my soul, why would you be depressed?
  Why would you sink into despair?
  Just keep hoping and waiting on God, your Savior.
  For no matter what, I will still sing with praise,
  for you are my saving grace!
⁶Here I am depressed and downcast.
  Yet I will still remember you as I ponder the place
  where your glory streams down from the mighty
    mountaintops, lofty and majestic—*the mountains
    of your awesome presence.*ᵃ
⁷My deep need calls out to the deep kindness of your
  love.
  Your waterfall of weeping sent waves of sorrow
  over my soul, carrying me away,
  cascading over me like a thundering cataract.
⁸All through the day Yahweh has commanded his
  endless love to pour over me.
  Through the night I sing his songs
  and my praisesᵇ to the living God.
⁹I will say to God, "You are my mountain of strength;
  how could you forget me?
  Why must I suffer this vile oppression of my enemies—
  these heartless tormentors who are out to kill me?"
¹⁰Their wounding words pierce my heart
  over and over while they say,
  "Where is this God of yours?"

---

a 42:6 The Hebrew text contains "Mount Hermon" and "Mount Mizar,"
  considered to be sacred mountains in the Hebrew culture. *Hermon*
  means "lofty and majestic." *Mizar* means "littleness."
b 42:8 Or "my prayer."

[11]So I say to my soul,
"Don't be discouraged. Don't be disturbed.
For I know my God will break through for me."
Then I'll have plenty of reasons to praise him all
over again.
Yes, he is my saving grace!

43 LIGHT AND TRUTH

*For the Pure and Shining One by the prophetic singers
of Korah's clan[a]*
A contemplative poem for instruction

[1]God, clear my name.
Plead my case against the unjust charges
of these ungodly workers of wickedness.
Deliver me from these lying degenerates.
[2]For you are where my strength comes from[b] and my
protector,
so why would you leave me now?
Must I be covered with gloom
while the enemy comes after me, gloating with glee?
[3]Pour into me the brightness of your daybreak!
Pour into me your rays of revelation-truth!
Let them comfort and gently lead me onto the
shining path,
showing the way into your burning presence,
into your many sanctuaries of holiness.
[4]Then I will come closer to your very altar
until I come before you, the God of my ecstatic joy!
I will praise you with the harp that plays in my heart
to you,
my God, my magnificent God!

---

a 43 Originally there was no inscription for this psalm as it was part of
Ps. 42.
b 43:2 Or "God of my strength."

⁵Then I will say to my soul,
"Don't be discouraged; don't be disturbed,
for I fully expect my Savior-God to break through for
me.
Then I'll have plenty of reasons to praise him all
over again."
Yes, he is my saving grace!

44 WAKE UP, LORD, WE'RE IN TROUBLE

*For the Pure and Shining One by the prophetic singers
of Korah's clan
A contemplative poem for instruction*

The Past

¹⁻²God, we've heard about all the glorious miracles
you've done for our ancestors in days gone by.
They told us about the ancient times, how by your
power
you drove out the ungodly nations from this
land,
crushing all their strongholds and giving the land to
us.
Now the people of Israel cover the land
from one end to the other,
all because of your grace and power!
³Our forefathers didn't take the land by their own
strength
or their own skill or strategy.
But it was through the shining forth of your radiant
presence
and the display of your mighty power.
You loved to give them victory,
for you took great delight in them.
⁴You are my God, my King!
It's now time to decree majesties for Jacob!

⁵Through your glorious name and your awesome
power,
 we can push through to any victory and defeat
 every enemy.
⁶For I will not trust in the weapons of the world;ᵃ
 I know they will never save me.
⁷Only you will be our Savior from all our enemies.
 All those who hate us you have brought to shame.
⁸So now I constantly boast in you.
 I can never thank you enough!

Pause in his presence

The Present

⁹But you have turned your back on us; you walked off
and left us!
 You've rejected us, tossing us aside in humiliating
 shame.
 You don't go before us anymore in our battles.
¹⁰We retreat before our enemies in defeat,
 for you are no longer helping us.
 Those who hate us have invaded our land
 and plundered our people.
¹¹You have treated us like sheep in the slaughter pen,
 ready to be butchered.
 You've scattered us to the four winds.
¹²You have sold us as slaves for nothing!
 You have counted us, your precious ones, as
 worthless.
¹³You have caused our neighbors to despise and
 scorn us.
 All those around us mock and curse us.
¹⁴You have made us the butt of their jokes.
 Disliked by all, we are the laughingstock of the people.

---

a 44:6 Or "bow and sword."

15-16There's no escape from this constant curse, this
humiliation!
We are despised, jeered, overwhelmed by shame,
and overcome at every turn
by our hateful and heartless enemies.
17Despite all of this, we have not forgotten you;
we have not broken covenant with you.
18We have not betrayed you; our hearts are still yours.
Our steps have not strayed from your path.
19Yet you have crushed us,
leaving us in this wilderness place *of misery and
desperation.*^a
With nowhere else to turn,
death's dark door seems to be the only way out.
20-21If we had forsaken your holy name, wouldn't you
know it?
You'd be right in leaving us.
If we had worshiped before other gods,
no one would blame you for punishing us.
God, you know our every heart-secret.
You know we still want you!
22Because of you we face death threats every day.
Like martyrs we are dying daily.
We are seen as lambs lined up to be slaughtered as
sacrifices.

The Future
23So wake up, Lord God!
Why would you sleep when we're in trouble?
Are you forsaking us forever?
24You can't hide your face any longer from us!
How could you forget our agonizing sorrow?

---

a 44:19 Or "in this place of jackals."

²⁵Now we lay facedown, sinking into the dust of death,
the quicksand of the grave.
²⁶Arise, awake, and come to help us, O Lord.
Let your unfailing love save us from this sorrow!

45 THE WEDDING SONG

*For the Pure and Shining One by the prophetic
singers of Korah's clan
A contemplative song of instruction for the Loved One
To the melody of "Lilies"ᵃ*

¹My heart is on fire, boiling over with passion.
Bubbling up within me are these beautiful lyrics
as a lovely poem to be sung for the King.
Like a river bursting its banks, I'm overflowing with
words,
spilling out into this sacred story.ᵇ

His Royal Majesty
²Beautiful! Beautiful! Beyond the sons of men!ᶜ
Elegant grace pours out through every word you
speak.ᵈ
Truly God has anointed you, his favored one, for
eternity!
³Now strap your lightning-sword of judgment upon
your side,

ᵃ 45 Lilies in the Bible are metaphors of God's precious people. See
Song. 2:1–2; Hos. 14:5; Luke 12:27–28. Many believe this was the
wedding song composed for Solomon as he married the princess
of Egypt. But the language is so lofty and glorious that we see One
greater than Solomon in its verses. This is a song of the wedding of
Jesus and his bride, the church.

ᵇ 45:1 The Hebrew is literally "My tongue is the pen of a skillful
[inspired] scribe."

ᶜ 45:2 Or "You are the most wonderful and winsome of all men."

ᵈ 45:2 See John 6:68; 7:46.

O mighty warrior, so majestic!
You are full of beauty and splendor as you go out to
  war!
⁴In your glory and grandeur go forth in victory!
Through your faithfulness and meekness
the cause of truth and justice will stand.
Awe-inspiring miracles are accomplished by your
  power,
leaving everyone dazed and astonished!
⁵Your wounding leaves men's hearts defeated
as they fall before you broken.
⁶Your glory-kingdom, O God, endures forever,
for you are enthroned to rule with a justice-scepter
  in your hand!
⁷You are passionate for righteousness, and you hate
  lawlessness.
This is why God, your God,
crowns you with bliss above your fellow kings.
He has anointed you, more than any other,
with his oil of fervent joy,
the very fragrance of heaven's gladness.
⁸Your royal robes release the scent of suffering love[a]
for your bride;
the odor of aromatic incense[b] is upon you.
From the pure and shining place,[c] lovely music
that makes you glad is played for your pleasure.

---

a 45:8 The Hebrew word *myrrh* is taken from a root word that means
"suffering." Jewish rabbis refer to myrrh as "tears from a tree," a
symbol of suffering love.

b 45:8 The Hebrew text reads "aloes and cassia." Both are equated
with the anointing spice, the incense burned in the Holy Place.

c 45:8 Or "from the ivory palaces." This is an obvious reference to the
Holy Place, as our High Priest comes from the chamber of glory to
be with us. The word *ivory* is taken from a Hebrew word for "white
and glistening."

Her Royal Majesty

[9]The daughters of kings, women of honor,
are maidens in your courts.
And standing beside you,
glistening in your pure and golden glory,
is the beautiful bride-to-be![a]

[10]Now listen, daughter, pay attention, and forget about
your past.
Put behind you every attachment to the familiar,
even those who once were close to you!

[11]For your royal Bridegroom is ravished by your
beautiful brightness.
Bow in reverence before him, for he is your Lord!

[12]Wedding presents pour in from those of great
wealth.[b]
The royal friends of the Bridegroom shower you
with gifts.

[13]As the princess-bride enters the palace,
how glorious she appears within the holy chamber,
robed with a wedding dress embroidered with pure
gold!

[14]Lovely and stunning, she leads the procession with
all her bridesmaids[c]
as they come before you, her Bridegroom-King.

[15]What a grand, majestic entrance!
A joyful, glad procession as they enter the palace
gates!

[16]Your many sons will one day be kings, just like their
Father.
They will sit on royal thrones all around the world.

---

a 45:9 Or "queen."

b 45:12 The Hebrew text is literally "the daughter of Tyre." This was
symbolic of the merchants of the earth, those possessing great
wealth.

c 45:14 Or "virgins." (See Rev. 14:1–4; cf. 2 Cor. 11:2.)

¹⁷I will make sure the fame of your name
  is honored in every generation, as all the people
    praise you,
  giving you thanks forever and ever!

46 GOD ON OUR SIDE

*For the Pure and Shining One by the prophetic singers
of Korah's clan
A poetic song to the melody of "Hidden Things"ᵃ*

¹God, you're such a safe and powerful place to find
    refuge!
  You're a proven help in time of trouble—
  more than enough and always available whenever I
    need you.
²So we will never fear
  even if every structure of supportᵇ were to crumble
    away.
  We will not fear even when the earth quakes and
    shakes,
  moving mountains and casting them into the sea.
³For the raging roar of stormy winds and crashing
  waves
  cannot erode our faith in you.
                              Pause in his presence

⁴God has a constantly flowing river whose sparkling
    streams
  bring joy and delight to his people.

---

a 46 As translated in the Septuagint. Other versions read "for the
  maidens." Ps. 46 is known as one of the Songs of Zion. The others
  are Pss. 48; 76; 84; 87; 122. These are psalms that praise Jerusalem
  as God's dwelling place.
b 46:2 Or "earth itself."

His river flows right through the city of God Most
  High,
into his holy dwelling places.*
⁵God is in the midst of his city,* secure and never
  shaken.
At daybreak his help will be seen with the appearing
  of the dawn.
⁶When the nations are in uproar with their tottering
  kingdoms,
God simply raises his voice,
and the earth begins to disintegrate before him.
⁷*Here he comes*!
  The Commander!
  The mighty Lord of Angel Armies is on our side!
  The God of Jacob fights for us!

                              Pause in his presence

⁸⁻⁹Everyone look!
  Come and see the breathtaking wonders of our God.
  For he brings *both* ruin *and revival.*
  He's the one who makes conflicts end
  throughout the earth,
  breaking and burning every weapon of war.
¹⁰Surrender your anxiety.*
  Be still and realize that I am God.
  I am God above all the nations,
  and I am exalted throughout the whole earth.
¹¹Here he stands!
  The Commander!

---

a 46:4 The plural "dwelling places" points to believers today. Each
  believer is now the holy dwelling place of God. God's river flows into
  us and through us.
b 46:5 This is a reference to Jerusalem, but today God calls his church
  a "city" on a hill.
c 46:10 Or "Let go!" The Septuagint reads "relax."

The mighty Lord of Angel Armies is on our side!
The God of Jacob fights for us!

Pause in his presence

47 THE KING OVER ALL THE EARTH

*For the Pure and Shining One by the prophetic singers
of Korah's clan
A poetic song*

¹Go ahead and celebrate!
    Come on and clap your hands, everyone!
    Shout to God with the raucous sounds of joy!
²The Lord God Most High is astonishing, awesome
    beyond words!
    He's the formidable and powerful King over all the
        earth.
³He's the one who conquered the nations before us
    and placed them all under our feet.
⁴He's marked out our inheritance ahead of time,
    putting us in the front of the line, honoring Jacob,
        the one he loves.ᵃ

Pause in his presence

⁵God arises with the earsplitting shout of his people!
    God goes up with a trumpet blast!
⁶Sing and celebrate! Sing some more, celebrate some
    more!
    Sing your highest song of praise to our King!
⁷For God is the triumphant King; all the powers of the
    earth are his.
    So sing your celebration songs of highest praise
    to the glorious Enlightened One!

---

a 47:4 Or "the pride of Jacob." The Septuagint reads "the beauty of
Jacob."

[8]Our God reigns over every nation.
  He reigns on his holy throne over all.
[9]All the nobles and princes,
    the loving servants of the God of Abraham,
    they all gather to worship.
    Every warrior's shield is now lowered
    as surrendered trophies before this King.
    He has taken his throne, high and lofty, exalted over
      all!

48 BEAUTIFUL ZION
A poetic song by the prophetic singers of Korah's clan

[1]There are so many reasons to describe God as
    wonderful!
    So many reasons to praise him with unlimited
      praise![a]
[2]Zion-City is his home; he lives on his holy mountain—
    high and glorious, joy-filled and favored.
    Zion-Mountain looms in the farthest reaches of the
      north,[b]
    the city of our incomparable King!
[3]This is his divine abode, an impenetrable citadel,
    for he is known to dwell in the highest place.
[4-6]See how the mighty kings united to come against
    Zion,
    yet when they saw God manifest in front of their
      eyes,
    they were stunned.

---

a 48:1 This psalm was written to commemorate the defeat of the
Assyrian army in the days of King Hezekiah.

b 48:2 Or "the sides of the north," a metaphor to describe God's heavenly home. See Isa. 14:13.

Trembling, they all fled away, gripped with fear.*a*
Seized with panic, they doubled up in frightful
   anguish,
like a woman in the labor pains of childbirth.
⁷Like a hurricane blowing and breaking the invading
   ships,*b*
God blows upon them and breaks them to pieces.
⁸We have heard about these wonders,
   and then we saw them with our own eyes.
   For this is the city of the Commander of Angel
     Armies,
   the city of our God, safe and secure forever!

Pause in his presence

⁹Lord, as we worship you in your temple,
   we recall over and over your kindness to us
   and your unending love.
¹⁰The fame of your name echoes throughout the entire
   world,
   accompanied with praises.
   Your right hand is full of victory.
¹¹So let the people of Zion rejoice with gladness;
   let the daughters of praise*c* leap for joy!
   For God will see to it that you are judged fairly.
¹²⁻¹³Circle Zion; count her towers.
   Consider her walls, climb her palaces,
   and then go and tell the coming generation
   of the care and compassion of our God.
¹⁴Yes, this is our God, our great God forever.
   He will lead us onward until the end,

---

a 48:4–6 This no doubt refers to the night the angel of the Lord
descended into the ranks of the Assyrians and killed 185,000 men.
See Isa. 37:36.
b 48:7 Or "ships of Tarshish."
c 48:11 Or "the daughters of Judah."

through all time, beyond death,
and into eternity!

49 WISDOM BETTER THAN WEALTH
For the Pure and Shining One
A poetic song by the prophetic singers of Korah's
clan

¹⁻²Listen, one and all!
Both rich and poor together, all over the world—
everyone listen to what I have to say!
³For wisdom will come from my mouth;
words of insight and understanding will be heard
from the musings of my heart.
⁴I will break open mysteries with my music,
and my song will release riddles solved.
⁵There's no reason to fear when troubling times come,
even when you're surrounded with problems
and persecutors who chase at your heels.*ᵃ*
⁶⁻⁷They trust in their treasures and boast in their riches,
yet not one of them, though rich as a king,
could rescue his own brother from the guilt of his
sins.
No one could give God the ransom price
for the soul of another, let alone for himself.
⁸⁻⁹A soul's redemption is too costly and precious
for anyone to pay with earthly wealth.
The price to pay is never enough
to purchase eternal life for even one, to keep them
out of hell.
¹⁰⁻¹¹The brightest and best, along with the foolish and
senseless,

---

a 49:5 This phrase contains a variant form of the name Jacob, which
means "heel grabber."

God sees that they all will die one day,
leaving their houses and wealth to others.
Even though they name streets and lands after
themselves,*
hoping to have their memory endure beyond the
grave,
becoming legends in their own minds,
their home address is now the cemetery!
¹²The honor of man is short-lived and fleeting.
There's little difference between man and beast,
for both will one day perish.
¹³Such is the path of foolish men
and those who quote everything they say,
for they are here today and gone tomorrow!
Pause in his presence

¹⁴A shepherd called "Death" herds them,
leading them straight to hell like mindless sheep.
Yet at daybreak you will find the righteous ruling in
their place.
Every trace of them will be gone forever,
with all their "glory" lost in the darkness of their
doom.
¹⁵But I know the loving God will redeem my soul,
raising me up from the dark power of death,
taking me as his bridal partner.*
Pause in his presence

¹⁶So don't be disturbed when you see the rich
surround you with the "glory" of their wealth on full
display.

---

a 49:10–11 Or "They read their names in the ground."
b 49:15 Or "he will offer his hand to me in marriage."

¹⁷For when they die, they will carry nothing with them,
and their riches will not follow them beyond the
grave.
^{18–19}Though they have the greatest rewards of this
world
and all applaud them for their accomplishments,
they will follow those who have gone before them
and go straight into the realm of darkness,
where they will never ever see the light again.
²⁰So this is the way of mortal man—
honored for a moment, yet without eternal insight,
like a beast that will one day perish.

50 GOD HAS SPOKEN
A poetic song of Asaph, the gatherer[a]

¹The God of gods, the mighty Lord himself, has
spoken!
He shouts out over all the people of the earth
in every brilliant sunrise and every beautiful
sunset,
saying, "Listen to me!"
²God's glory-light shines out of the Zion-realm[b]
with the radiance of perfect beauty.
³With the rumble of thunder he approaches;
he will not be silent, for he comes with an
earsplitting sound!
All around him are furious flames of fire,
and preceding him is the dazzling blaze of his glory.

---

a 50 Asaph's name means "gatherer" or "fulfilled prophecy." Like
David, Asaph was anointed with the spirit of prophecy and wrote
twelve psalms (Pss. 50; 73–83).
b 50:2 The Aramaic text can be translated "Out of Zion God has shown
a glorious crown."

[4]Here he comes to judge his people!
   He summons his court with heaven and earth as his
      jury, saying,
[5]"Gather all my devoted lovers,
   my godly ones whose hearts are one with me—
   those who have entered into my holy covenant
   by sacrifices upon the altar."
[6]And the heavens declare his justice:
   "God himself will be their judge,
   and he will judge them with righteousness!"
                              Pause in his presence

[7]"Listen to me, O my people! Listen well, for I am your
   God!
   I am bringing you to trial, and here are my charges.[a]
[8]I do not rebuke you for your sacrifices,
   which you continually bring to my altar.
[9]Do I need your young bulls or goats from your fields
   as if I were hungry?
[10-11]Every animal of field and forest belongs to me, the
   Creator.
   I know every movement of the birds in the sky,
   and every animal of the field is in my thoughts.
   The entire world and everything it contains is
      mine.
[12-13]If I were hungry, do you think I would tell you?
   For all that I have created, the fullness of the earth,
      is mine.
   Am I fed by your sacrifices? Of course not!
[14]Why don't you bring me the sacrifices I desire?
   Bring me your true and sincere thanks,

---

a 50:7 This summons to judgment is not against the heathen nations
   but against God's people. See 1 Peter 4:17.

and show your gratitude by keeping your promises
   to me,
the Most High.
¹⁵Honor me by trusting in me in your day of trouble.
   Cry aloud to me, and I will be there to rescue you.
¹⁶And now I speak to the wicked. Listen to what I have
   to say to you!
   What right do you have to presume to speak for me
   and claim my covenant promises as yours?
¹⁷For you have hated my instruction and disregarded
   my words,
   throwing them away as worthless!
¹⁸You forget to condemn the thief or adulterer.
   You are their friend, running alongside them into
      darkness.
^{19–20}The sins of your mouth multiply evil.
   You have a lifestyle of lies;
   you are devoted to deceit as you speak against
      others,
   even slandering those of your own household!
²¹All this you have done and I kept silent,
   so you thought that I was just like you, sanctioning
      evil.
   But now I will bring you to my courtroom
   and spell out clearly my charges before you.
²²This is your last chance, my final warning. Your time
   is up!
   Turn away from all this evil, or *the next time you
      hear from me*
   will be when I am coming to pass judgment upon you.
   I will snatch you away, and no one will be there
   to help you escape my judgment.
²³The life that pleases me is a life lived in the gratitude
   of grace,
   always choosing to walk with me in what is right.

This is the sacrifice I desire from you.
If you do this, more of my salvation will unfold for
you."

51 PARDON AND PURITY
For the Pure and Shining One
A prayer of confession when the prophet Nathan
exposed King David's adultery with Bathsheba[a]

David's Confession
[1-2]God, give me mercy from your fountain of
forgiveness!
I know your abundant love is enough to wash away
my guilt.
Because your compassion is so great,
take away this shameful guilt of sin.
Forgive the full extent of my rebellious ways,
and erase this deep stain on my conscience.[b]
[3-4]For I'm so ashamed.
I feel such pain and anguish within me.
I can't get away from the sting of my sin against
you, Lord!
Everything I did, I did right in front of you, for you
saw it all.
Against you, and you above all, have I sinned.
Everything you say to me is infallibly true

---

a 51 This psalm is based on the incident that is recorded in 2 Sam.
12–13. This is a psalm of confession that has been sung for ages.
Imagine composing a song about your failure and making it public for all time. David was not so much concerned about what the
people thought but about what God thought. He wanted to be clean
before God.

b 51:1–2 Or "wash me." David used the Hebrew word *kabas*, which
was used for washing clothes, not for bathing. David was asking
for his royal robes to be cleansed from the stains of his actions and
publicly restored.

and your judgment conquers me.
[5]Lord, I have been a sinner from birth,
from the moment my mother conceived me.
[6]I know that you delight to set your truth deep in my
spirit.[a]
So come into the hidden places of my heart
and teach me wisdom.

David's Cleansing

[7]Purify my conscience! Make this leper clean again![b]
Wash me in your love until I am pure in heart.[c]
[8]Satisfy me in your sweetness, and my song of joy will
return.
The places you have crushed within me
will rejoice in your healing touch.[d]
[9]Hide my sins from your face;[e]
erase all my guilt by your saving grace.
[10]Keep creating in me a clean heart.[f]

---

a 51:6 The Hebrew word *bat-ṭuchâh*, although difficult to translate, can mean "something that is covered over, hidden, or concealed." This could be paraphrased as "you desire light in my darkness" or "you want truth to expose my secrets."

b 51:7 The Hebrew text contains the word *hyssop*. This was a bushy plant used for sprinkling blood on a healed leper to ceremonially cleanse him for the worship of God. See Lev. 14:3–7; Num. 19.

c 51:7 Or "Wash me with the snow from above so I can be whitened."

d 51:8 In this beautiful verse, the broken places ("places you have crushed") are literally "broken bones." Our bones speak allegorically of our inner being, our emotional strength.

e 51:9 David was ashamed not just of what others would think but also that he had been seen by God. A truly remorseful person has no thought for reputation but only for righteousness.

f 51:10 The word used for "create" takes us back to Gen. 1, and it means to create from nothing. David knew he had no goodness without God placing it within him. David wanted a new creation heart, not just the old one changed.

Fill me with pure thoughts and holy desires, ready
    to please you.[a]
[11]May you never reject me!
    May you never take from me your sacred Spirit!

David's Consecration
[12]Let my passion for life be restored,
    tasting joy[b] in every breakthrough you bring to me.
    Hold me close to you with a willing spirit
    that obeys whatever you say.
[13]Then I can show other guilty ones
    how loving and merciful you are.
    They will find their way back home to you,
    knowing that you will forgive them.
[14]O God, my saving God,
    deliver me fully from every sin,
    even the sin that brought bloodguilt.[c]
    Then my heart will once again be thrilled to sing
    the passionate songs of joy and deliverance!
[15]Lord God, unlock my heart, unlock my lips,
    and I will overcome with my joyous praise!
[16]For the source of your pleasure is not in my
    performance
    or the sacrifices I might offer to you.
[17]The fountain of your pleasure is found
    in the sacrifice of my shattered heart before you.
    You will not despise my tenderness
    as I bow down humbly at your feet.

---

a 51:10 Or "Renew a reliable spirit in my inner being."
b 51:12 The Hebrew word for "joy" comes from two Hebrew roots: one means "bright" and the other means "lily [whiteness]." David wanted to taste a joy that was bright, pure, and as beautiful as a lily.
c 51:14 Or simply "blood." David could have been asking God to spare his life from death (that is, deliverance from death because of his sin).

¹⁸Because you favor Zion, do what is good for her.
Be the protecting wall around Jerusalem.
¹⁹And when we are fully restored,
you will rejoice and take delight
in every offering of our lives
as we bring our sacrifices of righteousness before
you in love!^a

52 THE FATE OF CYNICS

For the Pure and Shining One
A song of instruction by King David composed when
Doeg the Edomite betrayed David to Saul, saying,
"David has come to the house of Ahimilech!"^b

¹You call yourself a mighty man, a big shot?
Why do you boast in the evil you have done?
Yet God's loyal love will protect me and carry the
day!
²Listen, O deceiver, trickster of others:
Your words are wicked, harming and hurting all
who hear them.
³You love evil and hate what is good and right.
You would rather lie than tell the truth.

Pause in his presence

---

a 51:19 Or "then they will offer up bulls on your altar."
b 52 For this episode in David's life, see 1 Sam. 21:1–9; 22:9–23. The Edomites, although close relatives to the Hebrews, were bitter enemies to God's people. In spite of Doeg's lineage, he became a high-ranking official in Saul's kingdom. Herod the Great, who slaughtered the babies of Bethlehem, was an Edomite. At the time David wrote this psalm, Saul had already attempted to kill him sixteen times. Ahimilech, the caretaker of the sword of Goliath, was a descendant of Eli.

⁴You love to distort, devour, and deceive,
   using your sly tongue to spin the truth.
⁵But the Almighty will strike you down forever!
   He will pull you up by your roots
   and drag you away to the darkness of death.
                              Pause in his presence

⁶The godly will see all this and will be awestruck.
   Then they will laugh at the wicked, saying,
⁷"See what happens to those great in their own eyes
   who don't trust in the Most High to save them!
   Look how they trusted only in their wealth
   and made their living from wickedness."*a*
⁸But I am like a flourishing olive tree, *anointed* in the
   house of God.*b*
   I trust in the unending love of God;
   his passion toward me is forever and ever.
⁹Because it is finished,*c*
   I will praise you forever and give you thanks.
   Before all your godly lovers I will proclaim your
      beautiful name!

---

a 52:7 Or "and [was] strong in [his] destruction."
b 52:8 The olive tree was the source of the sacred anointing oil.
c 52:9 Or "You have acted [finished it]." The words "It is finished" were
   the last words of Jesus on the cross.

53 THE WICKEDNESS OF THE WORLD

For the Pure and Shining One
A contemplative song of instruction To the tune of
"The Dancings of Mourning"[a]

¹Only the withering soul[b] would say to himself,
　"There's no God for me!"
　Anyone who thinks like that is corrupt and callous;
　depraved and detestable, they are devoid of what is
　　good.
²The Lord looks down in love, bending over heaven's
　balcony.
　God looks over all of Adam's sons and daughters,
　looking to see if there are any who are wise with
　　insight—
　any who search for him, wanting to please him.
³But no, all have wandered astray, walking stubbornly
　toward evil.
　Not one is good; he can't even find one!
⁴Look how they live in luxury while exploiting my
　people.
　Won't these workers of wickedness ever learn!

---

a 53 Or "The Dance of Mourning." This could have been a footnote
to Ps. 52 instead of an inscription for Ps. 53. If so, read Ps. 52 and
imagine the dancing that broke loose when David and his mighty
men knew that Doeg had been judged by God for his murderous
betrayal.

b 53:1 The word often translated as "fool" comes from a Hebrew word
meaning "withering." If we make no room for God, we have withered hearts (or souls), our moral sense of righteousness is put to
sleep, and the noble aspirations of the heart shrivel up and die. Ps.
53 clearly speaks of the downfall of those who oppose Israel. Ps. 14
and Ps. 53 are very similar psalms. Ps. 14 deals with God's verdict,
while Ps. 53 speaks of God's vengeance. If God says it once, it is to
believed. If he says it twice, it demands our utmost attention!

They never even think of praying to God.
⁵Soon, unheard-of terror will seize them while in their
   sins.
   God himself will one day scatter the bones
   of those who rose up against you.*ª*
   Doomed and rejected, they will be put to shame,
   for God has despised them.
⁶Oh, I wish our time of rescue were already here.
   Oh, that God would come forth now*ᵇ*—
   arising from the midst of his Zion-people
   to save and restore his very own.
   When God fully restores his people,
   Jacob will rejoice, and Israel will be filled with
      gladness!

54 DEFEND ME

For the Pure and Shining One
David's contemplative song of instruction
*A song of derision*ᶜ *when the Ziphites betrayed David*
to Saul, saying, "David is hiding among us; come
and get him!"

¹God, deliver me by your mighty name!
   Come with your glorious power and save me!
²Listen to my prayer; turn your ears to my cry!

---

a 53:5 This could refer to the scattering of the armies of Sennacherib
   in the days of Hezekiah. See 2 Kings 18–19.
b 53:6 This is considered to be an ecphonesis, a rhetorical literary
   device that amplifies the emotion of the text. It is equivalent to an
   emotional outburst. Clearly, this is a passionate psalm.
c 54 The Hebrew word used here and translated in some versions as
   "stringed instrument" can also be rendered "a song of mocking."
   This is a psalm for anyone who feels betrayed, rejected, and stuck in
   a difficult situation with no one at his or her side.

³These violent men have risen up against me;
>   heartless, ruthless men*ᵃ* who care nothing about God
>   seek to take my life.

Pause in his presence

⁴But the Lord God has become my divine helper.
>   He leans into my heart and lays his hands upon*ᵇ* me!
⁵God will see to it that those who sow evil will reap evil.
>   So Lord, in your great faithfulness, destroy them
>   once and for all!
⁶Lord, I will offer myself freely, and everything I am I
>   give to you.
>   I will worship and praise your name, O Lord,
>   for it is precious to me.
⁷Through you I'm saved—rescued from every trouble.
>   I've seen with my eyes the defeat of my enemies.
>   I've triumphed over them all!

55 BETRAYED

To the Pure and Shining One
King David's song of derision for instruction

¹God, listen to my prayer!
>   Don't hide your heart from me when I cry out to you!
²⁻³Come close to me and give me your answer.
>   Here I am, moaning and restless.
>   I'm preoccupied with the threats of my enemies
>   and crushed by the pressure of their opposition.
>   They surround me with trouble and terror.
>   In their fury they rise up against me in an angry
>   uproar.

---

a 54:3 Or "foreigners."

b 54:4 The word used here can be translated "uphold" or "sustain." It comes from a root word that means "to lean upon" or "to lay hands upon." This translation includes both concepts in this verse.

⁴My heart is trembling inside my chest
  as the terror of death seizes me.
⁵Fear and dread overwhelm me. I shudder before the
  horror I face.
⁶I say to myself, "If only I could fly away from all of
  this!
  If only I could run away to the place of rest and
    peace.
⁷I would run far away where no one could find me,
  escaping to a wilderness retreat."

Pause in his presence

⁸I will hurry off to hide in the higher place,
  into my shelter, safe from this raging storm and
    tempest.
⁹God, confuse them until they quarrel with themselves.
  Destroy them with their own violent strife and
    slander.
  They have divided the city with their discord.
¹⁰Though they patrol the walls night and day against
  invaders,
  the real danger is within the city—
  the misery and strife in the hearts of its people.
¹¹Murder is in their midst.
  Wherever you turn, you find trouble and ruin.
¹²It wasn't an enemy who taunted me.
  If it was my enemy, filled with pride and hatred,
  then I could have endured it. I would have just run
    away.
¹³But it was you, my intimate friend—one like a brother
  to me.
  It was you, my adviser,ᵃ the companion

---

a 55:13 The Greek word in the Septuagint can be translated as "a seer
[prophet]."

I walked with and worked with!

[14]We once had sweet fellowship with each other.
We worshiped in unity as one,
celebrating together with God's people.[a]

[15]Now desolation and darkness has come upon you.
May you and all those like you descend into the pit
of destruction!
Since evil has been your home, may evil now bury
you alive!

[16]But as for me, I will call upon the Lord to save me,
and I know he will!

[17]Every evening I will explain my need to him.
Every morning I will move my soul toward him.
Every waking hour I will worship only him,
and he will hear and respond to my cry.

[18]Though many wish to fight and the tide of battle
turns against me,
by your power I will be safe and secure;
peace will be my portion.

[19]God himself will hear me!
God-Enthroned through everlasting ages,
the God of unchanging faithfulness—
he will put them in their place,
all those who refuse to love and revere him!

Pause in his presence

[20]I was betrayed by my friend, though I lived in peace
with him.
While he was stretching out his hand of friendship,
he was secretly breaking every promise he had ever
made to me!

---

a 55:14 David was speaking of Ahithophel, who had once been his
friend and adviser, only to betray him. This is foreshadowing of
what would happen between Jesus and Judas.

²¹His words were smooth and charming.
   Yet his heart was disloyal and full of hatred—
   his words soft as silk while all the time scheming my
      demise.
²²So here's what I've learned through it all:
   Leave all your cares and anxieties at the feet of the
      Lord,
   and measureless grace will strengthen you.
²³He will watch over his devoted lovers,
   never letting them slip or be overthrown.
   He will send all my enemies to the pit of destruction.
   Murderers, liars, and betrayers will face an untimely
      death.
   My life's hope and trust is in you, and you'll never
      fail to rescue me!

56 TRUSTING IN GOD

For the Pure and Shining One
King David's golden song of instruction composed
when the Philistines captured him in Gath To the
tune of "The Oppression of the Princes to Come"ᵃ

¹Lord, show me your kindness and mercy,
   for these men oppose and oppress me all day long.
²Not a day goes by without somebody harassing me.
   So many in their pride trample me under their feet.ᵇ
³But in the day that I'm afraid, I lay all my fears before
      you
   and trust in you with all my heart.
⁴What harm could a man bring to me?
   With God on my side, I will not be afraid of what
      comes.

---

a 56 Or "the distant dove of silence." David was no more than twenty-
   two years old when he composed this psalm.
b 56:2 The Septuagint reads "They war with me in the high places."

The roaring praises of God fill my heart
as I trust his promises.
⁵Day after day cruel critics distort my words;
constantly they plot my collapse.
⁶They lurk in the dark, waiting, spying on my
movements in secret
to take me by surprise, ready to take my life.
⁷They don't deserve to get away with this!
Look at their wickedness, their injustice, Lord.
In your fierce anger cast them down to defeat.
⁸You've kept track of all my wandering and my
weeping.
You've stored my many tears in your bottle—not one
will be lost.
For they are all recorded in your book of
remembrance.ᵃ
⁹The very moment I call to you for *a father's* help
the tide of battle turns and my enemies flee.
This one thing I know: God is on my side!
¹⁰I trust in the Lord. And I praise him!
I trust in the Word of God. And I praise him!
¹¹What harm could man do to me?
With God on my side, I will not be afraid of what
comes.
My heart overflows with praise to God and for his
promises.
I will always trust in him.
¹²So I'm thanking you with all my heart,
with gratitude for all you've done.
I will do everything I've promised you, Lord.
¹³For you have saved my soul from death
and my feet from stumbling

---

a 56:8 See Mal. 3:16.

so that I can walk before the Lord
bathed in his life-giving light.[a]

57 Triumphant Faith
To the Pure and Shining One
King David's golden song of instruction composed
when he hid from Saul in a cave[b]
To the tune of "Do Not Destroy"

[1]Please, God, show me mercy!
Open your grace-fountain for me,
for you are my soul's true shelter.
I will hide beneath the shadow of your embrace,
under the wings of your cherubim,
until this terrible trouble is past.
[2]I will cry out to you, the God of the highest heaven,
the mighty God, who performs all these wonders for
me.
[3]From heaven he will *send a father's help to* save me.
He will trample down those who trample me.

Pause in his presence

He will always show me love
by his gracious and constant care.
[4]I am surrounded by these fierce and brutal men.
They are like lions just wanting to tear me to shreds.
Why must I continue to live among these seething
terrorists,
breathing out their angry threats and insults against
me?
[5]Lord God, be exalted as you soar throughout the
heavens.

---

a 56:13 Or "in his fields of life."
b 57 This incident is recorded in 1 Sam. 24.

May your shining glory be seen in the skies!
Let it be seen high above over all the earth!
⁶For they have set a trap for me.ᵃ
Frantic fear has me overwhelmed.
But look! The very trap they set for me
has sprung shut upon themselves instead of me!

Pause in his presence

⁷My heart, O God, is quiet and confident.
Now I can sing with passion your wonderful praises!
⁸Awake, O my soul, with the music of his
splendor-song!
Arise, my soul, and sing his praises!
My worship will awaken the dawn,
greeting the daybreak with my songs *of praise*!
⁹Wherever I go, I will thank you, my God.
Among all the nations they will hear my praise
songs to you.
¹⁰Your love is so extravagant it reaches to the heavens;
your faithfulness so astonishing it stretches to the sky!
¹¹Lord God, be exalted as you soar throughout the
heavens.
May your shining glory be shown in the skies!
Let it be seen high above all the earth!

58 JUDGE OF THE JUDGES
For the Pure and Shining One
King David's golden song of instruction
To the tune of "Do Not Destroy"

¹⁻²God's justice? You high and mighty politicians
know nothing about it!

---

a 57:6 The Septuagint reads "They have dug a cesspool in front of
me."

Which one of you has walked in justice toward
　others?
Which one of you has treated everyone right and
　fair?
Not one! You only give "justice" in exchange for a
　bribe.
For the right price you let others get away with
　murder.
³⁻⁴Wicked wanderers even from the womb—that's who
you are!
　You lie with your words, and your teaching is
　　poison.ᵃ
⁵Like cobras closing their ears to the most expert of the
　charmers,
　you strike out against all who are near.
⁶O God, break their fangs;
　shatter the teeth of these ravenous lions!
⁷Let them disappear like water falling on thirsty
　ground.
　Let all their weapons be useless.
⁸Let them be like snails dissolving into the slime.
　Let them be cut off, never seeing the light of day!
⁹God will sweep them away so fast
　that they'll never know what hit them.ᵇ
¹⁰The godly will celebrate in the triumph of good over
　evil,
　and the lovers of God will trample
　the wickedness of the wicked under their feet!
¹¹Then everyone will say, "There is a God who judges
　the judges"
　and "There is a great reward in loving God!"

---

a 58:3–4 The Hebrew reads "venom of a serpent," which is a clear
metaphor for wrong teaching.

b 58:9 The Hebrew here is recognized by nearly every scholar to be
one of the most difficult verses in the Psalms to translate.

59 PROTECT ME

For the Pure and Shining One
King David's song of instruction composed when
Saul set an ambush for him at his home[a]
To the tune of "Do Not Destroy"

¹My God, protect me!
  Keep me safe from all my enemies, for they're
    coming to kill me.
  Put me in a high place out of their reach—
  a place so high that these assassins will never find me.
²Save me from these murdering men, these
  bloodthirsty killers.
³See how they set an ambush for my life.
  They're fierce men ready to launch their attack
    against me.
  O Lord, I'm innocent; *protect me!*
⁴I've done nothing to deserve this,
  yet they are already plotting together to kill me.
  Arise, Lord, see what they're scheming, and come
    and meet with me.
⁵Awaken, O God of Israel!
  Commander of Angel Armies,
  arise to punish these treacherous people who
    oppose you!
  Don't go soft on these hard-core killers!

                                    Pause in his presence

⁶After dark they came to spy, sneaking around the city,
  snarling, prowling like a pack of stray dogs in the
    night—
⁷boiling over with rage, shouting out their curses,
  convinced that they'll never get caught.

---

a 59 This incident is recorded in 1 Sam. 19:11–18.

[8]But you, Lord, break out laughing at their plans,
   amused by their arrogance, scoffing at their sinful
      ways.
[9]My strength is found when I wait upon you.
   Watch over me, God, for you are my mountain fortress;
   you set me on high!
[10]The God of passionate love will meet with me.
   My God will empower me to rise in triumph over my
      foes.
[11]Don't kill them; stagger them all with a vivid display
   of power
   and scatter them with your armies of angels,
   O mighty God, our protector!
   Use your awesome power to make them wanderers
      and vagabonds
   and then bring them down.
[12]They are nothing but proud, cursing liars.
   They sin in every word they speak, boasting in their
      blasphemies!
[13]May your wrath be kindled to destroy them; finish
   them off!
   Make an end of them and their deeds until they are
      no more!
   Let them all know and learn
   that God is the ruler over Jacob,
   the God-King over all the earth!

                                   Pause in his presence

[14]Here they come again—
   prowling, growling like a pack of stray dogs in the city.
[15]Drifting, devouring, and coming in for the kill,
   they refuse to sleep until they've eaten their fill.
[16]But as for me, your strength shall be my song of joy.
   At each and every sunrise, my lyrics of your love
      will fill the air!

For you have been my glory-fortress,
a stronghold in my day of distress.
[17]O my strength, I sing with joy your praises.
O my stronghold, I sing with joy your song!
O my Savior, I sing with joy the lyrics of your
faithful love for me!

60 HAS GOD FORGOTTEN US?

To the Pure and Shining One
King David's poem for instruction[a] composed when
he fought against the Syrians with the outcome
still uncertain and Joab turned back to kill twelve
thousand descendants of Esau in the Valley of Salt
To the tune of "Lily of the Covenant"

[1]God, it seems like you walked off and left us!
Why have you turned against us?
You have been angry with us.
O Lord, we plead, come back and help us *as a*
father.
[2]The earth quivers and quakes before you,
splitting open and breaking apart.
Now come and heal it, for it is shaken to its depths.
[3]You have taught us hard lessons
and made us drink the wine of bewilderment.
[4]You have given miraculous signs to those who love
you.
As we follow you, we fly the flag of truth,
and all who love the truth will rally to it.

Pause in his presence

---

a 60 Or "According to Shushan Eduth. A Mikhtam of David, to teach."
There is no scholarly consensus about what *Shushan Eduth* means.
Some have concluded it refers to a specific tune or possibly an
instrument, but it remains a mystery.

⁵Come to your beloved ones and gently draw us out.
  For Lord, you save those whom you love.
  Come with your might and strength!
⁶⁻⁷Then I heard the Lord speak in his holy splendor.
  From his sanctuary I heard the Lord promise:
  "In my triumph I will be the one to measure out
  the portion of my inheritance to my people,
  and I will secure the land as I promised you.
  Shechem, Succoth, Gilead, Manasseh,
  they are all still mine!" he says.
  "Judah will continue to produce kings and
    lawgivers,
  and Ephraim will produce great warriors.
⁸Moab will become my lowly servant.
  Edom will likewise serve my purposes.
  I will lift up a shout of victory over the land of
    Philistia!
⁹But who will bring my triumph into the strong city?
  Who will lead me into Edom's*a* fortresses?"
¹⁰Have you really rejected us, refusing to fight our
  battles?
¹¹Give us a father's help when we face our enemies.
  For to trust in any man is an empty hope.
¹²With God's help we will fight like heroes,
  and he will trample down our every foe!

61 PRAYER FOR PROTECTION
To the Pure and Shining One
A song for the guitar by King David

¹O God, hear my prayer. Listen to my heart's cry.
²For no matter where I am, even when I'm far from
  home,

---

a 60:9 Edom is a variant form of the name Adam.

I will cry out to you for a father's help.
When I'm feeble and overwhelmed by life,
guide me into your glory, where I am safe and
    sheltered.
³Lord, you are a paradise of protection to me.
    You lift me high above the fray.
    None of my foes can touch me
    when I'm held firmly in your wraparound presence!
⁴Keep me in this glory.
    Let me live continually under your splendor-shadow,
    hiding my life in you forever.

Pause in his presence

⁵You have heard my sweet resolutions
    to love and serve you, for I am your beloved.
    And you have given me an inheritance of rich
        treasures,
    which you give to all your devoted lovers.
⁶You treat me like a king, giving me a full and
    abundant life,
    years and years of reigning,[a]
    like many generations rolled into one.
⁷I will live enthroned with you forever!
    Guard me, God, with your unending, unfailing love.
    Let me live my days walking in grace and truth
        before you.
⁸And my praises will fill the heavens forever,
    fulfilling my vow to make every day a love-gift to
        you!

---

a 61:6 Or "add to the days of the king."

62 Unshakable Faith

To the Pure and Shining One
By David, for the one who praises[a]

¹I stand silently to listen for the one I love,
    waiting as long as it takes for the Lord to rescue me.
    For God alone has become my Savior.
²He alone is my safe place;
    his wraparound presence always protects me.
    For he is my champion defender;
    there's no risk of failure with God.
    So why would I let worry paralyze me,
    even when troubles multiply around me?
³But look at these who want me dead,
    shouting their vicious threats at me!
    The moment they discover my weakness,
    they all begin plotting to take me down.
⁴Liars, hypocrites, with nothing good to say—
    all their energies are spent
    on moving me from this exalted place.
                    Pause in his presence

⁵I am standing in absolute stillness, silent before the
    one I love,
    waiting as long as it takes for him to rescue me.
    Only God is my Savior, and he will not fail me.
⁶For he alone is my safe place.
    His wraparound presence always protects me
    as my champion defender.
    There's no risk of failure with God!
    So why would I let worry paralyze me,
    even when troubles multiply around me?

---

a 62 The inscription includes the name Jeduthun, which means "one
who praises."

⁷God's glory is all around me!
His wraparound presence is all I need,
for the Lord is my Savior, my hero, and my life-
giving strength.
⁸Trust only in God every moment!
Tell him all your troubles and pour out your heart-
longings to him.
Believe me when I tell you—he will help you!

Pause in his presence

⁹Before God all the people of the earth, high or low,
are like smoke that disappears,
like a vapor that quickly vanishes away.
Compared to God they're nothing but vanity, nothing
at all!
¹⁰The wealth of the world is nothing to God.
So if your wealth increases, don't be boastful or
put your trust in your money.
And don't you think for a moment that
you can get away with stealing by overcharging
others
just to get more for yourself!
¹¹God said to me once and for all,
"All the strength and power you need flows from me!"
And again I heard it clearly said,
¹²"All the love you need is found in me!"
And it's true that you repay people for what they do.

63 THIRSTING FOR GOD

For the Pure and Shining One
King David's song when he was exiled in the Judean
wilderness

¹O God of my life, I'm lovesick for you in this weary
wilderness.

I thirst with the deepest longings to love you more,
with cravings in my heart that can't be described.
Such yearning grips my soul for you, my God!
²I'm energized every time I enter
your heavenly sanctuary to seek more of your power
and drink in more of your glory.
³For your tender mercies mean more to me than life
itself.
How I love and praise you, God!
⁴Daily I will worship you passionately and with all my
heart.
My arms will wave to you like banners of praise.
⁵I overflow with praise when I come before you,
for the anointing of your presence satisfies me like
nothing else.
You are such a rich banquet of pleasure to my soul.
⁶⁻⁷I lie awake each night thinking of you
and reflecting on how you help me like a father.
I sing through the night under your
splendor-shadow,
offering up to you my songs of delight and joy!
⁸With passion I pursue and cling to you.
Because I feel your grip on my life,
I keep my soul close to your heart.
⁹Those who plot to destroy me shall descend into the
darkness of hell.
¹⁰They will be consumed by their own evil
and become nothing more than dust under our feet.*a*
¹¹These liars will be silenced forever!
But with the anointing of a king I will dance and
rejoice
along with all his devoted lovers who trust in him.

---

a 63:10 Or "food for foxes."

64 Victory over Evildoers

For the Pure and Shining One
King David's song

1-2Lord, can't you hear my cry, my bitter complaint?
  Keep me safe from this band of criminals and
  from the conspiracy of these wicked men.
  They gather in their secret counsel to destroy me.
3-4Can't you hear their slander, their lies?
  Their words are like poison-tipped arrows
  shot from the shadows.
  They are unafraid and have no fear of consequences.
5They persist with their evil plans
  and plot together to hide their traps.
  They boast, "No one can see us or stop us!"
6They search out opportunities to pervert justice
  as they plan the "perfect crime."
  How unsearchable is their endless evil!
  They try desperately to hide the deep darkness of
    their hearts.[a]
7But all the while God has his own fire-tipped arrows!
  Suddenly, without warning,
  they will be pierced and struck down.
8Staggering backward, they will be destroyed
  by the very ones they spoke against.
  All who see this will view them with scorn.
9Then all will stand awestruck over what God has done,
  seeing how he vindicated the victims of these crimes.
10The lovers of God will be glad, rejoicing in the Lord.
  They will be found in his glorious wraparound
    presence,
  singing songs of praise to God!

---

a 64:6 Scholars are unanimous in agreement that the meaning of the
  Hebrew text of this verse is uncertain.

65 WHAT A SAVIOR
For the Pure and Shining One
King David's poetic song

¹⁻²O God in Zion, to you even silence is praise!
　You who answers prayer,[a]
　all of humanity comes before you *with their requests.*
³Though we are overcome by our many sins,
　your sacrifice covers over them all.
⁴How blessed is the one you choose
　to live near you in your courts.
　The beauty of your house, your holy temple,
　　satisfies us.
⁵You answer our prayers with amazing wonders
　and with awe-inspiring displays of power.
　You are the righteous God who helps us like a father.
　Everyone everywhere looks to you,
　for you are the confidence of all the earth,
　even to the farthest islands of the sea.
⁶What jaw-dropping, astounding power is yours!
　You are the mountain maker who sets them all in
　　place.
⁷You muzzle the roar of the mighty seas
　and the rage of mobs with their noisy riots.
⁸O God, to the farthest corners of the planet
　people will stand in awe,
　startled and stunned by your signs and wonders.
　Sunrise brilliance and sunset beauty

---

a 65:1–2 The root of the Hebrew word for "prayer" is *palal*, which also means "tent peg." Jewish tradition views *palal* prayer (intercession) as a means of attaching yourself to God. In the same way a tent peg establishes a tent and fastens it securely, so *palal* prayer fastens the soul to God. *Palal* prayer is when you grab hold of God and attach yourself to him in surrender and humility. Hold on to God like a tent peg holds on to a tent.

both take turns singing their songs of joy to you.
⁹Your visitations of glory bless the earth;[a]
   the rivers of God overflow and enrich it.
   You paint the wheat fields golden as you provide
      rich harvests.
¹⁰Every field is watered with the abundance of rain—
   showers soaking the earth and softening its clods,
   causing seeds to sprout throughout the land.
¹¹You crown the earth with the fruits of your goodness.
   Wherever you go, the tracks of your chariot wheels
      drip with oil.
¹²Luxuriant green pastures boast of your bounty
   as you make every hillside blossom with joy.
¹³The grazing meadows are covered with flocks,
   and the fertile valleys are clothed with grain,
   each one dancing and shouting for joy, creation's
      celebration!
   They're all singing their songs of praise to you!

66 THANK YOU, LORD
For the Pure and Shining One
A song of awakening[b]

¹Everyone everywhere, lift up your joyful shout to God!
²Sing your songs tuned to his glory!
   Tell the world how wonderful he is.
³For he's the awe-inspiring God, great and glorious in
   power!
   We've never seen anything like him!
   Mighty in miracles, you cause your enemies to
      tremble.

---

a 65:9 The Septuagint reads "You've made the earth drunk with your
visitations."

b 66 As translated from the inscription found in the Septuagint.

No wonder they all surrender and bow before you!
⁴All the earth will bow down to worship;
   all the earth will sing your glories forever!
Pause in his presence

⁵Everyone will say, "Come and see the incredible
   things God has done;
   it will take your breath away!
   He multiplies miracles for his people!"ᵃ
⁶He made a highway going right through the Red Sea
   as the Hebrews passed through on dry ground,
   exploding with joyous excitement over the miracles
     of God.
⁷In his great and mighty power he rules forever,
   watching over every movement of every nation.
   So beware, rebel lands; he knows how to humble
     you!
Pause in his presence

⁸Praise God, all you peoples.
   Praise him everywhere and let everyone know you
     love him!
⁹There's no doubt about it: God holds our lives safely
   in his hands.
   He's the one who keeps us faithfully following him.
¹⁰O Lord, we have passed through your fire;
   like precious metal made pure,
   you've proved us, perfected us, and made us holy.
¹¹You've captured us, ensnared us in your net.
   Then, like prisoners, you *placed chains around our
     necks.*ᵇ

---

a 66:5 The Septuagint reads "His works are more to be feared than the
  decisions of men."
b 66:11 Or "you attached suffering to our hips."

¹²You've allowed our enemies to prevail against us.
    We've passed through fire and flood,
        yet in the end you always bring us out better than
            we were before,
        saturated with your goodness.*
¹³I come before your presence with my sacrifice.
    I'll give you all that I've promised, everything I
        have.
¹⁴When I was overcome in my anguish,
    I promised to give you my sacrifice.
    Here it is! All that I said I would offer you is yours.
¹⁵I'll throw it all—the best I have to bring—into the fire
    as the fragrance of my sacrifice ascends unto you.*

Pause in his presence

¹⁶All you lovers of God who want to please him,
    come and listen, and I'll tell you what he did for me.
¹⁷I cried aloud to him with all my heart, and he
    answered me!
    Now my mouth overflows with the highest praise.
¹⁸Yet if I had closed my eyes to my sin,*
    the Lord God would have closed his ears to my
        prayer.
¹⁹But praises rise to God,
    for he paid attention to my prayer and answered my
        cry to him!
²⁰I will forever praise this God who didn't close his
    heart when I prayed
    and never said no when I asked him for help.
    He never once refused to show me his tender love.

---

a 66:12 Or "you brought us out into a wide-open space [a place of rest]."

b 66:15 The literal Hebrew describes the sacrifice as "burnt offerings of fat beasts and the smoke of rams, bulls, and male goats."

c 66:18 Or "If I had cherished iniquity in my heart."

67 It's Time to Praise Him
For the Pure and Shining One
A poetic song of praise for guitar

¹God, keep us near your mercy-fountain and bless us!
  And when you look down on us, may your face
    beam with joy!ᵃ
                              Pause in his presence

²Send us out all over the world so that everyone
  everywhere
  will discover your ways and know who you are
  and see your power to save.
³Let all the nations burst forth with praise;
  let everyone everywhere love and enjoy you!
⁴Then how glad the nations will be when you are their
  King.
  They will sing, they will shout, for you give true
    justice to the people.
  Yes! You, Lord, are the shepherd of the nations!
                              Pause in his presence

⁵No wonder the peoples praise you!
  Let all the people praise you more!ᵇ
⁶The harvest of the earth is here!
  God, the very God we worship,
  keeps us satisfied at his banquet of blessings.
⁷And the blessings keep coming!
  All the ends of the earth will give him
  the honor he deserves and be in awe of him!

---

a 67:1 Or "May he cause his face to shine with us" or "May he smile
on us."
b 67:5 The Septuagint reads "Let all the people come to know you."

68 A SONG OF TRIUMPH
For the Pure and Shining One
David's poetic song of praise

¹God! Arise with awesome power,
and every one of your enemies will scatter in fear!
²Chase them away—all these God-haters.
Blow them away as a puff of smoke.
Melt them away like wax in the fire.
One good look at you and the wicked vanish.
³But let all the righteous be glad!
Yes, let them all rejoice in your presence
and be carried away with gladness.*ᵃ*
Let them laugh and be radiant with joy!
⁴Let them sing their celebration-songs
for the coming of the cloud rider whose name is
Yah!*ᵇ*
⁵⁻⁶To the fatherless he is a father.
To the widow he is a champion friend.
The lonely he makes part of a family.
The prisoners*ᶜ* he leads into prosperity until they
sing for joy.
This is our Holy God in his Holy Place!
But for the rebels there is heartache and despair.*ᵈ*
⁷O Lord, it was you who marched in front of your
people,
leading them through the wasteland.

Pause in his presence

---

a 68:3 As translated from the Septuagint. The Aramaic is "they rejoice in his sweetness."

b 68:4 More than an abbreviation, the name Yah is associated with the God of heaven, the God of highest glory and power.

c 68:5–6 The Septuagint reads "the bitter ones."

d 68:5–6 Or "they will live in a sun-scorched land."

⁸The earth shook beneath your feet; the heavens filled
   with clouds
      before the presence of the God of Sinai.
      The sacred mountain shook at the sight of the face
         of Israel's God.
⁹You, O God, sent the reviving rain upon your weary
   inheritance,
      showers of blessing to refresh it.
¹⁰So there your people settled.ᵃ
      And in your kindness you providedᵇ the poor with
         abundance.
¹¹God Almighty declares the word of the gospel with
   power,ᶜ
      and the warring women of Zion deliver its message:ᵈ
¹²"The conquering legions have themselves been
   conquered.
      Look at them flee!"
      Now Zion's women are left to gather the spoils.
¹³When you sleep between sharpened stakes,ᵉ
      I see you sparkling like silver and glistening like
         gold,
      covered by the beautiful wings of a dove!ᶠ

---

a 68:10 Or "For you live among them [in community]." The Hebrew is
   uncertain.
b 68:10 Or "sustain." God anticipates our needs and has gone before
   us to provide for and sustain us in our journey.
c 68:11 As translated from the Aramaic.
d 68:11 As translated from the Masoretic Text.
e 68:13 The Aramaic word *shaphya* can be translated "sharpened
   stakes" or "thorns." This is an obvious prophecy of the cross and our
   union with Christ as he was crucified.
f 68:13 As translated from the Aramaic text, this verse contains
   prophetic hints of Calvary, where Jesus "slept" the sleep of death
   between the "sharpened stakes" of the cross. The word *you* is plural
   and points us to our co-crucifixion with Christ.

[14]When the Almighty found a king for himself,
it became white as snow in his shade.[a]
[15-16]O huge, magnificent mountain,
you are the mighty kingdom of God![b]
All the other peaks, though impressive and
imposing,
look with envy on you, Mount Zion!
For Zion is the mountain where God has chosen to
live forever.
[17]Look! The mighty chariots of God!
Ten thousands upon ten thousands,
more than anyone could ever number.
God is at the front,
leading them all from Mount Sinai into his sanctuary
with the radiance of holiness upon him.[c]
[18]He ascends into the heavenly heights,
taking his many captured ones with him,
leading them in triumphal procession.
And gifts were given to men, even the once
rebellious,
so that they may dwell with Yah.
[19]What a glorious God![d]
He gives us salvation over and over,[e]
then daily he carries our burdens![f]

Pause in his presence

---

a 68:14 Every scholar consulted concludes that this verse is difficult,
if not impossible, to interpret properly and translate accurately. The
last words are literally "Snow fell in Zalmon." Zalmon (or Salmon)
was a wooded area and means "shady."

b 68:15–16 The Septuagint reads "mountain of provision."

c 68:17 The Septuagint reads "The Lord sends his provisions from his
Holy Place on Mount Sinai."

d 68:19 The Aramaic is *Maryah*, the Aramaic form of YHWH or Lord
Yahweh.

e 68:19 *Salvation* is in the plural form in the Hebrew text ("salvations").

f 68:19 Or "daily loads us with benefits."

²⁰Our God is a mighty God who saves us over and over!
   For the Lord, Yahweh, rescues us
   from the ways of death many times.
²¹But he will crush every enemy, shattering their
   strength.
   He will make heads roll
   for they refuse to repent of their stubborn, sinful ways.
²²I hear the Lord God saying to all the enemies of his
   people,
   "You'd better come out of your hiding places,
   all of you who are doing your best to stay far away
      from me.ᵃ
   Don't you know there's no place to hide?
²³For my people will be the conquerors;
   they will soon have you under their feet.
   They will crush you until there is nothing left!"ᵇ
²⁴O God, my King, your triumphal processions
   keep moving onward in holiness;
   you're moving onward toward the Holy Place!
²⁵Leaders in front,ᶜ then musicians,
   with young maidens in between, striking their
      tambourines.
²⁶And they sing, "Let all God's princely people rejoice!
   Let all the congregations bring their blessing to God,
      saying,
   'The Lord of the fountain! The Lord of the fountain
      of life!
   The Lord of the fountain of Israel!' "

ᵃ 68:22 The Hebrew text makes reference to Bashan (a high mountain) and to the depths of the sea. In other words, there's no place to hide.

ᵇ 68:23 The Hebrew text is literally "Your enemies will be food for the dogs."

ᶜ 68:25 As translated from the Septuagint. The Hebrew is "Singers in front."

²⁷Astonishingly, it's the favored youth leading the way:[a]
princes of praise in their royal robes
and exalted princes are among them,
along with princes who have wrestled with God.
²⁸⁻²⁹Display your strength, God, and we'll be strong![b]
For your miracles have made us who we are.
Lord, do it again
and parade from your temple your mighty power.
By your command even kings will bring gifts to you.
³⁰God, rebuke the beast-life that hides within us![c]
Rebuke those who claim to be "strong ones,"[d]
who lurk within the congregation
and abuse the people out of their love for money.
God scatters the people who are spoiling for a fight.
³¹Africa will send her noble envoys to you, O God.
They will come running, stretching out their hands
in love to you.
³²Let all the nations of the earth sing songs of praise
to Almighty God!
Go ahead, all you nations—sing your praise to the
Lord!

Pause in his presence

---

a   68:27 The Hebrew includes the names of four sons of Jacob, rep-
resenting four tribes. Benjamin, the youngest son, means "son of
my right hand" or "the favored one." Judah means "praise." Zebu-
lon's name is the word for "exalted." Naphtali means "obtained by
wrestling." Each name speaks of a princely group and is used here
poetically not only for Israel but for all of God's "princely people" in
this holy procession of worship.

b   68:28–29 The Great Bible translated by Miles Coverdale (1488–1569)
translates this as "Your God has sent forth strength for you."

c   68:30 Literal Hebrew is "rebuke the beasts in the reeds."

d   68:30 This verse has puzzled scholars, and many conclude that the
Hebrew text is nearly incomprehensible, with tremendous variations
in the translation.

³³Make music for the one who strides the ancient skies.
  Listen to his thunderous voice of might split open
    the heavens.
³⁴Give it up for God, for he alone has all the strength
  and power!
  Proclaim his majesty! For his glory shines down on
    Israel.
  His mighty strength soars in the clouds of glory.
³⁵God, we are consumed with awe, trembling before
  you
  as your glory streams from your Holy Place.
  The God of power shares his mighty strength with
    Israel
  and with all his people.
  God, we give our highest praise to you!

69 A Cry of Distress[a]

To the Pure and Shining One
David's poetic song of praise To the tune of "Lilies"

¹⁻²God, my God, come and save me!
  These floods of trouble have risen higher and
    higher.
  The water is up to my neck![b]
  I'm sinking into the mud with no place to stand,
  and I'm about to drown in this storm.
³I'm weary, exhausted with weeping.
  My throat is dry, my voice is gone, my eyes are
    swollen with sorrow,
  and I'm waiting for you, God, *to come through for me.*

---

a 69 Psalm 69 is considered one of the most outstanding messianic
  psalms, with obvious prophetic references to the sufferings and
  cross of Jesus Christ.
b 69:1–2 Or "throat."

⁴I can't even count all those who hate me for no
  reason.
  Many influential men want me silenced,
  yet I've done nothing against them.
  Must I restore what I never took away?
⁵God, my life is an open book to you.
  You know every sin I've ever done.
  For nothing within me is hidden from your sight!
⁶Lord Yahweh of Angel Armies,
  keep me from ever being a stumbling block to
    others,
  to those who love you.
  Lord God of Israel, don't let what happens to me
  be the source of confusion to those who are
    passionate for you.
⁷Because of my love for you, Lord,
  I have been mocked, cursed, and disgraced.
⁸Even my own brothers, those of my family,
  act as though they don't want anything to do with me.
⁹My love for you has my heart on fire!
  My passion for your house consumes me!
  Nothing will turn me away,
  even though I endure all the insults of those who
    insult you.
¹⁰When they see me seeking for more of you with
  weeping*a* and fasting,
  they all just scoff and scorn at my passion.
¹¹When I humble myself with sorrow over my sin,
  it gives them a reason to mock me even more.
¹²The leaders, the influential ones—how they scorn my
  passion for you!
  I've become the talk of the town, the theme of
    drunkards' songs.

---

a 69:10 Or "When I pour out my soul" or "When I weep soul-tears."

¹³But I keep calling out to you, Yahweh!
I know you will bend down to listen to me,
for now is the season of favor.
Because of your faithful love for me,
your answer to my prayer will be my sure salvation.
¹⁴Pull me out of this mess! Don't let me sink!
Rescue me from those who hate me and from all this
trouble I'm in!
¹⁵Don't let this flood drown me.
Save me from these deep waters
or I'll go down to the pit of destruction.
¹⁶⁻¹⁷Oh, Lord God, answer my prayers!
I need to see your tender kindness, your grace,
your compassion, and your constant love.
Just let me see your face, and turn your heart
toward me.
Come running quickly to your servant.
In this deep distress, come and answer my prayer.
¹⁸Come closer as a friend and redeem me.
Set me free so my enemies cannot say that you are
powerless.
¹⁹See how they dishonor me in shame and disgrace?
You know, Lord, what I'm going through, and you
see it all.
²⁰I'm heartsick and heartbroken by it all.
Their contempt has crushed my soul.
I looked for sympathy and compassion
but found only empty stares.
²¹I was hungry and they gave me bitter food.
I was thirsty and they offered me vinegar.ᵃ
²²Let their "feasts" turn to ashes.
Let their "peace and security" become their downfall.

---

a 69:21 This was fulfilled with Jesus being offered vinegar on the cross. See Luke 23:36.

²³Make them blind as bats, groping in the dark.
Let them be feeble, trembling continually.
²⁴⁻²⁵Pour out your fury on them all!
Consume them with the fire of your anger!
Burn down the walled palace where they live!
Leave them homeless and desolate!
²⁶For they come against the one you yourself have
struck,
and they scorn the pain of those you've pierced.
²⁷Pile on them the guilt of their sins.
Don't let them ever go free.
²⁸Leave them out of your list of the living!
Blot them out of your Book of Life!
Never name them as your own!
²⁹I am burdened and broken by this pain.
When your miracle rescue comes to me,
it will lift me to the highest place.
³⁰Then my song will be a burst of praise to you.
My glory-shouts will make your fame even more
glorious
to all who hear my praises!
³¹For I know, Yahweh, that my praises mean more to
you
than all my gifts and sacrifices.
³²All who seek you will see God do this for them,
and they'll overflow with gladness.
Let this revive your hearts, all you lovers of God!
³³For Yahweh does listen to the poor and needy
and will not abandon his prisoners of love.ᵃ
³⁴Let all the universe praise him!
The high heavens and everyone on earth, praise him!
Let the oceans deep, with everything in them, keep
it up!

---

a 69:33 Or "those wearing shackles."

³⁵God will come to save his Zion-people.
God will build up his cities of Judah,
for there his people will live in peace.
³⁶All their children will inherit the land,
and the lovers of his name will live there safe and
secure.

70 A Cry for Help
To the Pure and Shining One
David's poetic lament to always remember

¹Please, Lord! Come quickly and rescue me!
God, show me your favor and restore me.
²Let all who seek my life be humiliated and confused.
God, send them sprawling, all who wish me evil;
they just want me dead.
³Scoff at every scoffer and cause them all to be utter
failures!
Let them be ashamed and horrified over their
complete defeat.
⁴But let all who passionately seek you erupt with
excitement and joy
over what you've done!
Let all your devoted lovers, who continually rejoice
in the Savior,[a]
say aloud, "How great and glorious is our God!"
⁵Lord, in my place of weakness and need,
won't you turn your heart toward me and hurry to
help me?
For you are my Savior, and I'm always in your
thoughts.
So don't delay to deliver me now, for you are my
God.

---

a 70:4 This verse contains the Hebrew root word for Yeshua.

71 The Psalm of Old Age

¹Lord, you are my secure shelter. Don't ever let me
  down!
²Let your justice be my breakthrough.
  Bend low to my whispered cry
  and save me from all my enemies!
³You're the only place of protection for me.
  I keep coming back to hide myself in you,
  for you are like a mountain-cliff fortress where I'm
    kept safe.
⁴Let me escape from these cruel and wicked men,
  and save me from the hands of the evil one.
⁵For you are my only hope, Lord!
  I've hung on to you, trusting in you all my life.
⁶⁻⁷It was you who supported me from the day I was
  born,
  loving me, helping me through my life's journey.
  You've made me into a miracle;
  no wonder I trust you and praise you forever!
  Many marvel at my success,
  but I know it is all because of you, my mighty
    protector!
⁸I'm overflowing with your praise for all you've
  done,
  and your splendor thrills me all day long.
⁹Now that I'm old, don't set me aside.
  Don't let go of me when my strength is spent.
¹⁰⁻¹¹For all my enemies whisper behind my back.
  They're waiting for me to fall so they can finish me
    off.
  They're convinced you've left me
  and that you'll never come to my rescue.
  They're saying, "Let's get him now! He has no
    savior!"

¹²O God, stay close to me!
  Don't just watch from a distance! Hurry to help me,
    my God!
¹³Cover these accusers of mine with shame and failure!
  Destroy them all, for they only want to kill me!
¹⁴No matter what, I'll trust in you to help me.
  Nothing will stop me from praising you to magnify
    your glory!
¹⁵I couldn't begin to count the times you've been there
  for me.
  With the skill of a poet I'll never run out of things to
    say
  about how you faithfully kept me from danger.
¹⁶I will come forth in your mighty strength, O my Lord
  God.ᵃ
  I'll tell everyone that you alone are the perfect one.
¹⁷From my childhood you've been my teacher,
  and I'm still telling everyone of your
    miracle-wonders!
¹⁸God, now that I'm old and gray, don't walk away.
  Give me grace to demonstrate to the next generation
  all your mighty miracles and your excitement,
  to show them your magnificent power!
¹⁹For your glorious righteousness reaches up to the
  high heavens.
  No one could ever be compared to you!
  Who is your equal, O God of marvels and wonders?
²⁰Even though you've let us sink down with trials and
  troubles,
  I know you will revive us again,
  lifting us up from the dust of death.
²¹Give us even more greatness than before.
  Turn and comfort us once again.

---

a 71:16 Or "I will enter into the manliness of Lord Yahweh."

²²My loving God, the harp in my heart will praise you.
Your faithful heart toward us will be the theme of
my song.
Melodies and music will rise to you, the Holy One of
Israel.
²³I will shout and sing your praises for all you are to
me—
Savior, lover of my soul!
²⁴I'll never stop telling others how perfect you are,
while all those who seek my harm slink away
ashamed and defeated!

72 THE RIGHTEOUS KING
*Solomon's psalm*ᵃ

¹O God, make the king a godly judge like you
and give the king's son the gift of justice too.
²Help him to give true justice to your people,
honorably and equally to all.
³Then the mountains of influence will be fruitful,
and from your righteousness
prosperity and peace will flow to all the people.
⁴May the poor and humble have an advocate with the
king.
May he consider the children of the poor
and crush the cruel oppressor.
⁵The sun and moon will stop shining
before your devoted lovers will stop worshiping;
for ages upon ages the people will love and adore
you!

---

a 72 The Septuagint indicates this could be a psalm written by David
for his son Solomon. This royal psalm is a prayer for the king. Read
through it as though it is referring to King Jesus—One who is greater
than Solomon.

⁶Your favor will fall like rain upon our surrendered
   lives,*
   like showers reviving the earth.
⁷In the days of his reign the righteous will spring forth
   with the abundance of peace and prosperity
      forevermore.
⁸May he subdue and take dominion from sea to sea;
   may he rule from the river to the rim.
⁹Desert nomads are bowing at his feet;
   every enemy is falling facedown, biting the dust!
¹⁰Distant kings* will surrender and come with their
   gifts
   from every continent and coastland;
   they will offer their tribute to you.
¹¹O King of kings, they will all bow before you.
   O King of kings, every nation will one day serve
      you.
¹²⁻¹³He will care for the needy and neglected
   when they cry to him for help.
   The humble and helpless will know his kindness,
   for with a father's compassion he will save their
      souls.
¹⁴They will be rescued from tyranny and torture,
   for their lifeblood is precious in his eyes.
¹⁵Long live this King!
   May the wealth of the world* be laid before him.
   May there be ceaseless praise and prayer to him.
   May all the blessing be brought to him.
¹⁶Bless us with a bountiful harvest,
   with golden grain swaying on the mountain fields!

---

a 72:6 Or "like rain on mown grass."
b 72:10 Included in the Hebrew text are kings of Tarshish (Spain) and
   kings of Sheba and Seba (Ethiopia).
c 72:15 Or "the gold of Sheba."

May the cities be full of praising people, fruitful and
filled—
[17]so that his name may be honored forever!
May the fame of his name spring forth!
May it shine on, like the sunshine!
In him all will be blessed to bless others,
and may all the people bless the One who blessed
them.
[18]Praise Yahweh forever, the God of Israel!
He is the one and only God of wonders,
surpassing every expectation.
[19]The blazing glory of his name will be praised forever!
May all the earth overflow with his glory!
Faithful is our King! Amen!
[20]This concludes the poetry sung by David, Jesse's son.

BOOK 3
THE LEVITICUS PSALMS
Psalms of worship and God's house

73 GOD'S JUSTICE
Asaph's psalm[a]

[1]No one can deny it—God is really good to Israel
and to all those with pure hearts.
But I nearly missed seeing it for myself.

---

a 73 Asaph was one of three Levites that David set over the worship of Yahweh. However, it is possible that Asaph was an office
not an individual—Asaphites who were part of a prophetic company of composers. The name Asaph means "a harvest" or "fulfilled
prophecy." Asaph possibly comes from a Semitic root word for "portal." Perhaps the Asaphites were named such because their music
opened a portal into the heavenly realm.

²Here's my story: I narrowly missed losing it all.

³I was stumbling over what I saw the wicked doing.

For when I saw the boasters with such wealth and
prosperity,

I became jealous over their smug security.

⁴⁻⁵Indulging in whatever they wanted, going where
they wanted,

doing what they wanted, and with no care in the
world,

no pain, no problems—they seemed to have it made.

They lived as though life would never end.

⁶They didn't even try to hide their pride and opulence.

Cruelty and violence are parts of their lifestyle.

⁷Pampered and pompous, vice oozes from their souls;

they overflow with vanity.

⁸They're such snobs—looking down their noses.

They even scoff at God!

They are nothing but bullies threatening God's people.

⁹They are loudmouths with no fear of God, pretending
to know it all—

windbags full of hot air, impressing only themselves.

¹⁰Yet the people keep coming back to listen

to more of their nonsense.

¹¹They tell their cohorts, "God will never know.

See, he has no clue of what we're doing."

¹²These are the wicked ones I'm talking about!

They never have to lift a finger,

living a life of ease while their riches multiply.

¹³Have I been foolish to play by the rules and keep my
life pure?

¹⁴Here I am suffering under your discipline day after
day.

I feel like I'm being punished all day long.

¹⁵If I had given in to my pain and spoken of what I
was really feeling,

it would have sounded like unfaithfulness to the
next generation.
¹⁶When I tried to understand it all, I just couldn't.
It was too puzzling—too much of a riddle to me.
¹⁷But then one day I was brought into the sanctuaries
of God,
and in the light of glory, my distorted perspective
vanished.
Then I understood that the destiny of the wicked
was near!
¹⁸They're the ones who are on the slippery path,
and God will suddenly let them slide off into
destruction
to be consumed with terrors forever!
¹⁹It will be an instant end to all their life of ease;
a blink of the eye and they're swept away by sudden
calamity!
They're all nothing more than momentary
monarchs—
²⁰soon to disappear like a dream when one awakes.
When the rooster crows,
Lord God, you'll despise their life of fantasies.^a
²¹When I saw all of this, what turmoil filled my heart,
piercing my opinions with your truth.
²²I was so stupid. I was senseless and ignorant,
acting like a brute beast before you, Lord.
²³Yet, in spite of all this, I still belong to you;
you hold me by my right hand.
²⁴You lead me with your secret wisdom.
And following you brings me into your brightness
and glory!
²⁵Whom have I in heaven but you? You're all I want!
No one on earth means as much to me as you.

---

a 73:20 Or "shadows."

²⁶Lord, so many times I fail; I fall into disgrace.
> But when I trust in you, I have a strong and glorious
> > presence
> protecting and anointing me. Forever you're all I need!
²⁷Those who abandon the worship of God will perish.
> The false and unfaithful will be silenced, never
> > heard from again.
²⁸But I'll keep coming closer and closer to you, Lord
> Yahweh,
> for your name is good to me. I'll keep telling the
> > world of
> your awesome works, my faithful and glorious God!

74 WE NEED YOU NOW
Asaph's poem of instruction

¹Are you really going to leave us, God?
> Would you turn your back on us, rejecting your
> > people?
> We are yours, your very own.^{*a*}
> Will your anger smolder against us forever?
²Don't forget that we are your beloved ones.
> Wrap us back into your heart again, for you chose us.
> You brought us out of our slavery and bondage
> and made us your favored ones, your Zion-people,
> your home on earth.
³Turn your steps toward this devastation.
> Come running to bring your restoring grace to these
> > ruins,^{*b*}
> to what the enemy has done to devastate your Holy
> > Place.

---

a 74:1 Or "the sheep of your pasture."

b 74:3 This verse reads differently in the Aramaic: "Lift up your servants with your might above those who take them captive, for those who oppress us are enemies to your holiness."

⁴They have come into the very midst of your dwelling
place,
  roaring like beasts, setting up their banners to flaunt
    their conquest.
⁵Now everything is in shambles! They've totally
destroyed it.
  Like a forest chopped down to the ground,
  there's nothing left.
⁶All of the beauty of the craftsmanship
  of the inner place has been ruined,
  smashed, broken, and shattered.ᵃ
⁷They've burned it all to the ground.
  They've violated your sanctuary,
    the very dwelling place of your glory and your
      name.
⁸They boasted, "Let's completely crush them!
  Let's wipe out every trace of this God.
  Let's burn up every sacred place where they worship
    this God."
⁹We don't see any miraculous signs anymore.
  There's no longer a prophet among us
  who can tell us how long this devastation will
    continue.
¹⁰God, how much longer will you let this go on
  and allow these barbarians to blaspheme your
    name?
  Will you stand back and watch them get away with
    this forever?
¹¹Why don't you do something?
  You have the power to break in,

---

a 74:6 This psalm describes physical destruction as well as what the
enemy of our souls has done spiritually to mar the image of God
in the "inner place" of man's spirit. God will fully restore all things,
including his image within us, as our hearts become his Holy Place
on the earth.

so why would you hide your great power from us?
Don't hold back! Unleash your might and give them
a final blow.
¹²You have always been, and always will be, my King.
You are the mighty conqueror, working wonders all
over the world.
¹³It was you who split the sea in two by your glorious
strength.
You smashed the power of Tannin, the sea monster.
¹⁴You crushed the might of Leviathan,ᵃ the great
dragon,
then you took the crumbs and fed them to the sharks.
¹⁵With your glory you opened up springs and
fountains,
then you spoke, and the ever-flowing springs of
Jordan
dried up so we could cross over.
¹⁶You own the day and the night.
Sunlight and starlight call you Creator.
¹⁷The four corners of the earth were formed by your
hands,
and every changing season owes its beauty to you.
¹⁸O Yahweh, don't ever forget how these arrogant
enemies,
like fools, have mocked your name.
¹⁹Lord, aren't we your beloved dove that praises you?ᵇ
Protect us from these wild beasts who want to harm
us.
Don't leave us as lambs among wolves!
You can't abandon us after all we've been through!

---

a 74:14 Leviathan is mentioned six times in Job 41. Leviathan means
"twisted" or "coiled" and is considered to be a sea monster. See Gen.
1:21.

b 74:19 As translated from the Septuagint, Syriac, and one Hebrew
manuscript.

²⁰Remember your promises to us,
　for darkness covers the land,
　giving the violent ones a hiding place.
²¹Don't let these insults continue.
　Can't you see that we are your downtrodden
　and oppressed people?
　Make the poor and needy into a choir of praise to
　　you!
²²Don't ignore these ignorant words, this continual
　mocking.
　Rise up, God; it's time to defend yourself from all this.
²³Never forget what your adversaries are saying.
　For their rage and uproar rise continually against you.
　It's time to stand up to them!

75 A Cup in God's Hand

To the Pure and Shining One
Asaph's poetic song To the tune of "Do Not Destroy"

¹God, our hearts spill over with praise to you!
　We overflow with thanks, for your name is the "Near
　　One."
　All we want to talk about is your wonderful works!
　And we hear your reply:
²"When the time is ripe I will arise,
　and I will judge the world with perfect
　　righteousness.
³Though I have set the earth firmly on its pillars,
　I will shake it until it totters, and everyone's hearts
　　will tremble."

　　　　　　　　　　　　　　Pause in his presence

⁴God warns the proud, "Stop your arrogant boasting!"
　And he warns the wicked,
　"Don't think for a moment you can resist me!

⁵Why would you speak with such stubborn pride?
Don't you dare raise your fist against me!"
⁶⁻⁷This I know:
the favor that brings promotion and power
doesn't come from anywhere on earth,
for no one exalts a person but God, the true judge of
all.
He alone determines where favor rests.
He anoints one for greatness
and brings another down to his knees.
⁸A foaming cup filled with judgment mixed with
fury
is in the hands of the Lord Yahweh,
full to the brim and ready to run over.
He filled it up for the wicked, and they will drink it
down to the very last drop!
⁹But I will proclaim the victory of the God of Jacob.
My melodies of praise will make him known.
¹⁰My praises will break the powers of wickedness,
while the righteous will be promoted and become
powerful!

76 AWE-INSPIRING POWER
To the Pure and Shining One
Asaph's poetic tune, a song of smiting

¹God is well known in the land of Judah.
He is famous throughout Israel,
²making his home in Jerusalem,ᵃ living here on Mount
Zion.
³That's where he smashes every weapon of war
that comes against him.

---

a 76:2 Or "Salem," the ancient name of Jerusalem.

That's where he uses the broken arrows
as kindling for his mighty bonfire.

Pause in his presence

⁴God, you are so resplendent and radiant!*ᵃ*
    Your majesty shines from your everlasting
        mountain.
    Nothing could be compared to you in glory!
⁵Even the mightiest of men have been paralyzed by
    your presence.
    They were so stunned and lifeless,
    not even the strongest one could lift a hand.
⁶When Jacob's God roared his rebuke,
    soldiers and their steeds all fell to the ground,
    stunned and lying still.
⁷No wonder you are greatly feared! You are the awe-
    inspiring God!
    For who could ever stand before your face
    when your fierce anger burns and live to tell
        about it.
⁸As the earth itself holds its breath in awe before you,
    judgment is decreed from heaven.
⁹You arise to punish evil and defend the gentle upon
    the earth.

Pause in his presence

¹⁰You have power to transform man's futile anger into
    praise.*ᵇ*
    The fury of your enemies only causes your fame to
        increase.*ᶜ*

---

a 76:4 The word used here is often translated as "anointed" when
    taken from either the Hebrew or the Aramaic.
b 76:10 Or "The counsel of men will praise you."
c 76:10 The Septuagint reads "Survivors of your wrath keep your
    festivals."

[11]So you'd better keep every promise you've ever made
  to the Awesome One, Yahweh!
    Let all people bring their extravagant gifts to him
      alone.
[12]He is famous for breaking the spirit of the powers
  that be.
    And the kings of the earth will know him as the
      Fearsome One!

77 A CRY TO GOD
To the Pure and Shining One
Asaph's song of love's celebration

[1]I poured out my complaint to you, God.
  I lifted up my voice, shouting out for your help.
[2]When I was in deep distress, in my day of trouble,
  I reached out for you with hands stretched out to
    heaven.
  Over and over I kept looking for you, God,
  but your comforting grace was nowhere to be
    found.
[3]As I thought of you I moaned, "God, where are you?"[a]
  I'm overwhelmed with despair as I wait for your
    help to arrive.
                                    Pause in his presence

[4]I can't get a wink of sleep until you come and comfort
  me.
  Now I'm too burdened to even pray!
[5]My mind wandered, thinking of days gone by—
  the years long since passed.
[6]Then I remembered the worship songs I used to sing
  in the night seasons,

---

a 77:3 Or "When I am in heaviness [depressed], I will think upon God."

and my heart began to fill again with thoughts of
　you.
　So my spirit went out once more in search of you.
⁷Would you really walk off and leave me forever, my
　Lord God?
　Won't you show me your kind favor, delighting in
　　me again?
⁸Has your well of sweet mercy dried up?
　Will your promises never come true?
⁹Have you somehow forgotten to show me love?
　Are you so angry that you've closed
　your heart of compassion toward me?

Pause in his presence

¹⁰Lord, what wounds me most is that it's somehow my
　fault that
　you've changed your heart toward me
　and I no longer see the years of the Mighty One
　or your right hand of power.*ᵃ*
¹¹Yet I could never forget all your miracles, my God,
　as I remember all your wonders of old.
¹²I ponder all you've done, Lord, musing on all your
　miracles.
¹³It's here in your presence, in your sanctuary,
　where I learn more of your ways,*ᵇ*
　for holiness is revealed in everything you do.
　Lord, you're the one and only, the great and glorious
　　God!
¹⁴Your display of wonders, miracles, and power
　makes the nations acknowledge you.

---

a 77:10 This difficult verse has a number of alternate translations,
　including "Your right hand has changed [or withered]." The implica-
　tion is that God's power and protection are no longer being seen.
b 77:13 This is an alternative translation.

[15]By your glory-bursts you've rescued us over and over.
   Just ask the sons of Jacob or
   the sons of Joseph, and they will tell you!
   And all of us, your beloved ones, know that it's true!
                              Pause in his presence

[16]When the many waters of the Red Sea took one look
   at you,[a]
      they were afraid and ran away to hide—
      trembling to its depths!
[17]Storm clouds filled with water high in the skies;
   cloudbursts and thunderclaps announced your
      approach.
   Lightning-flashes lit up the landscape.
[18]Rolling whirlwinds exploded with sonic booms of
   thunder,
      rumbling as the skies shouted out your story
      with light and sound and wind.
   Everything on earth shook and trembled as you
      drew near.
[19]Your steps formed a highway through the seas
   with footprints on a pathway no one even knew was
      there.[b]
[20]You led your people forward by your loving hand,
   blessed by the leadership of Moses and Aaron.

78 LESSONS FROM HISTORY
Asaph's poetic song of instruction

[1]Beloved ones, listen to this instruction.
   Open your heart to the revelation
   of this mystery that I share with you.

---

a 77:16 Although the Red Sea is not mentioned in the verse, it is implied in the context.
b 77:19 This could be a prophecy of Jesus one day walking on water.

²A parable and a proverb are hidden in what I say—
an intriguing riddle[a] from the past.
³⁻⁴We've heard true stories from our fathers about our
rich heritage.
We will continue to tell our children
and not hide from the rising generation
the great marvels of our God—
his miracles and power that have brought us all this
far.
⁵The story of Israel is a lesson in God's ways.
He established decrees for Jacob and established
the law in Israel,
and he commanded our forefathers to teach them to
their children.
⁶For perpetuity God's ways will be passed down
from one generation to the next, even to those not
yet born.
⁷In this way, *every generation* will set its hope in God
and not forget his *wonderful* works but keep his
commandments.
⁸By following his ways they will break the past
bondage
of their fickle fathers, who were a stubborn,
rebellious generation
and whose spirits strayed from the eternal God.
They refused to love him with all their hearts.
⁹Take, for example, the sons of Ephraim.
Though they were all equipped warriors, each with
weapons,
when the battle began they retreated and ran away
in fear.

---

a 78:2 The Hebrew word for "riddle" (*chidoth*) comes from the verb
meaning "to tie a knot." It is something that must be untied and
unraveled by the Spirit of God. One of these riddles or wordplays is
the name of Jesus hidden in plain sight (see v. 22 and footnote).

[10]They didn't really believe the promises of God;
  they refused to trust him and move forward in faith.
[11]They forgot his wonderful works and the miracles of
  the past,
[12]even their exodus from Egypt, the epic miracle of his
  might.
  They forgot the glories of his power at the place of
    passing over.[a]
[13]God split the sea wide open, and
  the waters stood at attention on either side
  as the people passed on through!
[14]By day the moving glory-cloud led them forward.
  And all through the night the fire-cloud stood as a
    sentry of light.
[15-16]In the days of desert dryness, he split open the
  mighty rock,
  and the waters flowed like a river before their very
    eyes.
  He gave them all they wanted to drink from his
    living springs.
[17]Yet they kept their rebellion alive against God Most
  High,
  and their sins against God continued to be counted.
[18]In their hearts they tested God just to get what they
  wanted,
  asking for the food their hearts craved.
[19-20]Like spoiled children they grumbled against God,
  demanding he prove his love by saying,
  "Can't God provide for us in this barren wilderness?
  Will he give us food, or will he only give us water?
  Where's our meal?"

---

a 78:12 Or "the fields of Zoan." *Zoan* means "crossing place" or "place
of departure." (See v. 43.)

²¹Then God heard all their complaining and was
   furious!
   His anger flared up against his people.
²²For they turned away from faith and walked away in
   fear;
      they failed to trust in his power to save[a] them when
      he was near.
²³⁻²⁴Still he spoke on their behalf, and the skies opened
   up;
      the windows of heaven poured out food,
      the mercy bread-manna.
   The grain of grace fell from the clouds.
²⁵Humans ate angels' food—the meal of the mighty
   ones.[b]
   His grace gave them more than enough!
²⁶⁻²⁷The heavenly winds of miracle power blew in their
   favor,
      and food rained down upon them;
      succulent quail quieted their hunger as they ate all
      they wanted.
²⁸Food fell from the skies, thick as clouds;
   their provision floated down right in front of their
   eyes!
²⁹He gave them all they desired, and they ate to their
   fill.
³⁰⁻³¹But before they had even finished,
   even with their food still in their mouths,
   God's fiery anger arose against them,
   killing the finest of their mighty men.

---

a 78:22 The word for "save" looks and sounds like Yeshua (Jesus).

b 78:25 The word for "angels" is 'abirim which means "brave," "noble,"
   or "strong." The psalmist was saying that God gave them the best, most
   delicious food imaginable, a meal eaten by the mighty ones, and yet
   the people grew tired of it and began to complain and demanded some
   variety.

³²Yet in spite of all this, they kept right on sinning.
   Even when they saw God's marvels,
   they refused to believe God could care for them.
³³So God cut their lives short with sudden disaster,
   with nothing to show for their lives but fear and
      failure.
³⁴*When he cared for them they ignored him*,
   but when he began to kill them, ending their lives in
      a moment,
   they came running back to God, pleading for
      mercy.
³⁵They remembered that God, the Mighty One,
   was their strong protector,
   the Hero-God who would come to their rescue.
³⁶⁻³⁷But their repentance lasted only as long as they
      were in danger;
   they lied through their teeth to the true God of the
      Covenant.
   So quickly they wandered away from his promises,
   following God with their words and not their
      hearts!
   Their worship was only flattery.
³⁸But amazingly, God—so full of compassion—still
      forgave them.
   He covered over their sins with his love,
   refusing to destroy them all.
   Over and over he held back his anger,
   restraining wrath to show them mercy.
³⁹He knew that they were made from mere dust—
   frail, fragile, and short-lived, here today and gone
      tomorrow.
⁴⁰How many times they rebelled in their desert days!
   How they grieved him with their grumblings.
⁴¹Again and again they limited God, preventing him
   from blessing them.

Continually they turned back from him
and provoked[a] the Holy One of Israel!
⁴²They forgot his great love, how he took them by his
hand,
and *with redemption's kiss* he delivered them from
their enemies.
⁴³They disregarded all the epic signs and marvels they
saw
when they escaped from Egypt's bondage.
They forgot the judgment of the plagues that set
them free.
⁴⁴God turned their rivers into blood, leaving the people
thirsty.
⁴⁵He sent them vast swarms of filthy flies that sucked
their blood.
He sent hordes of frogs, ruining their lives.
⁴⁶Grasshoppers consumed all their crops.
⁴⁷Every garden and every orchard
was flattened with blasts of hailstones,
their fruit trees ruined by a killing frost.
⁴⁸Even their cattle fell prey, pounded by the falling
hail;
their livestock were struck with bolts of lightning.
⁴⁹Finally, he unleashed upon them the fierceness of his
anger.
Such fury!
He sent them sorrow and devastating trouble
by his mighty band of destroying angels;
messengers of death were dispatched against them.
⁵⁰⁻⁵¹He lifted his mercy and let loose his fearful anger
and did not spare their lives.

---

a 78:41 The Hebrew verb for "provoked" is a hapax legomenon and
comes from a root word for "marked." It is as though Israel's behav-
ior wounded the heart of God.

He released the judgment-plagues to rage through
    their land.
God struck down in death all the firstborn sons of
    Egypt—
the pride and joy of each family.
⁵²Then, like a shepherd leading his sheep, God led his
    people
    out of tyranny, guiding them through the wilderness
        like a flock.
⁵³Safely and carefully God led them out, with nothing
    to fear.
    But their enemies he led into the sea.
    He took care of them there once and for all!
⁵⁴Eventually God brought his people to the
    Holy Land,
    to a land of hills that he had prepared for them.ᵃ
⁵⁵He drove out and scattered all the peoples occupying
    the land,
    staking out an inheritance, a portion for each of
        Israel's tribes.
⁵⁶Yet for all of this, they still rebelled and refused to
    follow his ways,
    provoking to anger the God Most High.
⁵⁷⁻⁵⁸Like traitors turning back, they forsook him.
    They were even worse than their fathers!
    They became treacherous deceivers, crooked and
        corrupt,
    and worshiped false gods in the high places,
    bringing low the name of God with every idol they
        erected.
    No wonder he was filled with jealousy and furious
        with anger!

---

a 78:54 The Aramaic reads "He brought them to the border of his
holiness, the mountain possessed by his right hand."

⁵⁹Enraged with anger, God turned his wrath on them,
  and he rejected his people with disgust.
⁶⁰God walked away from them and left his dwelling
  place at Shiloh,
    abandoning the place where he had lived among
    them,
⁶¹allowing his emblem of strength, his glory-ark, to be
  captured.
    Enemies stole the very source of Israel's power.
⁶²God vented his rage, allowing his people to be
  butchered
    when they went out to battle,
    for his anger was intense against his very own.
⁶³Their young men fell on the battlefield and never
  came back.
    Their daughters never heard their wedding songs,
    since there was no one left to marry!
⁶⁴Their priests were slaughtered and their widows
  were killed
    before they had time to weep.
⁶⁵Then all at once the Almighty awakened
  as though he had been asleep.
    Like a mighty man he arose, roaring into action!
⁶⁶He blasted into battle, driving back every foe,
    defeating them and disgracing them for time and
    eternity.
⁶⁷He rejected Joseph's family, the tribe of Ephraim.
⁶⁸He chose instead the tribe of Judah*a*
  and Mount Zion, which he loves.
⁶⁹There he built his towering temple,
  strong and enduring as the earth itself.

---

a 78:68 The place of God's dwelling was moved from the land of
Ephraim (Shiloh) to the land of Judah (Jerusalem).

⁷⁰God also chose his beloved one, David.
   He promoted him from caring for sheep
   and made him his prophetic servant.
⁷¹⁻⁷²God prepared David and took this gentle
   shepherd-king
   and presented him before the people
   as the one who would love and care for them
   with integrity, a pure heart, and the anointing
   to lead Israel, his holy inheritance.

79 Prayer in a Time of National Disaster
Asaph's poetic song

¹God, won't you do something?
   Barbarians have invaded your inheritance.
   Your temple of holiness has been violated,
   and Jerusalem has been left in ruins.
²The corpses of your loving people are lying in the
   open—
   food for the beasts and the birds.
³The shed blood of your servants has soaked the city,
   with no one left to bury the dead.
⁴Now the nearby nations heap their scorn upon us,
   scoffing, mocking us incessantly.
⁵How much longer, O Yahweh, must we endure this?
   Does your anger have no end?
   Will your jealousy burn like a raging fire?
⁶If you're going to pour out your anger,
   pour it out on all these nations around us, not on us!
   They're the ones who do not love you like we do!
⁷See how they've attacked us, consuming the land,
   leaving it desolate.
⁸Please, God, don't hold the sins of our fathers against
   us.
   Don't make us pay for their sins.

Hurry to our side, and let your tenderhearted mercy
meet us in our need, for we are devastated beyond
belief.

[9]Our hero, come and rescue us!
O God of the breakthrough, for the glory of your
name,
come and help us!
Forgive and restore us; heal us and cover us in your
love.

[10]Why should all the nations sneer at us, saying,
"Where is this God of yours?"
Now is the time, Lord.
Show your people and all the world that
you will avenge this slaughter and bloodshed once
and for all!

[11]Listen, Lord! Hear the sighing of all the prisoners of war,
all those doomed to die. Demonstrate your glory-power,
and come and rescue your condemned children!

[12]Lord God, take what these mocking masses have
done to us
and pay it all back to them seven times over.

[13]Then we, your devoted lovers, will forever thank you,
praising your name from generation to generation!

80 RESCUE AND RESTORE

For the Pure and Shining One
Asaph's poetic song To the tune of "Your Decrees
Are like Lilies"

[1]God-Enthroned, be revealed in splendor
as you ride upon the cherubim!
How perfectly you lead us, a people set free.[a]

---

a 80:1 Or "You lead Joseph like a flock." Joseph, as a metaphor,
becomes a picture of the saga of God's people once imprisoned and
now set free to rule and reign.

Loving shepherd of Israel—listen to our hearts'
     cry!
Shine forth from your throne of dazzling light.
[2]In the sight of Benjamin, Ephraim, and Manasseh,[a]
     stir up your mighty power in full display before our
          eyes.
     Break through and reveal yourself by coming to our
          rescue.
[3]Revive us, O God! Let your beaming face shine upon
     us
     with the sunrise rays of glory;
     then nothing will be able to stop us.
[4]O God, the mighty Commander of Angel Armies,
     how much longer will you smolder in anger?
     How much longer will you be disgusted with your
          people
     even when they pray?
[5]You have fed us with sorrow and grief
     and made us drink our tears by the bowlful.
[6]You've made us a thorn in the side of all the
     neighboring lands,
     and now they just laugh at us with their mocking
          scorn.
[7]Come back, come back, O God, and restore us!
     You are the Commander of Angel Armies.
     Let your beaming face shine upon us with the
          sunrise rays of glory,
     and then nothing will be able to stop us!

---

a 80:2 The Hebrew text includes the names Ephraim ("doubly fruitful"), Benjamin ("son of my right hand"), and Manasseh ("you made
me forget"). These three sons of Rachel marched together behind
the ark of glory (see Num. 2:17–24) and became representatives of
all who follow the glory of God. They will be "doubly fruitful," "sons
of his right hand," and those who have "forgotten" their lives in
Adam.

[8-9]Remember how you transplanted us here
   like a tender vine from Egypt.
   You cleared the land for your vineyard,
   evicting the nations from your land and planting us
      here.
   The roots of your vineyard went deep into the soil
   and filled the land with fruit.
[10-11]Because of your favor on your vineyard,
   blessing extended to every mountain of influence.
   Through this flourishing vineyard mighty ones were
      raised up.
   The nations were blessed by your fruitful vineyard
      of Israel,
   all the way from the Mediterranean Sea[a] to the
      Euphrates.
[12-13]So Lord, why have you broken down
   your fence of favor around us?
   Trespassers can steal the fruit from off our vines,
   and now every wild beast comes
   breaking through our wall to ravage us.
   You've left us without protection!
[14]Come back, come back, O God to restore us!
   You are the Commander of Angel Armies.
   Look down from heaven and see our crisis.
   Come down and care for your lovely vineyard once
      again.
[15]Nurture our root and our fruit with your loving
   care.
   Raise up the Branch-Man, the Son whom you've
      made strong.

---

a 80:10–11 This translation makes explicit the symbols in the text. The
   "vineyard" is Israel, the mountains are the high places of influence
   in culture, the cedars ("mighty ones") are the mighty and powerful
   of men, and the "Sea" speaks of the nations (sea of humanity).

¹⁶Enemies chopped down our vine and set it on fire;
   now show them your anger and let them perish by
      your frown.
¹⁷Strengthen this Branch-Man, the Son of your love,
   the Son of Man who dwells at your right hand.
¹⁸Then we will never turn back from you.
   Revive us again, that we may trust in you.
¹⁹O God, the mighty Commander of Angel Armies,
   come back and rescue us!
   Let your beaming face shine upon us
   with the sunrise rays of glory.
   Then nothing will ever stop us again!

81 FOR THE FEAST OF HARVEST

For the Pure and Shining One
Asaph's poetic song set to the melody of "For the Feast
of Harvest"

¹Lord, just singing about you makes me strong!
   So I'll keep shouting for joy to Jacob's God, my
      champion.
²Let the celebration begin!
   I will sing with drum accompaniment and with the
      sweet sound
   of the harp and guitar strumming.
³Go ahead! Blow the jubilee trumpet to begin the feast!
   Blow it before every joyous celebration and festival.*ᵃ*
⁴For God has given us these seasons of joy,
   days that the God of Jacob decreed for us to
      celebrate and rejoice.
⁵He has given these feasts to remind us of his triumph
   over Egypt,
   when he went out to wage war against them.

---

a 81:3 Or "on the day of the new moon and the day of the full moon."

I heard the message in an unknown tongue as he
said to me,
[6]"I have removed your backbreaking burdens
and have freed your hands from the hard labor and
toil.[a]
[7]You called out to me in your time of trouble, and I
rescued you.
I came down from the realm of the secret place of
thunder,
where mysteries hide.
I came down to save you.
I tested your hearts at the place where there was no
water to drink,
the place of your bitter argument with me."[b]

Pause in his presence

[8]"Listen to me, my dear people.
For I'm warning you, and you'd better listen well!
For I hold something against you.
[9]Don't ever be guilty of worshiping any other god but
me.
[10]I am your only God, the living God.
Wasn't I the one who broke the strongholds over
you
and raised you up out of bondage?
Open your mouth with a mighty decree;
I will fulfill it now, you'll see!
The words that you speak, so shall it be!
[11]But my people still wouldn't listen;
my princely people would not yield to me.

---

a 81:6 Or "from holding the baskets," which alludes to the Hebrews
carrying basket loads of burdens for their Egyptian masters.
b 81:7 The Hebrew includes the word *Meribah*, which means "the
place of strife and contention."

¹²So I lifted my grace from off of their lives, and I
    surrendered them
    to the stubbornness of their hearts.
    For they were living according to their own selfish
        fantasies.
¹³O that my people would once and for all listen to me
    and walk faithfully in my footsteps, following my ways.
¹⁴Then and only then will I conquer your every foe
    and tell every one of them, 'You must go!'
¹⁵Those who hate my ways will cringe before me
    and their punishment will be eternal.
¹⁶But I will feed you with my spiritual bread.
    You will feast and be satisfied with me,
    feeding on my revelation-truth like honey
    dripping from the cliffs of the high place."

82 TRUE JUSTICE
Asaph's poetic song

¹All rise! For God now comes to judge
    as he convenes heaven's courtroom.*
    He judges every judge and rules in the midst of the
        gods, saying,
²"How long will you judges refuse to listen
    to the voice of true justice and continue to corrupt
        what is right
    by judging in favor of the wrong?"

                                    Pause in his presence

³"Defend the defenseless, the fatherless and the
    forgotten,
    the disenfranchised and the destitute.

---

a 82:1 Or "the council of El." The Aramaic reads "God now stands in
    the assembly of the angels, and he will judge in their midst."

⁴Your duty is to deliver the poor and the powerless;
  liberate them from the grasp of the wicked.
⁵But you continue in your darkness and ignorance
  while the foundations of society are shaken to the
    core!
⁶Didn't I commission you as judges, saying,
  'You are all like gods, since you judge on my behalf.
  You are all like sons of the Most High, my
    representatives.'
⁷Nevertheless, in death you are nothing but mere men!
  You will be laid in the ground like any prince and
    you will die."
⁸All rise! For God now takes his place as judge of all
  the earth.
  Don't you know that everything and everyone
    belongs to him?
  The nations will be sifted in his hands!

83 GOD, DON'T BE SILENT[a]
Asaph's poetic song

¹God, you have to do something![b] Don't be silent and
  just sit idly by.
²⁻³Can't you see what they're doing?
  All your enemies are stirred up in an uproar!
  They despise you, Lord.
  In their defiant arrogance they rise up
  to host their secret council against your people.
  They conspire together to come and harm
  your cherished ones—your hidden ones.

---

a 83 The historical background to this psalm may be found in 2 Chron. 20:14–36.

b 83:1 Both the Aramaic and the Septuagint add a line in verse 1: "God, who is like you?"

[4]Our enemies keep saying,
"Now is the time to wipe Israel off the map.
We'll destroy even the memory of her existence!"
[5]They've made their pact, consulting and conspiring,
aligning together in their covenant against God.
[6-8]All the sons of Ishmael, the desert sheiks and the
nomadic tribes, Amalekites, Canaanites, Moabites,
and all the nations that surround us,
Philistines, Phoenicians, Gadarenes, and
Samaritans;[a]
allied together they're ready to attack!

Pause in his presence

[9]Do to them all what you did to the Midianites
who were defeated by Gideon.
Or what you did to Sisera and Jabin
when Deborah and Barak defeated them by the
Kishon River.
[10]Do to your enemies what you did at Endor,
whose rotting corpses fertilized the land.
[11-12]Repeat history, God! Make all their "noble ones"
die like Oreb, Zebah, and Zalmunna, who said in
their pride,
"We will seize God's people along with all their
pleasant lands!"

---

a 83:6–8 As translated from the Aramaic. The Greek is "It includes
the tents of Edom and Ishmael [Palestinians and those of southern
Jordan], Moab [Palestinians and those of central Jordan] and Hag-
rites [Egyptians or possibly northern Jordanians], Gebal [Byblos and
northern Lebanon], Ammon [Palestinians and northern Jordanians]
and Amalek [Arabs of the Sinai Peninsula], Philistia [Gaza], and the
inhabitants of Tyre [southern Lebanese]. Even Assyria [Syrians and
northern Iraqis] has become their ally as an arm [military might] for
the sons of Lot." This comprises virtually every neighbor surrounding Israel.

¹³Blow them away, God, like straw in the wind,
   like a tumbleweed in the wilderness!
¹⁴Burn them up like a raging fire roaring down the
   mountainside;
   consume them all until only charred sticks remain!
¹⁵Chase them away like before a mighty storm and
   terrifying tempest.
¹⁶O Lord, disgrace them until their faces fill with
   shame,
   and make them acknowledge the glory of your
      name.
¹⁷Make them utter failures in everything they do
   until they perish in total disgrace and humiliation,
¹⁸so they will know that you, and you alone,
   are Yahweh, the only Most High God exalted over all
      the earth!

84 Longing for God

For the Pure and Shining One
A prophetic song written by the prophetic singers of
Korah's clan
Set to the melody of "For the Feast of Harvest"ᵃ

¹God of Heaven's Armies, you find so much beauty in
   your people!
   They're like lovelyᵇ sanctuaries of your presence.
²Deep within me are these lovesick longings,
   desires and daydreams of living in union with you.
   When I'm near you, my heart and my soul
   will sing and worship with my joyful songs of you,
   my true source and spring of life!

---

a 84 The Septuagint reads "For the wine vats."
b 84:1 The Hebrew word for "lovely" used here can also mean
   "beloved." This translation includes both of these concepts in this
   verse.

³O Lord of Heaven's Armies, my King and my God,
    even the sparrows and swallows are welcome to
       build a nest
    among your altars to raise their young.
⁴What pleasure fills those who live every day in your
    temple,
    enjoying you as they worship in your presence!
                                Pause in his presence

⁵How enriched are they who find their strength in the
    Lord;*ᵃ*
    within their hearts are the highways of holiness!*ᵇ*
⁶Even when their paths wind through the dark valley
    of tears,
    they dig deep to find a pleasant pool *where others*
       find only pain.
    He gives to them a brook of blessing
    filled from the rain of an outpouring.
⁷They grow stronger and stronger with every step
    forward,
    and the God of all gods will appear before them in
      Zion.
⁸Hear my cry, O God of Heaven's Armies!
    God of Jacob, listen to my loving prayer.
                                  Pause in his presence

⁹God, your wraparound presence is our defense.
    In your kindness look upon the faces of your
      anointed ones.*ᶜ*

---

a 84:5 The Aramaic reads "How blessed is the Son of Man with you as
   his helper."
b 84:5 The Hebrew is literally "Roads are in their hearts." It implies the
   ways [roads or "highways"] that lead us to God's holy presence.
c 84:9 Or "the face of your Anointed [Christ]."

¹⁰For just one day of intimacy with you*a* is like
    a thousand days of joy rolled into one!
    I'd rather stand at the threshold in front of the Gate
      Beautiful,
    ready to go in and worship my God,
    than to live my life without you
    in the most beautiful palace of the wicked.
¹¹For the Lord God is brighter than the brilliance of a
    sunrise!
    Wrapping himself around me like a shield,
    he is so generous with his gifts of grace and glory.
    Those who walk along his paths with integrity
    will never lack one thing they need, for he provides
      it all!
¹²O Lord of Heaven's Armies,
    what euphoria fills those who forever trust in you!

85 MERCY AND TRUTH
For the Pure and Shining One
A prophetic song composed by the prophetic singers
of Korah's clan

¹Lord, your love has poured out
    so many amazing blessings on our land!
    You've restored Jacob's destiny from captivity.
²You've forgiven our many sins and covered
    every one of them in your love.

                        Pause in his presence

³So now it's obvious that your blazing anger has
    ended and
    the furious fire of wrath has been extinguished *by*
      your mercy.

---

a 84:10 Or "in your [temple] courts."

⁴So bring us back to loving you, God our Savior.
  Restore our hearts so that we'll never again
  feel your anger rise against us.
⁵Will you forever hold a grudge?
  Will your anger endure for all time?
⁶Revive us again, O God! I know you will! Give us a
  fresh start!
  Then all your people will taste your joy and
    gladness.
⁷Pour out even more of your love on us!
  Reveal more of your kindness and restore us back to
    you!
⁸Now I'll listen carefully for your voice
  and wait to hear whatever you say.
  Let me hear your promise of peace—
  the message every one of your godly lovers longs to
    hear.
  Don't let us in our ignorance turn back from
    following you.
⁹For I know your power and presence shines on all
  your devoted lovers.
  Your glory always hovers over all who bow low
    before you.
¹⁰Your mercy and your truth have married each other.
  Your righteousness and peace have kissed.
¹¹Flowers of your faithfulness are blooming on the earth.
  Righteousness shines down from the sky.
¹²Yes, the Lord keeps raining down blessing after
  blessing,
  and prosperity will drench the land with a bountiful
    harvest.
¹³For deliverance*a* goes before him,
  preparing a path for his steps.

---

a 85:13 Or "righteousness."

86 A Prayer of Faith
King David's prayer

¹Lord, bend down to listen to my prayer.
   I am in deep trouble. I'm broken and humbled,
   and I desperately need your help.
²Guard my life, for I'm your faithful friend, your loyal
   servant for life.
   I turn to you in faith, my God, my hero; come and
      rescue me!
³Lord God, hear my constant cry for help;
   show me your favor and bring me to your fountain
      of grace!
⁴Restore joy to your loving servant once again,
   for all I am is yours, O God.
⁵Lord, you are so good to me, so kind in every way[a]
   and ready to forgive,
   for your grace-fountain keeps overflowing,
   drenching all your devoted lovers who pray to you.
⁶God, won't you pay attention to this urgent cry?
   Lord, bend down to listen to my prayer.
⁷Whenever trouble strikes, I will keep crying out to
   you,
   for I know your help is on the way.
⁸God, there's no one like you;
   there's no other god as famous as you.
   You outshine all others, and your miracles make it
      easy to know you.
⁹Lord Almighty, you are the one who created all the
   nations.
   Look at them—they're all on their way!
   Yes, the day will come when they all will worship you
   and put your glory on display.

---

a 86:5 The Septuagint reads "You're my provider."

[10]You are the one and only God.
   What miracles! What wonders! What greatness
      belongs to you!
[11]Teach me more about you, how you work and how
   you move,
      so that I can walk onward in your truth
      until everything within me brings honor to your
         name.
[12]With all my heart and passion I will thank you, my God!
   I will give glory to your name, always and forever!
[13]You love me so much, and you have placed your
   greatness upon me.[a]
      You rescued me from the deepest place of darkness,
      and you have delivered me from a certain death.
[14]God, look at how these arrogant ones have defied me.
   Like a vicious band of violent men, they have tried
      to kill me.
   They wouldn't worry for a moment that they were
      sinning against you!
[15]But Lord, your nurturing love is tender and gentle.
   You are slow to get angry yet so swift to show your
      faithful love.
   You are full of abounding grace and truth.[b]
[16]Bring me to your grace-fountain
   so that your strength becomes mine.
   Be my hero and come rescue your servant once
      again!
[17]Send me a miraculous sign to show me how much
   you love me,
      so that those who hate me will see it and be ashamed.
      Don't they know that you, Lord, are my comforter,
      the one who comes to help me?

---

a 86:13 As translated from the Aramaic.
b 86:15 As translated from the Aramaic and the Septuagint.

87 FOUNTAINS OF DELIGHT

A prophetic song composed by the prophetic singers of Korah's clan

¹High upon his hills of holiness stands God's city.*ᵃ*
²How God loves the gates of Zion, his favorite place on
　　earth.*ᵇ*
³So many glorious things have been proclaimed
　　over Zion, God's holy city!

Pause in his presence

⁴For the Lord says, "Here are the nations
　　who will acknowledge me as God:*ᶜ*
　　Egypt,*ᵈ* Iraq,*ᵉ* Palestine,*ᶠ* and the Mediterranean people,*ᵍ*
　　even distant Ethiopia.
　　They will all boast, 'I was born in Zion!' "
⁵But over Zion it will be said,
　　"The mighty Man was born there, and he will
　　　　establish it."*ʰ*
　　For the God Most High will truly bless Jerusalem.
⁶And when he counts her citizens, recording them in
　　his registry,
　　he will write by their names: "This one was born
　　　　again here!"

Pause in his presence

---

a 87:1 The Aramaic reads "His foundations are in his holy mountains."
b 87:2 Or "The Lord loves Zion's gates more than all the dwelling places of Jacob."
c 87:4 This is in anticipation of the nations of the earth coming to know Christ as the eternal King. See Ps. 86:9.
d 87:4 Or "the proud one," which is a title given to Egypt.
e 87:4 Or "Babylon," which means "gate of God."
f 87:4 Or "Philistia," which means "land of sojourners."
g 87:4 Or "Tyre," which means "a rock."
h 87:5 As translated from the Aramaic. The Hebrew reads "Each one is born in Zion, and the Most High makes her secure."

[7]And the princes of God's feasts will sing and dance,[a]
  singing,
    "Every fountain of delight springs up from your life
      within me!"

88 SAVE ME FROM THIS SORROW[b]
To the Pure and Shining One
A song, a psalm[c] by the prophetic singers of Korah's
clan
To the tune of "Pierced," for instruction by Heman
the Ezrahite[d]

[1]Yahweh is the God who continually saves me.
  I weep before you night and day.
[2]Please bend down and listen to my sobbing,
  for my life is riddled with troubles
  and death is just around the corner!
[3]Everyone sees my life ebbing out.
  They consider me a hopeless case and see me as a
    dead man.

---

a 87:7 As translated from the Aramaic.

b 88 This psalm has traditionally been used by Christians for reading
  on Good Friday. Many insights can be found here of the crucifixion
  of Jesus Christ.

c 88 Psalm 88 is both a song and a psalm. The Hebrew for "song" can
  also mean "wall." There are times that our purest music will come
  when we feel like we are up against a "wall."

d 88 Heman the Ezrahite was considered comparable to Solomon in
  his wisdom (1 Kings 4:31). Jewish literature states that he was also
  a gifted musician and vocalist. But it also teaches that Heman was a
  leper, an outcast from society who lived in poverty, was shunned by
  all, and could not sing in the temple because of his disease. Read Ps.
  88 with this background in mind. *To the tune of "Pierced"* can also be
  translated "He has been humbled more than any man." The Hebrew
  word for "instruction" (*maschil*) comes from a word that means "to
  prosper" or "to understand."

⁴They've all left me here to die, helpless,
   like one who is doomed for death.
⁵They're convinced you've forsaken me,
   certain that you've forgotten me completely—
   abandoned, pierced, with nothing to look forward to
      but death.
⁶They have discarded me*a* and thrown me down
   into the deepest darkness as into a bottomless pit.
⁷I feel your wrath, and it's a heavy weight upon me,
   drowning me beneath a sea of sorrow.

                              Pause in his presence

⁸Why did you turn all my friends against me?
   You've made me like a cursed man in their eyes.
   No one wants to be with me now.
   You've caught me in a trap with no way out.
⁹Every day I beg for your help. Can't you see my
   tears?
   My eyes are swollen with weeping.
   My arms are wide, longing for mercy,*b*
   but you're nowhere to be found.
¹⁰How can those who are cut off from your care
   even know that you are there?
   Do departed spirits*c* rise up to praise you?

                              Pause in his presence

---

a 88:6 As translated from the Septuagint. The Hebrew reads "You have discarded me."

b 88:9 As translated from the Septuagint. The Greek reads "My hands are stretched out to you."

c 88:10 Or "Rephaites." The Rephaites were giants that inhabited the region of Bashan east of the Jordan. See Deut. 2:11; 3:11; Josh. 12:4–5.

¹¹Who can give thanks for your love in the graveyard?
  Who preaches your faithfulness in the place of
    destruction?
¹²Does death's darkness declare your miracles?
  How can anyone who's in the grave, where all is
    forgotten,
  remember how you keep your promises?
¹³Lord, you know my prayer before I even whisper it.*
  At each and every sunrise you will
  continue to hear my cry until you answer.
¹⁴O Lord, why have you thrown my life away?
  Will you keep turning the other way every time I call
    out to you?
¹⁵I've had to live in poverty and trouble all my life.*
  Now I'm humiliated, broken, and helpless before
    your terrors
  and I can't take it anymore.
¹⁶I'm overwhelmed by your burning anger.
  I've taken the worst you could give me,
  and I'm speechless before you.
¹⁷I'm drowning beneath the waves of this sorrow,
  cut off with no one to help.
¹⁸All my loved ones and friends keep far away from
    me,
  leaving me all alone with only darkness as my
    friend.

---

a 88:13 As translated from the Septuagint.
b 88:15 As translated from the Septuagint. The Greek reads "close to
  death all my life."

89 WILL YOU REJECT US FOREVER?
Poems by Ethan the Ezrahite for instruction[a]

First Poem – God's Promises to David

[1]This forever-song I sing[b] of the gentle love of God!
　　Young and old alike will hear about
　　your faithful, steadfast love—never failing!
[2]Here's my chorus: "Your mercy grows through the
　　ages.[c]
　　Your faithfulness is firm, rising up to the skies."
[3]I heard the Lord say, "My covenant has been made,
　　and I'm committed forever to my chosen one, David.
[4]I have made my oath that there will be sons of David
　　forever,
　　sons that are kings through every generation."
Pause in his presence

[5-6]Can you hear it? Heaven is filled with your praises,
　　O Lord!
　　All the holy ones are praising you for your miracles.
　　The sons of God are all praising you for your mighty
　　wonders.

---

a 89 Many scholars believe Ps. 89 contains four poems or stanzas.
This translation signifies each poem with an inscription.

b 89:1 The Hebrew word for "sing" has multiple homonyms. *Shuwr* can
also mean "wall." When we feel like we are up against a wall, it is
time to sing and see ourselves break through by faith. But *shuwr* can
also mean "to behold" or "to perceive." As we sing to God in abandoned worship, we perceive that his glory is greater than the wall that
stands before us. The root word of the word used here for "sing" is
sur, which is also the same word used for "having dominion over." So
many times when we sing in worship, exalting the loving-kindness of
God, we establish dominion over any thoughts that God might not be
faithful or that he may fail us. Sing when you feel defeated and watch
as the walls come down and you rise to take dominion over your foes.

c 89:2 As translated from the Septuagint.

We could search the skies forever and never find
   one like you.
All the mighty angels could not be compared to you.
⁷You are a God who is greatly to be feared
   as you preside over the council of holy ones.
You are surrounded by trembling ones
who are overwhelmed with fear and dread,
stunned as they stand in awe of you!
⁸So awesome are you, O Yahweh, Lord God of Angel
   Armies!
Where could we find anyone as glorious as you?
Your faithfulness shines all around you!
⁹You rule over oceans and the swelling seas.
   When their stormy waves rise, you speak, and they
      lie still.ᵃ
¹⁰You crushed the strongholds of Egypt,
   and all your enemies were scattered
   at the mighty display of your glory-power.
¹¹All the heavens and everything on earth belong to
   you,
for you are the Creator of all that is seen and
   unseen.
¹²The four corners of the earth were put in place by you.
   You made the majestic mountains
   that are still shouting their praises to your name.
¹³Breathtaking and awesome is your power!
   Astounding and unbelievable
   is your might and strength when it goes on display!
¹⁴Your glorious throne rests on a foundation
   of righteousness and just verdicts.
Grace and truth are the attendants who go before
   you.

ᵃ 89:9 This is a prophecy of Jesus, who would one day calm the
stormy seas. See Matt. 8:23–27.

[15]O Lord, how blessed are the people
who know the triumphant shout,[a]
for they walk in the radiance of your presence.[b]
[16]We can do nothing but leap for joy all day long,
for we know who you are and what you do,
and you've exalted us on high.
[17]The glory of your splendor is our strength,
and your marvelous favor makes us even stronger,
lifting us even higher!
[18]You are our King, the holiest one of all;
your wraparound presence is our protection.

Second Poem – God Keeps His Promises

[19-20]You spoke to your prophets in visions, saying,
"I have found a mighty hero for my people.
I have chosen David as my loving servant and
exalted him.
I have anointed him as king with the oil of my
holiness.
[21]I will be strength to him, and I will give him
my grace to sustain him no matter what comes.
[22]None of his enemies will get the best of him,
nor will the wicked one overpower him.
[23]For I will crush his every adversary
and do away with all who hate him.
[24]Because I love him and treasure him,
my faithfulness will always protect him.
I will place my great favor upon him,
and I will cause his power and fame to increase.
[25]I will set his hand over the sea
and his right hand over the rivers.

---

a 89:15 The Hebrew word for "triumphant shout" is *teruah*, a homonym of the word for "brokenness." Our triumphant shout can be powerful even in the midst of our brokenness.

b 89:15 Or "in the radiance of your face."

²⁶And he will come before me, saying,
   'You truly are my Father,ᵃ my only God, and my
      strong deliverer!'
²⁷I am setting him apart, favoring him as my firstborn
   son.
   I will make him the most high king in all the earth!
²⁸I will love him forever and always show him
   kindness.
   My covenant with him will never be broken.
²⁹For I have decreed that he will always have an heir—
   a dynasty that will release the days of heaven on
      earth.
³⁰⁻³²But if his children turn from me and forsake my
   words,
   refusing to walk in my truth, renouncing and
      violating my laws,
   then I will surely punish them for their sins
   with my stern discipline until they regret it.
³³But I will never, no never, lift my faithful love from
   off their lives.
   My kindness will prevail and I will never disown
      them.
³⁴⁻³⁵How could I revoke my covenant of love that I
   promised David?
   For I have given him my word, my holy, irrevocable
      word.
   How could I lie to my loving servant David?
³⁶⁻³⁷Sons of David will continue to reign on his throne,
   and their kingdom will endure as long as the sun is
      in the sky.
   This covenant will be an unbreakable promise that
   I have established for all time."

Pause in his presence

ᵃ 89:26 David was the first man in the Bible to address God as "my
Father."

Third Poem – Why Has Our King Been Defeated?

³⁸Why have you rejected me, the one you anointed?
Why would you cast me away?
Why would you lose your temper with me?
³⁹You have torn up the contract you made with me,
your servant.
You have stripped away my crown*a* and thrown it to
the ground.
⁴⁰You have torn down all my walls of defense
and have made my every hiding place into ruins.
⁴¹All the passersby attack and rob me while my
neighbors mock!
⁴²Instead of fighting for me, you take the side of my
enemies,
even giving them strength to subdue me,
and then watched them celebrate their victory!
⁴³You are no longer helping me in battle.
You've forsaken me to the swords of those
who would strike me down.
⁴⁴You've made my regal splendor to decrease
and allowed my rule to be overthrown.
⁴⁵Because of you, I've become old before my time,
and I'm publicly disgraced!

Pause in his presence

Fourth Poem – Save Us, God

⁴⁶How long will you hide your love from me?
Have you left me for good?
How long will your anger continue to burn against
me?
⁴⁷Remember, Lord, I am nothing but dust,
here today and so soon blown away.

---

a 89:39 In place of the word *crown*, some translations render "my
dignity."

Is this all you've created us for? For nothing but
this?
48Which one of us will live forever?
We are all mortal, terminal, for we will all one day
die.
Which one of us would ever escape our appointment
with death
and dodge our own funeral?

Pause in his presence

49So God, where is all this love and kindness you
promised us?
What happened to your covenant with David?
50Have you forgotten how your own servants are being
slandered?
Lord God, it seems like I'm carrying in my heart
all the pain and abuse of many people.
51They have relentlessly insulted and persecuted us,
your anointed ones.
52Nevertheless, blessed be our God forever and ever.
Amen! Faithful is our King!

BOOK 4
THE NUMBERS PSALMS
Psalms of our pilgrimage on earth

90 GOD, THE ETERNAL
A prayer of Moses, God's prophet

1Lord, you have always been our eternal home,
our hiding place from generation to generation.
2Long before you gave birth to the earth
and before the mountains were born,

you have been from everlasting to everlasting,[a]
the one and only true God.
[3]When you speak the words "Life, return to me!"
man turns back to dust.
[4]One thousand years pass before your eyes
like yesterday that quickly faded away,
like a night's sleep soon forgotten.[b]
[5-6]One day we will each be swept away into the sleep
of death.
We glide along through the tides of time—
so quickly gone, like a dream that fades at dawn,[c]
like glistening grass that springs up one day
and is dry and withered the next, ready to be cut
down!
[7]Terrified by your anger, confined beneath the curse,
we live our lives knowing your wrath.[d]
[8]For all of our faults and flaws are in full view to you.[e]
Everything we want to hide, you search out
and expose by the radiance of your face.
[9]We are banished to live in the shadow of your anger.
Our days soon become years until our lifetime
comes to an end,
finished with nothing but a sigh.[f]
[10]You've limited our life span to a mere seventy years,
yet some you give grace to live still longer.[g]

---

a 90:2 The Hebrew word often rendered "eternity" ["everlasting"] is
'olam, which can be translated "beyond the horizon."

b 90:4 Or "like divisions [watches] of the night."

c 90:5–6 A poetic description of what is implied in the context.

d 90:7 Or "worn out by your rage." Jesus has come and broken the
curse and lifted the unbearable burden of our sins.

e 90:8 The Septuagint reads "The laws we have broken all stand
before you."

f 90:9 The Septuagint reads "All our days have been filled with
failures."

g 90:10 Or "if in strength eighty years."

But even the best of years are marred by tears and toils
and in the end are nothing more than a gravestone
  in a graveyard![a]
We're gone so quickly, so swiftly;
we pass away and simply disappear.
[11]Lord, who fully knows the power of your passion
and the intensity of your emotions?[b]
[12]Help us to remember that our days are numbered,
and help us to interpret our lives correctly.
Set your wisdom deeply in our hearts
so that we may accept your correction.[c]
[13]Return to us again, O God!
How much longer will it take until you show us
your abundant compassion?
[14]Let the sunrise of your love end our dark night.
Break through our clouded dawn again!
Only you can satisfy our hearts,
filling us with songs of joy to the end of our days.
[15]We've been overwhelmed with grief;
come now and overwhelm us with gladness.
Replace our years of trouble with decades of delight.
[16]Let us see your miracles again, and let the rising
generation
see the glorious wonders you're famous for.
[17]O Lord our God, let your sweet beauty[d] rest upon us.
Come work with us, and then our works will endure;
you will give us success in all we do.

---

a 90:10 A poetic description of what is implied in the context. The Septuagint has the phrase "until we mellow and accept your correction."

b 90:11 As translated from the Aramaic. The Hebrew can be translated "Who could experience the strength of your anger? Who could endure the fear your fury can bring, and who truly comprehends the fear of God?"

c 90:12 As translated from the Septuagint.

d 90:17 Or "favor."

91 SAFE AND SECURE

¹When you abide under the shadow of Shaddai,[a]
    you are hidden[b] in the strength of God Most High.
²He's the hope that holds me and the stronghold to
    shelter me,
    the only God for me, and my great confidence.
³He will rescue you from every hidden trap of the
    enemy,[c]
    and he will protect you from false accusation
    and any deadly curse.[d]
⁴His massive arms[e] are wrapped around you,
    protecting you.
    You can run under his covering of majesty and hide.
    His arms of faithfulness are a shield keeping you
        from harm.
⁵You will never worry about an attack of demonic
    forces at night
    nor have to fear a spirit of darkness coming against
        you.

---

a 91:1 Shaddai (*šadday*) is taken from a Hebrew root word with many
expressive meanings. It can mean "God of the Mountain," "God the
Destroyer of Enemies," "God the Self-Sufficient One," "God the Nur-
turer of Babies," or "God the Almighty." Moses the lawgiver is the
author of this psalm, yet every verse seems to breathe the unlimited
grace and mercy of God.

b 91:1 Or "[I] endure through the night." See Job 39:28, where the
same Hebrew word is used for an eagle passing the night on the
high cliffs.

c 91:3 Or "hunter."

d 91:3 As translated from the most ancient Hebrew manuscripts and
the Septuagint. The Hebrew word can mean "poisoned arrows."

e 91:4 Or "wings." Also found in the next sentence, "under his wings,"
which speaks not of God having wings, but of the wings of the
cherubim resting on the mercy seat. The implication is that we can
always come to the mercy seat and rest without fear.

⁶Don't fear a thing!
Whether by night or by day, demonic danger will not
trouble you,ᵃ
nor will the powers of evil be launched against you.
⁷Even in a time of disaster, with thousands and
thousands being killed,
you will remain unscathed and unharmed.
⁸You will be a spectator as the wicked perish in
judgment,
for they will be paid back for what they have done!
⁹⁻¹⁰When we live our lives within the shadow of God
Most High,
our secret hiding place, we will always be shielded
from harm.
How then could evil prevail against us or disease
infect us?
¹¹God sends angels with special orders to protect you
wherever you go,
defending you from all harm.
¹²If you walk into a trap, they'll be there for you
and keep you from stumbling.
¹³You'll even walk unharmed among the fiercest
powers of darkness,ᵇ
trampling every one of them beneath your feet!

---

a 91:6 Verses 5–6 are seen by many Jewish scholars as a reference
not merely to pestilence and natural dangers but to the realm of
spiritual darkness that would come against God's servants. These
spirits are equated to "arrows that fly in daytime" or "a pestilence
that walks" in the darkness. God's sheltered ones are kept from the
harm that could come from natural sources or supernatural sources.
What a wonderful place to hide and be secure!

b 91:13 The Hebrew includes the words for "lions," "snakes," and
"dragons" as the three great symbols of satanic power.

¹⁴For here is what the Lord has spoken to me:
"Because you loved me, delighted in me, and have
been loyal to my name,
I will greatly protect you.
¹⁵I will answer your cry for help every time you pray,
and you will feel my presence
in your time of trouble.
I will deliver you and bring you honor.
¹⁶I will satisfy you with a full life and with all that I do
for you.
For you will enjoy the fullness of my salvation!"

92 A SONG OF PRAISE
A song for the day of worship[a]

¹It's so enjoyable to come before you
with uncontainable praises spilling from our hearts!
How we love to sing our praises over and over to
you,
to the matchless God, high and exalted over all!
²At each and every sunrise we will be thanking you
for your kindness and your love.
As the sun sets and all through the night,
we will keep proclaiming, "You are so faithful!"
³Melodies of praise will fill the air as every musical
instrument,[b]
joined with every heart, overflows with worship.
⁴No wonder I'm so glad; I can't keep it in!
Lord, I'm shouting with glee over all you've done,
for all you've done for me:

---

a 92 Ancient Jewish tradition holds that Adam composed this psalm
on the first Sabbath of creation, and it was to be sung by the Levites
on the Sabbath in the temple.
b 92:3 Or "a ten-stringed harp and lyre."

⁵what mighty miracles and your power at work—just
    to name a few!
    Depths of purpose and layers of meaning
    saturate everything you do.
⁶Such amazing mysteries are found within every
    miracle
    that nearly everyone seems to miss.
    Those with no discernment can never really discover
    the deep and glorious secrets hidden in your ways.
⁷It's true the wicked flourish, but only for a moment;
    they foolishly forget their destiny with death,
    that they will all one day be destroyed forevermore.
⁸But you, O Lord, are exalted forever
    in the highest place of endless glory,
⁹while your opponents, the workers of wickedness,
    will all perish, forever separated from you.
¹⁰Your anointing has made me strong and mighty.
    *You've empowered my life for triumph*ᵃ
    by pouring fresh oil over me.
¹¹You've said that those lying in wait to pounce on me
    would be defeated,
    and now it's happened right in front of my eyes,
    and I've heard their cries of surrender!
¹²Yes! Look how you've made all your devoted lovers
    to flourish like palm trees,
    each one growing in victory, standing with strength!ᵇ
¹³You've transplanted them into your heavenly
    courtyard,
    where they are thriving before you,

---

a 92:10 The Septuagint reads "I will raise my horn high like a rhinoc-
eros [Hb. translated as "wild ox"], and in my old age I will still have
plenty of oil [anointing]."

b 92:12 Or "growing high like a cedar in Lebanon." God makes us
immortal and immovable.

¹⁴for in your presence they will still overflow and be
anointed.
Even in their old age they will stay fresh,
bearing luscious fruit and abiding faithfully.
¹⁵Listen to them! With pleasure they still proclaim:
"You're so good! You're my beautiful strength!
You've never made a mistake with me."[a]

93 THE MAJESTY OF GOD

*A Friday song composed by King David after being
resettled in the land*[b]

¹Look! Yahweh now reigns as King!
He has covered himself with majesty and strength,
wearing them as his splendor-garments.
Regal power surrounds him as he sits securely on
his throne.
He's in charge of it all, the entire world,
and he knows what he's doing!
²Lord, you have reigned as King from the very
beginning of time.
Eternity is your home.
³⁻⁴Chaos once challenged you.
The raging waves lifted themselves over and over,
high above the ocean's depths, letting out their
mighty roar!
Yet at the sound of your voice they were all stilled
by your might.
What a majestic King, filled with power!
⁵Nothing could ever change your royal decrees;
they will last forever!

---

a 92:15 Or "You are just and never unfair."

b 93 This inscription is found in the Septuagint. Jews called this psalm
"The Friday psalm." The Talmud indicates that this psalm was sung
every Friday in the temple by the Levites.

Holiness is the beauty that fills your house;[a]
you are the one who abides forevermore!

94 GOD OF VENGEANCE
A Wednesday song composed by King David[b]

[1]Lord God Almighty, you are the God
who takes vengeance on your enemies.
It's time for you to punish evil!
Let your rays of revelation-light shine from your
people and
pierce the conscience of the wicked and punish
them.
[2]It's time to arise as judge of all the earth;
arise to punish the proud with the penalty they
deserve!
[3]How much longer will you sit back and watch the
wicked
triumph in their evil, boasting in all that is wrong?
[4-5]Listen to them bragging among themselves,
big in their own eyes, all because of the crimes
they've committed against your people!
See how they're crushing those who love you, God,
cruelly oppressing those who belong to you.[c]
[6]Heartlessly they murder the widows, the foreigners,
and even the orphaned children.
[7]They say to themselves, "The Lord God doesn't see
this.
Their God, the God of Jacob, he doesn't even care!"

---

a 93:5 Believers are now God's house, made holy by the blood of
Jesus. See 1 Cor. 3:16 and Heb. 3:6.

b 94 This inscription is taken from the Septuagint. The Mishnah states
that this psalm was sung by the Levites on the fourth day of the
week, each Wednesday, in the temple.

c 94:4–5 Or "[the people of] his inheritance." (See also v. 14.)

[8]But you'd better watch out, you stupid fools!
  You'd better wise up! Why would you act like God
    doesn't exist?
  Do you really think that God can't hear their cries?
[9]God isn't hard of hearing; he'll hear all their cries.
  God isn't blind. He who made the eye has superb
    vision,
  and he's watching all you do.
[10]Won't the God who knows all things know what
    you've done?
  The God who punishes nations will surely punish
    you!
[11]The Lord has fully examined every thought of man
  and found them all to be empty and futile.
[12]Lord Yah, there's such a blessing that comes
  when you teach us your Word and your ways.[a]
  Even the sting of your correction can be sweet.
[13]It rescues us from our days of trouble
  until you are ready to punish the wicked.[b]
[14]For the Lord will never walk away from his cherished
    ones,
  nor would he forsake his chosen ones who belong
    to him.[c]
[15]Whenever you pronounce judgments, they reveal
    righteousness.[d]
  All your devoted lovers will be pleased.[e]
[16]Lord, who will protect me from these wicked ones?
  If you don't stand to defend me, who will? I have no
    one but you!

---

a 94:12 Or "from your Torah."
b 94:13 Or "until a pit is dug for the wicked."
c 94:14 Or "[the people of] his inheritance."
d 94:15 Or "justice will prevail."
e 94:15 The Hebrew reads "and after it [judgment] are the pure in
   heart."

¹⁷I would have been killed so many times
   if you had not been there for me.
¹⁸When I screamed out, "Lord, I'm doomed!"
   your fiery love was stirred, and you raced to my
     rescue.
¹⁹Whenever my busy thoughts were out of control,
   the soothing comfort of your presence
   calmed me down and overwhelmed me with delight.
²⁰It's obvious to all; you will have nothing to do
   with corrupt rulers who pass laws that empower evil
   and defeat what is right.
²¹For they gang up against the lovers of righteousness
   and condemn the innocent to death.
²²⁻²³But I know that all their evil plans will boomerang
   back onto them.
   Every plot they hatch will simply seal their own
     doom.
   For you, my God, you will destroy them,
   giving them what they deserve.
   For you are my true tower of strength,
   my safe place, my hideout, and my true shelter.

95 It's Time to Sing

¹Come on, everyone! Let's sing for joy to the Lord!
   Let's shout our loudest praises to our God who saved
     us!
²Everyone come meet his face with a thankful heart.
   Don't hold back your praises;
   make him great by your shouts of joy!
³For the Lord is the greatest of all,
   King-God over all other gods!
⁴In one hand he holds the mysteries of the earth,
   and in the other he holds the highest mountain
     peaks.

⁵He's the owner of every ocean,
   the engineer and sculptor of earth itself!
⁶Come and kneel before this Creator-God;
   come and bow before the mighty God, our majestic
      maker!
⁷⁻⁹For we are those he cares for, and he is the God we
      worship.
   So drop everything else and listen to his voice!
   For this is what he's saying:
   "Today, when I speak,
   don't even think about turning a deaf ear to me
   like they did when they tested me at Meribah and
      Massah,ª
   the place where they argued with me, their Creator.
   Your ancestors challenged me over and over with
      their complaining,
   even though I had convinced them of my power
      and love.
   They still doubted my care for them.
¹⁰So for forty long years I was grieved and disgusted
      by them.
   I described them as wicked wanderers
   whose hearts would not follow my ways or keep my
      words.
¹¹So I made a vow in my anger and declared,
   'They will not enter the resting place I've planned
      for them!'
   *So don't you ever be hard-hearted or stubborn like
      they were!"*

---

a 95:7–9 *Meribah* means "strife" or "argument." *Massah* means
   "testing."

96 King of the World

[1]Go ahead—sing your new song to the Lord!
   Let everyone in every language sing him a new song.[a]
[2-3]Don't stop! Keep on singing! Make his name famous!
   Tell everyone every day how wonderful he is.
   Give them the good news of our great Savior.
   Take the message of his glory and miracles to every
      nation.
   Tell them about all the amazing things he has done.
[4]For the Lord's greatness is beyond description,
   and he deserves all the praise that comes to him.
   He is our King-God, and it's right to be in holy awe
      of him.
[5]Other gods[b] are absolutely worthless.
   For the Lord God is Creator-God,
   who spread the splendor of the skies!
[6]Breathtaking brilliance and awe-inspiring majesty
   radiate from his shining presence.
   His stunning beauty overwhelms all who come
      before him.[c]
[7]Surrender to the Lord Yahweh, all you nations and
      peoples.
   Surrender to him all your pride and strength.
[8]Confess that Yahweh alone deserves all the glory and
      honor.
   Bring an offering and come celebrate in his courts.
[9]Come worship the Lord God wearing the splendor of
      holiness.
   Let everyone wait in wonder as they tremble in awe
      before him.

---

a 96:1 Every new thing God does requires a new song to make it
known.
b 96:5 The Septuagint reads "demons."
c 96:6 Or "Strength and beauty are in his sanctuary."

[10]Tell the nations plainly that Yahweh rules over all!
  He is doing a great job, and nothing will disrupt him,
  for he treats everyone fair and square.
[11-12]Let the skies sing for joy! Let the earth join in the
  chorus.
  Let oceans thunder and fields echo this ecstatic
    praise
  until every swaying tree of every forest joins in,
  lifting up their songs of joyous praise to him!
[13]For here he comes, the Lord God,
  and he's ready to judge the world.
  He will do what's right and can be trusted
  to always do what's fair.

97 GOD RULES OVER ALL

*A psalm of David when his kingdom was
established*[a]

[1]Yahweh now reigns as King! Let everyone rejoice!
  His rule extends everywhere, even to distant lands,
  and the islands of the sea, let them all be glad.
[2]Clouds both dark and mysterious now surround him.[b]
  His throne of glory rests upon
  a foundation of righteousness and justice.
[3]All around him burns a blazing glory-fire consuming
  all his foes.
[4]When his lightning strikes, it lights up the world.
  People are wide-eyed as they tremble and shake.
[5]Mountains melt away like wax in a fire
  when the Lord of all the earth draws near.
[6]Heaven's messengers preach righteousness, and
  people everywhere see God's glory in the sky!

---

a 97 This inscription is from the Septuagint.
b 97:2 See Deut. 4:11; 5:22.

⁷Shame covers all who boast in other gods, for they
  worship idols.
  For all the supernatural powers once worshiped
  the true and living God.
⁸But God's Zion-people are content,
  for they know and hear the truth.
  The people of praise rejoice over all your
    judgments, O Lord!
⁹For you are King-God, the Most High God over all the
  earth.
  You are exalted above every supernatural power!
¹⁰Listen, you lovers of God! Hate evil,
  for God can keep you from wrong
  and protect you from the power of wickedness.
¹¹For he sows seeds of light within his devoted lovers,
  and seeds of joy burst forth for the lovers of God!
¹²So be glad and continue to give him thanks,
  for God's holiness is seen in everything he does.

98 SING A NEW SONG
David's poetic praise[a]

¹Go ahead—sing your brand-new song to the Lord!
  He is famous for his miracles and marvels,
  for he is victorious through his mighty power and
    holy strength.
²Everyone knows how God has saved us,
  for he has displayed his justice throughout history.
³He never forgets to show us his love and faithfulness.
  How kind he has been to Israel!
  All the nations know how he stands behind his people
  and how he saves his own.

---

a 98 The Septuagint has David as the author. The Hebrew reads simply "A psalm."

⁴So go ahead, everyone, and shout out your praises
  with joy!
  Break out of the box and let loose
  with the most joyous sound of praise!
⁵Sing your melody of praise to the Lord
  and make music like never before!ᵃ
⁶Blow those trumpets and shofars!
  Shout with joyous triumph before King Yahweh!
⁷Let the ocean's waves join in the chorus with their
  roaring praise
  until everyone everywhere shouts out in unison,
  "Glory to the Lord!"
⁸Let the rivers and streams clap with applause
  as the mountains rise in a standing ovation
  to join the mighty choir of exaltation.
⁹Look! Here he comes! The Lord and judge of all the
  earth!
  He's coming to make things right and to do it fair
    and square.
  And everyone will see that he does all things well!

99 GOD OF HOLINESS

¹Yahweh is King over all! Everyone trembles in awe
  before him.
  He rules enthroned between the wings of the
    cherubim.
  So let the earth shake and quake in wonder before
    him!
²For Yahweh is great and glorious in the midst of his
  Zion-people.
  He is exalted above all!
³Let everyone praise this breathtaking God, for he is holy.

---

a 98:5 Or "accompanied by a harp and the sound of music."

⁴A lover of justice is our mighty King; he is right in all
his ways.
He insists on being fair to all,
promoting true justice and righteousness in Jacob.
⁵So everyone, exalt the Lord our God
facedown before his glory-throne, for he is great and
holy.
⁶*God has his praying priests*,
like Moses, Aaron, and Samuel, who all interceded,
asking God for help.
God heard their cries and came to their rescue.
⁷He spoke to them from the pillar of clouds,
and they followed his instructions,
doing everything he told them.
⁸God, the great forgiver, answered their prayers,
yet he would punish them when they went astray.
⁹Keep exalting the Lord our God
facedown before his glory-throne, for he is great and
holy!

100 PRAISE GOD
A poetic song for thanksgiving

¹Lift up a great shout of joy to Yahweh!
Go ahead and do it—everyone, everywhere!
²Worship Yahweh with gladness.
Sing your way into his presence with joy!
³And realize what this really means—
we have the privilege of worshiping Yahweh our
God.
For he is our Creator and we belong to him.
We are the people of his pleasure.ᵃ

---

a 100:3 Or "the sheep of his pasture."

⁴You can pass through his open gates*a* with the
password of praise.
Come right into his presence with thanksgiving.
Come bring your thank offering to him
and affectionately bless his beautiful name!
⁵For Yahweh is always good and ready to receive you.
He's so loving that it will amaze you—
so kind that it will astound you!
And he is famous for his faithfulness toward all.
Everyone knows our God can be trusted,
for he keeps his promises to every generation!

101 INTEGRITY
David's poetic praise

¹Lord, I will sing about your faithful love for me.
My song of praise will have your justice as its
theme.
²I'm trying my best to walk in the way of integrity,
especially in my own home.
But I need your help!
I'm wondering, Lord, when will you appear?
³I refuse to gaze on that which is vulgar.
I despise works of evil people
and anything that moves my heart away from you.
I will not let evil hold me in its grip.
⁴Every perverse and crooked way I have put away
from my heart,
for I will have nothing to do with the deeds of
darkness.*b*

---

a 100:4 The Hebrew word for "gate [doorway]" is *sha'ar* and has multiple meanings. It can also mean "storm." When you pass through
his gates you enter into the stormy, passionate love of God. See Rev.
3:20.

b 101:4 Or "evil people."

⁵I will silence those who secretly want to slander my
  friends,
  and I will not tolerate the proud and arrogant.
⁶My innermost circle*ᵃ* will only be those
  who I know are pure and godly.
  They will be the only ones I allow to minister to me.
⁷There's no room in my home for hypocrites,
  for I can't stand chronic liars who flatter and
    deceive.
⁸At each and every sunrise I will awake to do what's
  right
  and put to silence those who love wickedness,
  freeing God's people*ᵇ* from their evil grip.
  I will do all of this because of my great love for you!ᶜ

102 FROM TEARS TO PRAISE
*A prayer for those who are overwhelmed and for all
the discouraged who come to pour out their hearts
before the Lordᵈ*

¹Lord, listen to my prayer! Listen to my cry for help!
²You can't hide your face from me in the day of my
  distress.
  Stoop down to hear my prayer and answer me
    quickly, Lord!
³⁻⁴For my days of happiness have gone up in smoke.
  My body is raging with fever, my heart is sick,
  and I'm consumed by this illness—
  withered like a dead leaf. I can't even eat.

---

a 101:6 Or "The faithful of the land."
b 101:8 Or "the city of Yahweh."
c 101:8 This phrase, implied in the Hebrew text, brings conclusion to
  the psalm.
d 102 As translated from the Septuagint.

⁵I'm nothing but skin and bones.
   Nothing's left of me but whispered groans.
⁶I'm like a pelican of the wilderness,ᵃ
   like an owl among the ruins.
⁷I'm sleepless, shivering in the cold, forlorn, and friendless,
   like a lonely bird on the rooftop.
⁸My every enemy mocks and insults me incessantly.
   They even use my name as a curse to speak over others!
⁹⁻¹⁰Because of your great and furious anger against me,
   all I do is suffer with sorrow,
   with nothing to eat but a meal of mourning.ᵇ
   My crying fills my cup with salty tears!
   In your wrath you have rejected me,
   sweeping me away like dirt on the floor.
¹¹My days are marked by the lengthening shadows of death.
   I'm withering away and there's nothing left of me.
¹²But then I remember that you, O Lord,
   still sit enthroned as King over all!
   The fame of your name will be revealed to every generation.

---

a 102:6 Ancient expositors viewed the "pelican in the wilderness" as a reference to Christ. The famous legend and much medieval artwork taught that the pelican would give the gift of blood to her starving young by piercing her own breast with her beak, allowing her young to drink her blood and live. What an amazing example of sacrificial love. Augustine writes concerning this: "The mother wounds herself deeply and pours forth her blood over her young, bathed in which they recover life." See Augustine, "Exposition on the Book of Psalms," in *Nicene and Post-Nicene Fathers, First Series*, ed. A. Cleveland Coxe and Philip Schaff (Peabody, MA: Hendrickson, 1955), 8:497.

b 102:9–10 Or "I eat ashes as if they were bread." Ashes speak of mourning, for mourners would often throw dust and ashes over their heads.

¹³I know you are about to arise and show your tender
love to Zion.
Now is the time, Lord,
for your compassion and mercy to be poured out—
the appointed time has come
for your prophetic promises to be fulfilled!
¹⁴For your servants weep in sympathy over Zion's ruins
and feel love for her every stone.
¹⁵When you arise to intervene,
all the nations and kings will be stunned
and will fear your awesome name, trembling before
your glory!
¹⁶Yes, you will reveal yourself to Zion
and appear in the brightness of your glory
to restore her and give her children.
¹⁷He responds to the prayer of the poor and broken
and will not despise the cry of the homeless.
¹⁸Write all this down for the coming generation,
so re-created people*ᵃ* will read it and praise the Lord!
¹⁹Tell them how Yah*ᵇ* looked down from his high and
holy place,
gazing from his glory to survey the earth.
²⁰He listened to all the groaning of his people longing
to be free,
and he set loose the sons of death to experience life.
²¹Multitudes will stream to Jerusalem to
praise the Lord and declare his name in Zion!
²²Peoples from every land, their kings and kingdoms,
will gather together to worship the Lord.
²³But God has brought me to my knees, shortening my
life.

---

a 102:18 Or "those born anew [re-created]."
b 102:19 Taken from *Yah*weh. Yah is often used as the name of the
God of Power.

²⁴So I cry out to you, my God, Father of eternity,
    please don't let me die!
    I know my life is not yet finished.
²⁵With your hands you once formed the foundations of
    the earth
    and handcrafted the heavens above.
²⁶⁻²⁷They will all fade away one day like worn-out
    clothing,
    ready to be discarded, but you'll still be here.
    You will replace it all!
    Your first creation will be changed,
    but you alone will endure, the God of all eternity!
²⁸Generation after generation our descendants will live
    securely,
    for you are the one protecting us, keeping us for
        yourself.

103 Our Father's Love
King David's song of praise

¹With my whole heart, with my whole life,
    and with my innermost being,
    I bow in wonder and love before you, the holy God!
²Yahweh, you are my soul's celebration.
    How could I ever forget the miracles of kindness
    you've done for me?
³You kissed my heart with forgiveness, in spite of all
    I've done.*ª*
    You've healed me inside and out from every disease.
⁴You've rescued me from hell*ᵇ* and saved my life.
    You've crowned me with love and mercy.

---

a 103:3 From this verse through the rest of the psalm, the writer used
    the second person (you). This translation has left the psalm in the
    first person to enhance the poetic nuance for the English reader.
b 103:4 Or "redeemed me from the pit," a term often used for Sheol or hell.

⁵You satisfy my every desire with good things.[a]
   You've supercharged my life so that I soar again[b]
   like a flying eagle in the sky!
⁶You're a God who makes things right,
   giving justice to the defenseless.
⁷You unveiled to Moses your plans
   and showed Israel's sons what you could do.
⁸Lord, you're so kind and tenderhearted[c]
   and so patient with people who fail you!
   Your love is like a flooding river
   overflowing its banks with kindness.[d]
⁹You don't look at us only to find our faults,[e]
   just so that you can hold a grudge against us.
¹⁰You may discipline us for our many sins,
   but never as much as we really deserve.
   Nor do you get even with us for what we've done.
¹¹Higher than the highest heavens—
   that's how high your tender mercy extends!
   Greater than the grandeur of heaven above
   is the greatness of your loyal love, towering over
     all
   who fear you and bow down before you!
¹²Farther than from a sunrise to a sunset—
   that's how far you've removed our guilt from us.

---

a 103:5 The Hebrew text is somewhat difficult to understand. It is literally "who satisfies with good ornaments."

b 103:5 Or "your youth [implying both strength and beauty] he restores."

c 103:8 Or "Lord, you're so compassionate and merciful." The Hebrew word for "compassion" has a homonym that means "womb." The Lord carries his people like a mother carries a child in her womb.

d 103:8 See Ex. 34:6.

e 103:9 Or "You [he] will not always fight with us [like fighting with enemies]."

226 { PSALM 103

¹³The same way a loving father feels toward his
children—
that's but a sample of your tender feelings toward
us,^a
your beloved children, who live in awe of you.
¹⁴You know all about us, inside and out.^b
You are mindful that we're made from dust.
¹⁵Our days are so few, and our momentary beauty^c
so swiftly fades away!
¹⁶Then all of a sudden we're gone,
like grass clippings blown away in a gust of wind,
taken away to our appointment with death,
leaving nothing to show that we were here.
¹⁷But Lord, your endless love stretches
from one eternity to the other,
unbroken and unrelenting toward those who fear
you
and those who bow facedown in awe before you.
Your faithfulness to keep every gracious promise
you've made
passes from parents, to children, to grandchildren,
and beyond.

---

a 103:13 Or "like a father has deep compassion for his children." The
Hebrew word for "tender feelings" is *racham*, which has a homonym
that can be translated "womb." Our Father carries you in his womb.
What a beautiful word play that our Father has a mother's nurturing
love for his children.

b 103:14 The Hebrew word *yatsar* can be translated "form" or "frame."
God knows our frame. But *yatsar* also has a homonym that means
"to be in distress" or "to be frustrated." So this sentence could be
translated "You know all about our frustrations and distress." These
thoughts combined would mean that God hasn't forgotten that he
formed us from dust and we'll experience frustrations as human
beings. God is sympathetic to our difficulties.

c 103:15 The Hebrew word translated "beauty" actually means
"shining."

¹⁸You are faithful to all those who follow your ways
   and keep your word.
¹⁹Yahweh has established his throne in heaven;
   his kingdom rules the entire universe.
²⁰So bless the Lord, all his messengers of power,
   for you are his mighty heroes who listen intently
   to the voice of his word to do it.
²¹Bless and praise the Lord, you mighty warriors,
   ministers who serve him well and fulfill his desires.
²²I will bless and praise the Lord with my whole heart!
   Let all his works throughout the earth,
   wherever his dominion stretches—
   let everything bless the Lord!

104 OUR CREATOR'S COMPASSION*a*

¹Everything I am will praise and bless the Lord!
   O Lord, my God, your greatness takes my breath
      away,
   overwhelming me by your majesty, beauty, and
      splendor!*b*
²You wrap yourself with a shimmering, glistening light.
   You wear sunshine like a garment of glory.
   You stretch out the starry skies like a tapestry.
³You build your balconies with light beams
   and ride as King in a chariot you made from clouds.
   You fly upon the wings of the wind.
⁴You make your messengers into winds of the Spirit,
   and all your ministers become flames of fire.

---

a 104 This psalm, attributed to David in the Septuagint, can be seen as
an exposition of the days of creation: first day: vv. 1–2; second day:
vv. 3–4; third day: vv. 5–17; fourth day: vv. 18–23; fifth day: vv. 24–
26; sixth day: vv. 27–30.
b 104:1 See Job 40:10.

⁵You, our Creator, formed the earth,
and you hold it all together so it will never fall apart.
⁶You poured the ocean depths over the planet,
submerging mountains beneath.
⁷Yet at the sound of your thunder-shout
the waters all fled away, filling the deep with seas.
⁸The mountains rose and valleys sank
to the levels you decreed for them.
⁹Then you set a boundary line for the seas
and commanded them not to trespass.
¹⁰You sent springs cascading through the valleys,
flowing freely between the mountains and hills.
¹¹You provide drink for every living thing;
men and beasts*a* have their thirst quenched because
of you.
¹²The birds build nests near the tranquil streams,
chirping their joyous songs from the branches
above.
¹³From your kindness you send the rain to water the
mountains
from the upper rooms of your palace.
Your goodness*b* brings forth fruit for all to enjoy.
¹⁴Your compassion brings the earth's harvest, feeding
the hungry.
You cause the grass to grow for livestock,
along with the fruit, grains, and vegetables to feed
mankind.
¹⁵You provide sweet wine to gladden hearts.
You give us daily bread to sustain life,
giving us glowing health for our bodies.*c*

---

a 104:11 Or "wild donkeys."
b 104:13 Or "your works."
c 104:15 Or "oil for our faces to shine."

¹⁶The trees of the Lord drink until they're satisfied.
  Lebanon's lofty trees stand tall right where you
    planted them.
¹⁷Within their branches you provide for birds
  a place to build their nests;
  even herons find a home in the cypress trees.
¹⁸You make the high mountains a home for wild goats
  and the rocky crag where the rock badgers burrow.
¹⁹You made the moon to mark the months
  and the sun to measure the days.
²⁰You turn off the light and it becomes night,
  and all the beasts of the forest come out to prowl.
²¹The mighty lions roar for their dinner,
  but it's you, God, who feeds them all.
²²At sunrise they slink back to their dens
  to crouch down in the shadows.
²³Then man goes out to his labor and toil,
  working from dawn to dusk.
²⁴O Lord, what an amazing variety of all you have
  created!
  Wild and wonderful is this world you have made,
  while wisdom was there at your side.
  This world is full of so many creatures, yet each
    belongs to you!
²⁵And then there is the sea! So vast! So wide and deep—
  swarming with countless forms of sea life, both
    small and great.
²⁶Trading ships glide through the high seas.
  And look! There are the massive whales
  bounding upon the waves.
²⁷All the creatures wait expectantly for you
  to give them their food as you determine.
²⁸You come near and they all gather around,
  feasting from your open hands,
  and each is satisfied from your abundant supply.

²⁹But if you were to withhold from them and turn
away,
they all would panic.
And when you choose to take away their breath,
each one dies and returns to the dust.
³⁰When you release your Spirit-Wind, life is created,
ready to replenish life upon the earth.
³¹May God's glorious splendor endure forever!
May the Lord take joy and pleasure in all that he has
made.
³²For the earth's overseer has the power to make it
tremble;
just a touch of his finger and volcanoes erupt
as the earth shakes and melts.
³³I will sing my song to the Lord as long as I live!
Every day I will sing my praises to God.
³⁴May you be pleased with every sweet thought I have
about you,
for you are the source of my joy and gladness.
³⁵Now, let all the sinners be swept from the earth.
But I will keep on praising you, my Lord, with all
that is within me.
My joyous, blissful shouts of "Hallelujah" are all
because of you!

105 GOD'S WONDERFUL WORKS*a*

¹Go ahead and give God thanks
for all the glorious things he has done!
Go ahead and worship him!
Tell everyone about his wonders!

---

a 105 The first fifteen verses of this psalm were sung as the ark of
glory was brought up to Jerusalem. See 2 Sam. 6; 1 Chron. 13–16.

²Let's sing his praises! Sing, and put all of his miracles
to music!
³Shine and make your joyful boast in him, you lovers
of God.
Let's be happy and keep rejoicing no matter what.
⁴Seek more of his strength! Seek more of him!
Let's always be seeking the light of his face.
⁵Don't you ever forget his miracles and marvels.
Hold to your heart every judgment he has decreed.
⁶For you are his servants, the true seed of Abraham,
and you are the chosen ones, Jacob's sons.
⁷For he is the Lord our God,
and his wise authority[a] can be seen in all he does.
⁸⁻⁹For though a thousand generations may pass away,
he is still true to his word.
He has kept every promise[b] he made to Abraham
and to Isaac.
¹⁰His promises have become an everlasting covenant
to Jacob,
as a decree to Jacob.
¹¹He said to them, "I will give you all the land of Canaan
as your inheritance."
¹²They were very few in number
when God gave them that promise,
and they were all foreigners to that land.
¹³They were wandering from one land to another
and from one kingdom to another.[c]
¹⁴Yet God would not permit anyone to touch them,
punishing even kings who came against them.
¹⁵He said to them, "Don't you dare lay a hand on my
anointed ones,
and don't do a thing to hurt my prophets!"

---

a 105:7 Or "judgments."
b 105:8–9 Or "promise of the covenant [pact]."
c 105:13 Or "from a kingdom to another nation."

¹⁶So God decreed a famine upon Canaan-land,
   cutting off their food supply.
¹⁷But he had already sent a man ahead of his people
   to Egypt;
   it was Joseph, who was sold as a slave.
¹⁸His feet were bruised by strong shackles
   and his soul was held by iron.
¹⁹God's promise to Joseph purged his character
   until it was time for his dreams to come true.
²⁰Eventually, the king of Egypt sent for him, setting
   him free at last.
²¹Then Joseph was put in charge of everything under
   the king;
   he became the master of the palace
   over all the royal possessions.
²²Pharoah gave him authority over all the princes of
   the land,
   and Joseph became the teacher of wisdom to the
      king's advisers.
²³Then Jacob, with all of Joseph's family,
   came from Canaan to Egypt and settled in Goshen.ᵃ
²⁴God made them very fruitful, and they multiplied
   incredibly
   until they were greater in number than those who
      ruled them.
²⁵God turned their hearts to hate his people
   and to deal treacherously with his servants.
²⁶But he sent them his faithful servant, Moses, the
   deliverer,
   and chose Aaron to accompany him.
²⁷Their command brought down signs and wonders,
   working miracles in Egypt.

---

a 105:23 Or "lived as a foreigner in the land of Ham [Egypt]." Ham
was a son of Noah.

²⁸By God's direction, they spoke and released a plague
of thick darkness over the land.

²⁹God turned their rivers to blood, causing every fish to
die.

³⁰And the judgment-plague of frogs came in enormous
numbers,
swarming everywhere, even into Pharaoh's
bedroom!

³¹God spoke and another plague was released—
massive swarms of flies, vast clouds of insects,
covered the land.

³²God rained down hail and flaming fire upon Egypt.

³³Their gardens and vines were all destroyed,
shattering trees into splinters throughout the
territory.

³⁴God spoke, and devouring hordes of locusts swept
over the land,

³⁵picking the ground clean of vegetation and crops.

³⁶Then God struck down their firstborn sons,
the pride and joyᵃ of every Egyptian family.

³⁷At last, God freed all the Hebrews from their slavery
and sent them away laden with the silver and gold
of Egypt.
And not even one was feebleᵇ on their way out!

³⁸Egypt was relieved at their exodus, ready to see them
go,
for the terror of the Lord of the Hebrews had fallen
upon them!

³⁹God spread out a cloud as shade as they moved
ahead
and a cloud of fire to light up their night.

_a_ 105:36 Or "the beginning of all their strength."

_b_ 105:37 Or "Not one of his tribes was a pauper" or "Not one stumbled."

⁴⁰Moses prayed and God brought them quail to eat.
  He satisfied them with heaven's bread falling from
    the sky.
⁴¹He broke open the boulder
  and the waters poured out like a river in the
    desert.
⁴²For God could never forget
  his holy promise to his servant Abraham.
⁴³So God brought out his chosen ones with singing;
  with a joyful shout they were set free!
⁴⁴He gave them lands and nations, just like he
    promised.
  Fruitful lands of crops they had never planted were
    now theirs.
⁴⁵All this was done for them so that they would be
    faithful
  to keep the ways of God, obeying his laws and
    following his truths.
  Hallelujah! Praise the Lord!

106 GOD IS GOOD

¹Hallelujah! Praise the Lord!
  Everyone thank God, for he is good and easy to
    please.
  Your tender love for us, Lord, continues on
    forever.
²Who could ever fully describe your glorious
    miracles?
  Yahweh, who could ever praise you enough?
³The happiest one on earth is the one who keeps your
    word
  and clings to righteousness every moment.
⁴So remember me, Lord, as you take joy in your
    people.

And when you come to bring the blessings of
  salvation,
  don't forget me!
⁵Let me share in the wealth and beauty of all your
  devoted lovers,
    rejoice with your nation in all their joys,
    and let me share in the glory you give to your
      chosen ones.
⁶We have all sinned so much, just like our fathers.
  "Guilty" is written over our lives.
⁷Our fathers who were delivered from Egypt
  didn't fully understand your wonders,
  and they took you for granted.
    Over and over you showed them such tender love
      and mercy!
    Yet they were barely beyond the Red Sea
    when they rebelled against you.
⁸Nonetheless, you saved them more than once
  so they would know how powerful you are,
  showing them the honor of your name.
⁹You roared over the waters of the Red Sea,
  making a dry path for your people to cross
    through.
¹⁰You freed them from the strong power
  of those who oppressed them
  and rescued them from bondage.
¹¹Then the waters rushed over their enemies and
  drowned them all—
    not one survived.
¹²Seeing this, the people believed your words,
  and they all broke out with songs of praise!
¹³Yet how quickly they forgot your miracles of
  power.
    They wouldn't wait for you to act when they were
      hungry,

¹⁴but demanded you satisfy their cravings and give
    them food!
    They tested you to the breaking point.
¹⁵So you gave them what they wanted to eat,
    but their souls starved away to nothing.
¹⁶They became envious of Moses and Aaron, your holy
    ones.
¹⁷You split open the earth, and it swallowed up
    Dathan and Abiram along with their followers.
¹⁸Fire fell from heaven and burnt up all the band of
    rebels,
    turning them to ashes.
¹⁹They made an idol of a calf at Sinai
    and bowed to worship their man-made statue.
²⁰They preferred the image of a grass-eating ox
    to the presence of the glory-filled God.
²¹⁻²²They totally forgot it was you who saved them
    by the wonders and awesome miracles you worked
        in Egypt.
²³So you decided to destroy them.
    But Moses, your chosen leader,
    stood in the gap between you and the people
    and made intercession on their behalf
    to turn away your wrath from killing them all.
²⁴Yet they still didn't believe your words
    and they despised the land of delight you gave to
        them.
²⁵They grumbled and found fault with everything
    and closed their hearts to your voice.
²⁶So you solemnly swore to them
    that they would all die in the desert.
²⁷And you scattered their children to distant lands to
    die as exiles.
²⁸Then our fathers joined the worshipers
    of the false god named "Lord of the Pit."

They even ate the sacrifices offered to the dead!
²⁹All they did made you burn with anger.
It made you so angry that a plague broke out among
them!
³⁰It continued until Phineas intervened and executed
the guilty for causing judgment to fall upon them.ᵃ
³¹Because of this deed of righteousness
Phineas will be remembered forever.
³²Your people also provoked you to wrath
at the stream called Strife.ᵇ
This is where Moses got into serious trouble!
³³Because the people were rebellious against you,
Moses exploded in anger and spoke to them out of
his bitterness.
³⁴Neither did our fathers destroy the enemies in the
land,
as you had commanded them.
³⁵But they mingled themselves with their enemies
and learned to copy their works of darkness.
³⁶They began to serve their gods and bow before their
idols.
All of this led them away from you
and brought about their downfall.
³⁷They even sacrificed their little children to the demon
spirits,
³⁸⁻³⁹shedding the innocent blood of their sons and
daughters.
These dark practices greatly defiled the land and
their own souls,
through the murder and bloodshed of their own
babies!

---

a 106:30 This is implicit information found in the story of Phineas
(Num. 25:7–9).

b 106:32 The word used here is *Meribah*, the Hebrew word for "strife"
(Num. 20:1–13).

Their sins made them spiritual adulterers before
    you.
⁴⁰This is why you were furious.
    As your anger burned hot against them,
    you couldn't even stand to look
    at your very own people any longer!
⁴¹So you turned them over to the crushing hands of
    other nations,
    and those who hated them became tyrants over
        them.
⁴²Oppressive enemies subdued them,
    ruling over them with their tyranny.
⁴³Many times you would have come to rescue them,
    but they continued in their rebellious ways,
    choosing to ignore your warnings.
    Then they sank lower and lower, destroyed by their
        depravity.
⁴⁴⁻⁴⁵Yet even so, you waited and waited,
    watching to see if they would turn
    and cry out to you for *a father's* help.
    And then, when you heard their cry,
    you relented and you remembered your covenant,
    and you turned your heart toward them again,
    according to your abundant, overflowing, and
        limitless love.
⁴⁶Then you caused even their oppressors
    to pity them and show them compassion.
⁴⁷Do it again, Lord! Save us, O Lord, our God!
    Gather us from our exile and unite us together
    so that we will give our great and joyous thanks to
        you again
    and bring you glory by our praises.
⁴⁸Blessed be our Lord God forever and ever.
    And let everyone everywhere say, "Hallelujah!"
    Amen! Faithful is our King!

BOOK 5
THE DEUTERONOMY PSALMS
Psalms of praise and the Word

107 GOD'S CONSTANT LOVE

[1]Let everyone give all their praise and thanks to the
  Lord!
    Here's why—he's better than anyone could ever
      imagine.
    Yes, he's always loving and kind, and his faithful
      love never ends.
[2-3]So, go ahead—let everyone know it!
    Tell the world how he broke through
    and delivered you from the power of darkness and
    has gathered us together from all over the world.
    He has set us free to be his very own!
[4]Some of us once wandered in the wilderness like
  desert nomads,
    with no true direction or dwelling place.
[5]Starving, thirsting, staggering,
    we became desperate and filled with despair.
[6]Then we cried out, "Lord, help us! Rescue us!" And he
  did!
[7]He led us out by the right way
    until we reached a suitable city to dwell in.
[8]So lift your hands and thank God for his marvelous
  kindness
    and for all his miracles of mercy for those he loves.
[9]How he satisfies the souls of thirsty ones
    and fills the hungry with goodness!
[10]Some of us once sat in darkness,
    living in the dark shadows of death.
    We were prisoners to our pain, chained to our
      regrets.

[11]For we rebelled against God's Word
  and rejected the wise counsel of God Most High.
[12]So he humbled us through our circumstances,
    watching us as we stumbled, with no one there to
      pick us back up.
  Our own pain became our punishment.
[13]Then we cried out, "Lord, help us! Rescue us!" And
  he did!
[14]His light broke through the darkness and
  he led us out in freedom from death's dark shadow
  and snapped every one of our chains.
[15]So lift your hands and give thanks to God for his
    marvelous kindness
  and for his miracles of mercy for those he loves!
[16]For he smashed through heavy prison doors and
    shattered the steel bars that held us back, just to set
      us free!
[17]Some of us were such fools, bringing on ourselves
    sorrow and suffering all because of our sins.
[18]Sick and feeble, unable to stand the sight of food,
  we drew near to the gates of death.
[19]Then we cried out, "Lord, help us! Rescue us!" And
  he did!
[20]God spoke the words "Be healed," and we were
    healed,
  delivered from death's door!
[21]So lift your hands and give thanks to God for his
    marvelous kindness
  and for his miracles of mercy for those he loves!
[22]Bring your praise as an offering and your thanks as a
    sacrifice
  as you sing your story of miracles with a joyful
      song.
[23]Some of us set sail upon the sea to faraway ports,
  transporting our goods from ship to shore.

²⁴We were witnesses of God's power out in the ocean
   deep;
   we saw breathtaking wonders upon the high seas.
²⁵When God spoke he stirred up a storm,
   lifting high the waves with hurricane winds.
²⁶⁻²⁷Ships were tossed by the swelling sea, rising to the
   sky,
   then dropping down to the depths,
   reeling like drunkards, spinning like tops,
   everyone at their wits' end until even sailors
      despaired of life, cringing in terror.
²⁸Then we cried out, "Lord, help us! Rescue us!" And
   he did!
²⁹God stilled the storm, calmed the waves,
   and he hushed the hurricane winds to only a
      whisper.
³⁰We were so relieved, so glad as he guided us
   safely to harbor in a quiet haven.
³¹So lift your hands and give thanks to God for his
   marvelous kindness
   and for his miracles of mercy for those he loves!
³²Let's exalt him on high and lift up our praises in
   public;
   let all the people and the leaders of the nation
      know
   how great and wonderful is Yahweh, our God!
³³Whenever he chooses he can dry up a river
   and turn the land into a desert.
³⁴Or he can take a fruitful land and make it into a
   saltwater swamp,
   all because of the wickedness of those who dwell
      there.
³⁵But he also can turn a barren wilderness into an
   oasis with water!
   He can make springs flow into desert lands

[36]and turn them into fertile valleys so that cities spring up,
  and he gives it all to those who are hungry.
[37]They can plant their fields and vineyards there
  and reap a bumper crop and gather a fruitful harvest.
[38]God will bless them and cause them to multiply and prosper.
[39]But others will become poor,
  humbled because of their oppression, tyranny, and sorrows.
[40]For God pours contempt upon their arrogant abuse of power,
  heaping scorn upon their princes,
  and makes them wander among ruins.
[41]But he raises up the poor and lowly with his favor,
  giving them a safe place to live where no one can touch them.
  God will grant them a large family and bless them!
[42]The lovers of God will rejoice when they see this.
  Good men are glad when the evil ones are silenced.
[43]If you are truly wise, you'll learn from what I've told you.
  It's time for you to consider these profound lessons of God's great love and mercy!

108 A Prayer for God's Help
A poetic psalm by King David

[1]My heart, O God, is focused and determined.
  Now I can sing my song with passionate praises!
  Awake, O my soul, with the music of his splendor.
[2]Arise, my soul, and sing his praises!
  I will awaken the dawn with my worship,
  greeting the daybreak with my songs *of light*.

³Wherever I go, I will thank you.
  All the nations will hear my praise songs to you.
⁴Your love is so extravagant, it reaches higher than the
    heavens!
  Your faithfulness is so astonishing, it stretches to the
    skies!
⁵Lord God, be exalted as you soar throughout the
    heavens.
  May your shining glory be seen high above all the
    earth!
⁶Come to your beloved ones and gently draw us out.
  Answer our prayer for your saving help.
  Come with your might and strength, *for we need you,*
    Lord!
⁷⁻⁹Then I heard the Lord speak in his holy splendor,
  and from his sanctuary I heard the Lord promise:
  "In my triumph I will be the one to measure out
  the portion of my inheritance to my people,
  and I will secure the land as I promised you.
  Shechem, Succoth, Gilead, Manasseh*ᵃ*—
  they are all still mine!" he says.
  "Judah will continue to produce kings and
    lawgivers,
  and Ephraim will produce great warriors.
  Moab will become my lowly servant.
  Edom will likewise serve my purposes.
  I will lift up a shout of victory over the land of
    Philistia!

---

a 108:7–9 The Hebrew includes two geographical places in the text:
Shechem and Succoth. Shechem is where Jacob (Israel) first bought
title to the land, paying one hundred pieces of silver for the place
where he camped. Succoth is another place where Jacob temporar-
ily camped in the Land of Promise. These two places speak of God
being the one who brought them in and portioned out the land for
his people.

¹⁰But who will bring my triumph into Edom's
    fortresses?"ᵃ
¹¹Lord, have you really rejected us, refusing to fight
    our battles?
¹²Give us a father's help when we face our enemies.
    For to trust in any man is an empty hope.
¹³With God's help we will prevail with might and power.
    And with God's help we'll trample down our every
        foe!

109 God, It's Time for Vengeance

To the Pure and Shining One
A poetic song by King David

¹God of all my praise, don't stand silently by, aloof to
    my pain,
²while the wicked slander me with their lies.
    Even right in front of my face they lie through their
        teeth.
³I've done nothing to them, but they still surround me
    with their venomous words of hatred and vitriol.
⁴Though I love them, they stand accusing me like
    Satan
    for what I've never done.
    I will pray until I become prayer itself.ᵇ
⁵They continually repay me with evil when I show
    them good.
    They give me hatred when I show them love.
⁶⁻⁷Show him how it feels! Let accusing liars be raised
    up against him,
    like Satan himself standing right next to him.

---

a 108:10 *Edom* is a variant form of the word *Adam*.
b 109:4 In the face of accusation and slander, David wrote in Hebrew
    literally "I am prayer!"

And let him be declared guilty by a wicked
   judge.
May even his prayers be seen as sinful!
⁸Shorten his life and let another replace him!
⁹Make his wife a widow and his children orphans!
¹⁰Let them wander as beggars in the street,
   like homeless vagabonds, evicted from their
      ruins!
¹¹Let the creditors seize his entire estate,
   and strangers, like vultures, take all that's left!
¹²Let no one be kind to him by showing pity to his
   fatherless children!
¹³May all his posterity die with him! Cut down his
   family tree!
¹⁴⁻¹⁵And may all the sins of his ancestors be recorded,
   remembered before you, forever!
   Cut off even the memory of his family from the face
      of the earth,
¹⁶because he never once showed love or kindness to
   others,
   but persecuted the poor, the brokenhearted, and
      afflicted ones,
   even putting them to death!
¹⁷Since he enjoyed cursing them,
   may all his curses now come raining back on him
   until it all overwhelms him with misfortune!
   Since he refused to bless others,
   God, withhold every single blessing from him!
¹⁸Bitterness, such vile vindictiveness, was upon
   everything he did.
   Cursing was his lifestyle.
¹⁹⁻²⁰So smother him now with his own curses as his just
   reward.
   This will be the Lord's punishment upon him and
   all my lying accusers who speak evil against me.

²¹But now, O Yahweh-God, make yourself real to me
like you promised me you would.ᵃ
Because of your constant love and your heart-melting
kindness, come be my hero and deliver me!
²²I'm so broken, needy and hurting.
My heart is pierced through and I'm so wounded.
²³I'm slipping down a dark slope, shaken to the core,
and helpless.
²⁴All my fasting has left me so weak I can hardly stand.
Now I'm shriveled up, nothing but skin and bones.
²⁵I'm the example of failure and shame to all who see
me.
They just walk by me, shaking their heads.
²⁶You have to help me, O Lord God!
My true hero, come to my rescue and save me,
for you are loving and kind.
²⁷Then everyone will know that you have won my
victory,
and they will all say to the Lord, "You have finished it!"
²⁸So let them curse me if they want,
but I know you will bless me!
All their efforts to destroy me will fail,
but I will succeed and be glad.
²⁹So let my Satan-like accusers fail!
Make them look ridiculous if they try to come
against me.
Clothe them with a robe of guilty shame from this
day on!
³⁰But I will give my thanks to you over and over,
and everyone will hear my lavish praises.
³¹For you stand right next to the broken ones
as their saving hero to rescue them from all their
accusers!

---

a 109:21 The Hebrew text reads "for your name's sake."

110 MESSIAH, KING, AND PRIEST[a]
King David's psalm

¹Yahweh said to my Lord, the Messiah:
"Sit with me as enthroned ruler[b]
while I subdue your every enemy.
They will bow low before you
as I make them a footstool for your feet."[c]
²Messiah, I know God himself will establish your
kingdom
as you reign in Zion-glory.
For he says to you, "Rule in the midst of your
enemies!"
³Your people will be your love offerings.
In the day of your mighty power you will be exalted,
and in the brightness of your holy ones you will
shine
as an army arising from the womb of the dawn,
anointed with the dew of your youth![d]
⁴Yahweh has taken a solemn oath
and will never back away from it, saying,
"You are a priest for eternity, after the manner of
Melchizedek!"[e]

---

a 110 This psalm is applied to Christ in the New Testament, where it
is quoted more often than any other Old Testament passage.

b 110:1 Or "at my right hand." The right hand is the position of authority and honor.

c 110:1 A footstool symbolizes what is subdued. It is taken from the
Hebrew root word "to subdue."

d 110:3 Or "like dew, your youth will come to you."

e 110:4 Melchizedek was the name of a Canaanite king and priest
over the Jebusite kingdom that later became Jerusalem. The name
Melchizedek means "my king of righteousness."

⁵The Lord stands in full authority*a* to shatter to pieces
   the kings who stand against you
   on the day he displays his terrible wrath.
⁶He will judge every rebellious nation,
   filling their battlefields with corpses,
   and will shatter the strongholds of ruling powers.
⁷Yet he himself will drink from his inheritance
   as from a flowing brook;
   refreshed by love he will stand victorious!

111 CELEBRATE GOD'S GREATNESS

¹Shout hallelujah to Yahweh!
   May every one of his devoted lovers hear my
      passionate praise to him,
   even among the council of the holy ones.
²For God's mighty miracles astound me!
   His wonders are so delightfully mysterious
   that they leave all who seek them astonished.
³Everything he does is full of splendor and beauty!
   Each miracle demonstrates his eternal perfection.
⁴His unforgettable works of surpassing wonder
   reveal his grace and tender mercy.
⁵He satisfies all who love and trust him,
   and he keeps every promise he makes.
⁶He reveals mighty power and marvels to his people
   by handing them nations as a gift.
⁷All God accomplishes is flawless, faithful, and fair,
   and his every word proves trustworthy and true.
⁸They are steadfast forever and ever,
   formed from truth and righteousness.

---

a 110:5 The Hebrew word used here for "Lord" is *Adonai* or *Adonay*. It is the plural form of *Adhon*. Jesus is called Lord of lords, and we are the lords that he is Lord over. We are seated at his right hand (Benjamin) to rule with him.

[9]His forever-love paid a full ransom for his people
  so that now we're free to come before Yahweh
  to worship his holy and awesome name!
[10]Where can wisdom be found? It is born in the fear of
  God.
  Everyone who follows his ways
  will never lack his living-understanding.
  And the adoration of God will abide throughout
    eternity!

112 The Triumph of Faith

[1]Shout in celebration of praise to the Lord!
  Everyone who loves the Lord and delights in him
  will cherish his words and be blessed beyond
    expectation.
[2]Their descendants will be prosperous and influential.
  Every generation of the righteous will experience
    his favor.
[3]Great blessing and wealth fills the house *of the wise*,
  for their integrity endures forever.
[4]Even if darkness overtakes them,
  sunrise-brilliance will come bursting through
  because they are gracious to others, so tender and
    true.
[5]Life is good for the one who is generous and
  charitable,
  conducting affairs with honesty and truth.
[6]Their circumstances will never shake them
  and others will never forget their example.
[7]They will not live in fear or dread of what may come,
  for their hearts are firm, ever secure in their faith.
[8]Steady and strong, they will not be afraid,
  but will calmly face their every foe
  until they all go down in defeat.

⁹Never stingy and always generous to those in need,
they lived lives of influence and honor that will
never be forgotten,
for they were full of good deeds.
¹⁰But the wicked take one look at a life lived like this
and they grit their teeth in anger, not understanding
their bliss.
The wicked slink away speechless in the darkness
that falls,
where hope dies and all their dreams fade away to
nothing,
nothing at all!

113ᵃ GOD IS KIND

¹Hallelujah! Praise the Lord!
Go ahead, praise the Lord, all you loving servants of
God!
Keep it up! Praise him some more!
²For the glorious name of the Lord is blessed forever
and ever.
³From sunrise-brilliance to sunset-beauty,
lift up his praise from dawn to dusk!
⁴For he rules on high over the nations
with a glory that outshines even the heavens.
⁵No one can be compared to God, enthroned on high!
⁶He stoops down to look upon the sky and the earth.
⁷He promotes the poor, picking them up from the dirt,
and rescues the needy from the garbage dump.
⁸He turns paupers into princes and seats them
on their royal thrones of honor.

---

a 113 Psalms 113–114 were sung before the meal during the Jewish
family's celebration of Passover, while Pss. 115–118 were sung after
the meal (see Mark 14:26).

⁹God's grace provides for the barren ones a joyful
   home with children
   so that even childless couples find a family.
   He makes them happy parents surrounded by their
      pride and joy.
   That's the God we praise, so give it all to him!

114 A Song for Passover

¹Many years ago the Jewish people escaped Egypt's
   tyranny,
²so that Israel, God's people of praise,ᵃ
   would become his holy sanctuary,
   his kingdom on the earth.
³The Red Sea waters saw them coming and ran the
   other way!
   Then later, the Jordan River too
   moved aside so that they could all pass through.
⁴The land shuddered with fear.
   Mountains and hills shook with dread.ᵇ
⁵O sea, what happened to you to make you flee?
   O Jordan, what was it that made you turn and run?
⁶O mountains, what frightened you so?
   And you hills, what made you shiver?
⁷Tremble, O earth, for you are in the presence of the
   Lord,
   the presence of the God of Jacob.
⁸He splits open boulders and brings up bubbling
   water.
   Gushing streams burst forth *when he is near*!

---

a 114:2 Or *Judah*, which means "praise."

b 114:4 The literal Hebrew reads "Mountains skipped like rams, the
hills like lambs." This does not mean they skipped with joy, but that
they shook with fear, as the context reveals.

115 THE ONLY TRUE HERO

¹God, glorify your name!
    Yes, your name alone be glorified, not ours.
    For you are the one who loves us passionately,
    and you are faithful and true.
²Why should the unbelievers mock us, saying,
    "Where is this God of yours?"
³But we know our God rules from the heavens,
    and he takes delight in all that he does.
⁴The unbelievers worship what they make—
    their wealth and their work.
⁵⁻⁸They idolize what they own
    and what they make with their hands,
    but their things can't talk to them or answer their
        prayers.
    Their possessions will never satisfy.
    Their futile faith in dead idols and dead works
    can never bring life or meaning to their souls.
    Blind men can only create blind things.
    Those deaf to God can only make a deaf image.[a]
    Dead men can only create dead idols.
    And everyone who trusts in these powerless, dead
        things
    will be just like what they worship—powerless and
        dead.
⁹So trust in the Lord, all his people.
    For he is the only true hero,
    the wraparound God who is our shield!

---

a 115:5–8 Referring to the idols, the literal Hebrew could be translated
    "With mouths, but they cannot speak; with eyes, but they cannot see;
    with ears, but they cannot hear; with noses, but they cannot smell; with
    hands, but they cannot feel; with feet, but they cannot walk. Those who
    make them will become like them and everyone who trusts in them."

¹⁰You, his priests, trust in the Lord.
  For he is the only true hero,
  God-wrapped-around-us as our shield.
¹¹Yes, all his lovers who bow before him, trust in the
    Lord.
  For he is our only true hero,
  God-wrapped-around-us as our shield.
¹²The Lord will never forget us in our need; he will
    bless us indeed!
  He will bless the house of Israel;
  he will bless the house of Aaron, his priest.
¹³Yes! He will bless his devoted lovers who bow before
    him,
  no matter who they are.
¹⁴⁻¹⁵God himself will fill you with more.
  Blessings upon blessings will be heaped upon
      you
  and upon your children from the maker of heaven
      and earth,
  the very God who made you!
¹⁶The heavens belong to our God; they are his alone,
  but he has given us*a* the earth and put us in charge.
¹⁷⁻¹⁸Dead people cannot praise the Lord, but we can!
  Those who sink to the silence of the grave
  can no longer give glory to God, but we can!
  So let's praise the Lord and let it go on forever.
  Hallelujah, and praise the Lord!

116 I'M SAVED

¹I am passionately in love with God because he listens
    to me.
  He hears my prayers and answers them.

---

a 115:16 Or "Adam's sons."

²As long as I live I'll keep praying to him,
   for he stoops down to listen to my heart's cry.
³Death once stared me in the face,
   and I was close to slipping into its dark shadows.
   I was terrified and overcome with sorrow.
⁴I cried out to the Lord, "God, come and save me!"
⁵He was so kind, so gracious to me.
   Because of his passion toward me,
   he made everything right and he restored me.
⁶So I've learned from my experience
   that God protects the vulnerable.
   For I was broken and brought low,
   but he answered me and came to my rescue!
⁷Now I can say to myself and to all,
   "Relax and rest, be confident and serene,
   for the Lord rewards fully those who simply trust in
      him."
⁸God has rescued my soul from death's fear
   and dried my eyes of many tears.
   He's kept my feet firmly on his path
⁹and strengthened me so that I may please him*a*
   and walk before Yahweh in his fields of life.
¹⁰⁻¹¹Even when it seems I'm surrounded
   by many liars and my own fears,
   and though I'm hurting in my suffering and trauma,
   I still stay faithful to God and speak words of faith.
¹²So now, what can I ever give back to God
   to repay him for the blessings he's poured out on me?
¹³I will lift up his cup of salvation and praise him
   extravagantly
   for all that he's done for me.
¹⁴I will fulfill the promise I made to God
   in the presence of his gathered people.

---

a 116:9 As translated from the Septuagint.

¹⁵When one of God's holy lovers dies,
  it is costly to the Lord, touching his heart.
¹⁶Lord, because I am your loving servant,
  you have broken open my life and freed me from my
    chains.
¹⁷Now I'll worship you passionately and bring to you
  my sacrifice of praise, drenched with thanksgiving!
¹⁸I'll keep my promise to you, God,
  in the presence of your gathered people, just like I
    said I would.
¹⁹I will worship you here in your living presence,
  in the temple in Jerusalem.
  I will worship and sing hallelujah, for I praise you,
    Lord!

117 GLORIOUS PRAISE
A praise psalm

¹Let everyone everywhere shine with praise to
  Yahweh!^{*a*}
  Let it all out! Go ahead and praise him!
²For he has conquered us with his great love,
  and his kindness has melted our hearts.
  His faithfulness lasts forever, and he will never fail
    you.
  So go ahead, let it all out!
  Praise Yah!
  O Yah!^{*b*}

---

a 117:1 The word for "praise" is taken from the Hebrew words for "to
shine."

b 117:2 The name Yah is not an abbreviated form of Yahweh; it is the
name of God as he displays his power. Yahweh is found 6,830 times
in the Hebrew text, and Yah is found 49 times.

118 Glorious Thanksgiving
A praise psalm[a]

¹Keep on giving your thanks to God, for he is so good!
   His constant, tender love lasts forever!
²Let all his princely people sing,
   "His constant, tender love lasts forever!"
³Let all his holy priests sing,
   "His constant, tender love lasts forever!"
⁴Let all his lovers who bow low before him sing,
   "His constant, tender love lasts forever!"
⁵Out of my deep anguish and pain I prayed,
   and God, you helped me as a father.
   You came to my rescue and broke open the way
   into a beautiful and broad place.
⁶Now I know, Lord, that you are for me,
   and I will never fear what man can do to me.
⁷For you stand beside me as my hero who rescues me.
   I've seen with my own eyes the defeat of my
      enemies.
   I've triumphed over them all!
⁸Lord, it is so much better to trust in you to save me
   than to put my confidence in someone else.
⁹Yes, it is so much better to trust in the Lord to save me
   than to put my confidence in celebrities.
¹⁰Once I was hemmed in and surrounded by those
   who don't love you.
   But by Yahweh's supernatural power I overcame
      them all!
¹¹⁻¹²Yes, they surrounded me,
   like a swarm of killer bees swirling around me.

---

a 118 This is the psalm or hymn that Jesus likely sang after the Passover supper with his disciples, before making his way to Gethsemane and Calvary.

I was trapped like one trapped by a raging fire;
I was surrounded with no way out and at the point
　　of collapse.
But by Yahweh's supernatural power, I overcame
　　them all!
¹³They pushed me right up to the edge, and I was
　ready to fall,
　　but you helped me to triumph, and together we
　　　overcame them all.
¹⁴Lord, you are my true strength and my glory-song,
　my champion, my Savior!
¹⁵The joyful songs I now sing will be sung again
　in the hearts and homes of all your devoted lovers.
　My loud shouts of victory will echo throughout the
　　land.ᵃ
For Yahweh's right hand conquers valiantly!
¹⁶The right hand of Yahweh exalts!
　The right hand of Yahweh will never fail.
¹⁷You will not let them kill me,
　but I will live to tell the world what the Lord has
　　done for me.
¹⁸Yes, the Lord punished me as I deserved,
　but he'll never give me over to death.
¹⁹Swing wide, you gates of righteousness, and let me
　pass through,
　and I will enter into God's presence to worship only
　　him.
²⁰I have found the gateway to God,
　the pathway to his presence for all his devoted lovers.
²¹I will offer all my loving praise to you,
　and I thank you so much for answering my prayer
　and bringing me salvation!

---

a 118:15 Or "in the tents of the righteous."

²²The very stone the masons rejected as flawed
   has turned out to be the most important capstone of
      the arch,^a
   holding up the very house of God.
²³The Lord himself is the one who has done this,
   and it's so amazing, so marvelous to see!
²⁴This is the very day of the Lord that brings
   gladness and joy, filling our hearts with glee.
²⁵O God, please come and save us again;
   bring us your breakthrough-victory!
²⁶Blessed is this one who comes to us, the sent one of
   the Lord.
   And from within the temple we cry, "We bless you!"
²⁷⁻²⁸For the Lord our God has brought us his glory-light.
   I offer him my life in joyous sacrifice.
   Tied tightly to your altar, I will bring you praise.
   For you are the God of my life and I lift you high,
   exalting you to the highest place.
²⁹So let's keep on giving our thanks to God, for he is so
   good!
   His constant, tender love lasts forever!

---

a 118:22 The words "capstone of the arch" can also be translated
"head of the corner."

119 THE WORDS OF GOD^a

The Way to Happiness

¹You're only truly happy when you walk in total
   integrity,
     walking in the light of God's Word.^b
²What joy overwhelms everyone who keeps the ways
   of God,
     those who seek him as their heart's passion!
³They'll never do what's wrong
     but will always choose the paths of the Lord.
⁴God has prescribed the right way to live:
     obeying his laws with all our hearts.
⁵How I long for my life to bring you glory
     as I follow each and every one of your holy
       precepts!
⁶Then I'll never be ashamed,
     for I take strength from all your commandments.
⁷I will give my thanks to you from a heart of love and
   truth.
     And every time I learn more of your righteous
       judgments,
⁸I will be faithful to all that your Word reveals—
     so don't ever give up on me!

---

a 119 This psalm is an acrostic poem, a mathematical masterpiece.
It consists of twenty-two stanzas of eight lines each. Each stanza
begins with the same Hebrew letter at the beginning of every one
of its eight lines, going in succession, by strophes, from *alef*—the
first letter of the Hebrew alphabet, as the first letter of each line in
the first strophe—to *taw*—the last letter of the Hebrew alphabet, as
the first letter of each line in the last strophe. Like the eight lines of
each stanza, there are eight Hebrew words, all synonyms, used to
refer to the Word of God. Although many believe Ezra wrote Ps. 119,
the acrostic poetic style is unique to King David within the book of
Psalms, which points to his authorship of this psalm.

b 119:1 Or "perfection." The Hebrew reads "utterances."

True Joy

⁹How can a young man stay pure?
Only by living in the Word of God and walking in its
truth.
¹⁰I have longed for you with the passion of my heart;
don't let me stray from your directions!
¹¹I consider your Word to be my greatest treasure,
and I treasure it in my heart
to keep me from committing sin's treason against
you.
¹²My wonderful God, you are to be praised above all;
teach me the power of your decrees!
¹³I speak continually of your laws
as I recite out loud your counsel to me.
¹⁴I find more joy in following what you tell me to do
than in chasing after all the wealth of the world.
¹⁵I set my heart on your precepts
and pay close attention to all your ways.
¹⁶My delight is found in all your laws,
and I won't forget to walk in your words.

The Abundant Life

¹⁷Let me, your servant, walk in abundance of life
that I may always live to obey your truth.
¹⁸Open my eyes to see the miracle-wonders hidden in
Scripture.ᵃ
¹⁹My life on earth is so brief, so tutor me in the ways
of your wisdom.
²⁰I am continually consumed by these irresistible
longings,
these cravings to obey your every commandment!
²¹Your displeasure rests with those who are
arrogant,

ᵃ 119:18 Or "your law."

who think they know everything;
you rebuke the rebellious who refuse your laws.
²²Don't let them mock and scorn me for obeying you.
²³For even if the princes and my leaders choose to
criticize me,
I will continue to serve you and walk in your plans
for my life.
²⁴Your commandments are my counselors;
your Word is my light and delight!

Revived by the Word

²⁵Lord, I'm fading away. I'm discouraged and lying in
the dust;
revive me by your word, just like you promised you
would.
²⁶I've poured out my life before you,
and you've always been there for me.
So now I ask: teach me more of your holy decrees.
²⁷Open up my understanding to the ways of your
wisdom,
and I will meditate deeply on your splendor and
your wonders.
²⁸My life's strength melts away with grief and sadness;
come strengthen me and encourage me with your
words.
²⁹Keep me far away from what is false;
give me grace to stay true to your laws.
³⁰I've chosen to obey your truth
and walk in the splendor-light of all that you teach
me.
³¹Lord, don't allow me to make a mess of my life,
for I cling to your commands and follow them as
closely as I can.
³²I will run after you with delight in my heart,
for you will make me obedient to your instructions.

Understanding God's Ways

³³Give me revelation about the meaning of your ways
   so I can enjoy the reward of following them fully.
³⁴Give me an understanding heart so that I can
   passionately know and obey your truth.
³⁵Guide me into the paths that please you,
   for I take delight in all that you say.
³⁶Cause my heart to bow before your words of wisdom
   and not to the wealth of this world.
³⁷Help me turn my eyes away from illusions
   so that I pursue only that which is true;
   drench my soul with life as I walk in your paths.*a*
³⁸Reassure me of your promises, for I am your beloved,
   your servant who bows before you.
³⁹Defend me from the criticism I face
   for keeping your beautiful words.
⁴⁰See how I long with cravings for more of your ways?
   Let your righteousness revive my spirit!

Trust in the Lord

⁴¹May your tender love overwhelm me, O Lord,
   for you are my Savior and you keep your promises.
⁴²I'll always have an answer for those who mock me
   because I trust in your word.
⁴³May I never forget your truth, for I rely upon your
   precepts.
⁴⁴I will observe your laws every moment of the day
   and will never forget the words you say.
⁴⁵I will walk with you in complete freedom,
   for I seek to follow your every command.
⁴⁶When I stand before kings, I will tell them the truth
   and will never be ashamed.

---

a 119:37 The Masoretic Text and the Dead Sea Scrolls read "Preserve
my life according to your word."

⁴⁷My passion and delight is in your word,
　　for I love what you say to me!
⁴⁸I long for more revelation of your truth,
　　for I love the light of your word as I meditate on
　　　your decrees.

My Comfort
⁴⁹Lord, never forget the promises you've made to me,
　　for they are my hope and confidence.
⁵⁰In all of my affliction I find great comfort in your
　　promises,
　　for they have kept me alive!
⁵¹No matter how bitterly the proud mockers speak
　　against me,
　　I refuse to budge from your precepts.
⁵²Your revelation-light is eternal;
　　I'm encouraged every time I think about your truth!
⁵³Whenever I see the wicked breaking your laws, I feel
　　horrible.
⁵⁴As I journey through life, I put all your statutes to
　　music;
　　they become the theme of my joyous songs.
⁵⁵Throughout the night I think of you, dear God;
　　I treasure your every word to me.
⁵⁶All this joy is mine as I follow your ways!

My Heart Is Devoted to You
⁵⁷You are my satisfaction, Lord, and all that I need,
　　so I'm determined to do everything you say.
⁵⁸With all my heart I seek your favor;
　　pour out your grace on me as you promised!
⁵⁹When I realize that I'm going astray,
　　I turn back to obey your instructions.
⁶⁰I give my all to follow your revelation-light; I will not
　　delay to obey.

⁶¹Even when temptations encircle me with evil,
I won't forget for a moment to follow your
commands.
⁶²In the middle of the night I awake to give thanks to
you
because of all your revelation-light—so right and
true!
⁶³Anyone who loves you and bows in obedience to
your words
will be my friend.
⁶⁴Give me more revelation of your ways,
for I see your love and tender care everywhere.

My True Treasure
⁶⁵Your extravagant kindness to me
makes me want to follow your words even more!
⁶⁶Teach me how to make good decisions,
and give me revelation-light, for I believe in your
commands.
⁶⁷Before I was humbled I used to always wander
astray,
but now I see the wisdom of your words.
⁶⁸Everything you do is beautiful, flowing from your
goodness;
teach me the power of your wonderful words!
⁶⁹Proud boasters make up lies about me
because I am passionate to follow all that you say.
⁷⁰Their hearts are dull and void of feelings,
but I find my true treasure in your truth.
⁷¹The punishment you brought me through was the
best thing
that could have happened to me, for it taught me
your ways.
⁷²The words you speak to me are worth more
than all the riches and wealth in the whole world!

Growth through the Word

73Your very hands have held me and made me who I
am;
give me more revelation-light so I may learn to
please you more.
74May all your devoted lovers see how you treat me
and be glad,
for your words are entwined with my heart.
75Lord, I know that your judgments are always right.
Even when it's me you judge, you're still faithful and
true.
76Send your kind mercy-kiss to comfort me, your
servant,
just like you promised you would.
77Love me tenderly so I can go on,
for I delight in your life-giving truth.
78Shame upon the proud liars! See how they oppress me,
all because of my passion for your precepts!
79May all your devoted lovers follow me
as I follow the path of your instruction.
80Make me passionate and wholehearted to fulfill your
every wish,
so that I'll never have to be ashamed of myself.

Deliver Me

81I'm lovesick with yearnings for more of your
salvation,
for my heart is entwined with your Word.
82I'm consumed with longings for your promises,
so I ask, "When will they all come true?"
83My soul feels dry and shriveled, useless and forgotten,
but I will never forget your living truth.
84How much longer must I wait until you punish my
persecutors?
For I am your loving servant.

[85]Arrogant men who hate your truth and never obey
  your laws
    have laid a trap for my life.
[86]They don't know that everything you say is true,
    so they harass me with their lies. Help me, Lord!
[87]They've nearly destroyed my life, but I refuse to
  yield;
    I still live according to your Word.
[88]Revive me with your tender love and
    spare my life by your kindness, and I will continue
      to obey you.

Faith in the Word of God

[89]Standing firm in the heavens and fastened to
  eternity
    is the Word of God.
[90]Your faithfulness flows from one generation to the
  next;
    all that you created sits firmly in place to testify of
      you.
[91]By your decree everything stands at attention,
    for all that you have made serves you.
[92]Because your words are my deepest delight,
    I didn't give up when all else was lost.
[93]I can never forget the profound revelations you've
  taught me,
    for they have kept me alive more than once.
[94]Lord, I'm all yours, and you are my Savior;
    I have sought to live my life pleasing to you.
[95]Even though evil men wait in ambush to kill me,
    I will set my heart before you to understand more of
      your ways.
[96]I've learned that there is nothing perfect
    in this imperfect world except your words,
      for they bring such fantastic freedom into my life!

I Love the Word of God

[97]O how I love and treasure your law;
   throughout the day I fill my heart with its light!
[98]By considering your commands I have an edge over
   my enemies,
   for I take seriously everything you say.
[99]You have given me more understanding than those
   who teach me,
   for I've absorbed your eye-opening revelation.
[100]You have graced me with more insight than the old
   sages
   because I have not failed to walk in the light of your
      ways.
[101]I refused to bend my morals when temptation was
   before me
   so that I could become obedient to your Word.
[102]I refuse to turn away from difficult truths,
   for you yourself have taught me to love your words.
[103]How sweet are your living promises to me;
   sweeter than honey is your revelation-light.
[104]For your truth is the source of my understanding,
   not the falsehoods of those who don't know you,
      which I despise.

Truth's Shining Light

[105]Truth's shining light guides me in my choices and
   decisions;
   the revelation of your Word makes my pathway
      clear.
[106]To live my life by your righteous rules
   has been my holy and lifelong commitment.
[107]I'm bruised and broken, overwhelmed by it all;
   breathe life into me again by your living word.
[108]Lord, receive my grateful thanks
   and teach me more of how to please you.

¹⁰⁹Even though my life hangs in the balance,
   I'll keep following what you've taught me, no matter
      what.
¹¹⁰The ungodly have done their best to throw me off
   track,
   but I'll not deviate from what you've told me to do.
¹¹¹Everything you speak to me is like joyous treasure,
   filling my life with gladness.
¹¹²I have determined in my heart to obey whatever you
   say,
   fully and forever!

Trust and Obey

¹¹³I despise those who can't keep commitments,
   for I passionately love your revelation-light!
¹¹⁴You're my place of quiet retreat, and your
   wraparound presence
   becomes my shield as I wrap myself in your Word!
¹¹⁵Go away! Leave me, all you workers of wickedness,
   for you can't stop me from following every
      command of my God.
¹¹⁶Lord, strengthen my inner being by the promises of
   your Word
   so that I may live faithful and unashamed for you.
¹¹⁷Lift me up and I will be safe.
   Empower me to live every moment in the light of
      your ways.
¹¹⁸Lord, you reject those who reject your laws,
   for they fool no one but themselves!
¹¹⁹The wicked are thrown away, discarded and
   valueless.
   That's why I will keep loving all of your laws!
¹²⁰My body trembles in holy awe of you, leaving me
   speechless,
   for I'm frightened of your righteous judgments.

I Will Follow Your Ways

¹²¹Don't leave me to the mercies of those who hate me,
    for I live to do what is just and fair.
¹²²Let me hear your promise of blessing over my life,
    breaking me free from the proud oppressors.
¹²³As a lovesick lover, I yearn for more of your salvation
    and for your virtuous promises.
¹²⁴Let me feel your tender love, for I am yours.
    Give me more understanding of your wonderful ways.
¹²⁵I need more revelation from your Word
    to know more about you, for I'm in love with you!
¹²⁶Lord, the time has come for you to break through,
    for evil men keep breaking your laws.
¹²⁷Truly, your message of truth means more to me
    than a vault filled with the purest gold.
¹²⁸Every word you speak, every truth revealed, is
    always right
    and beautiful to me, for I hate what is phony or
      false.

I Long to Obey You

¹²⁹Your marvelous words are living miracles;
    no wonder I long to obey everything you say.
¹³⁰Break open your Word within me until revelation-
    light shines out!
    Those with open hearts are given insight into your
      plans.
¹³¹I open my mouth and inhale the Word of God
    because I crave the revelation of your commands.
¹³²Turn your heart to me, Lord, and show me your
    grace
    like you do to every one of your godly lovers.
¹³³Prepare before me a path filled with your promises,
    and don't allow even one sin to have dominion over
      me.

[134]Rescue me from the oppression of ungodly men
   so that I can keep all your precepts.
[135]Smile on me,[a] your loving servant.
   Instruct me in what is right in your eyes.
[136]When I witness the rebellious breaking your laws,
   it makes me weep uncontrollably!

His Word Is True

[137]Lord, your judgments reveal your righteousness,
   and your verdicts are always fair.
[138]The motive behind your every word is pure,
   and your teachings are remarkably faithful and true.
[139]I've been consumed with a furious passion to do
   what's right,
   all because of the way my enemies disrespect your
      laws.
[140]All your promises glow with fire;[b]
   that's why I'm a lover of your Word.
[141]Even though I'm considered insignificant and
   despised
   by the world, I'll never abandon your ways.
[142]Your righteousness has no end; it is everlasting,
   and your rules are perfectly fair.
[143]Even though my troubles overwhelm me with
   anguish,
   I still delight and cherish every message you speak
      to me.
[144]Give me more revelation so that I can live for you,
   for nothing is more pure and eternal than your
      truth.

---

a 119:135 Or "Cause your face to shine on me."
b 119:140 As translated from the Septuagint and implied in the
   Hebrew.

Save Me, God

[145]Answer my passionate prayer, O Lord,
and I'll obey everything you say.
[146]Save me, God, and I'll follow your every instruction.
[147]Before the day dawns, I'll be crying out for help
and wrapping your words into my life.
[148]I lie awake every night pondering your promises to
me.
[149]Lord, listen to my heart's cry, for I know your love is
real for me;
breathe life into me again by the revelation of your
justice.
[150]Here they come—these lawless rebels are coming
near,
but they are all so far away from your laws.
[151]God, you are near me always, so close to me;
every one of your commands reveals truth.
[152]I've known all along how true and unchanging
is every word you speak, established forever!

Breathe Life into Me Again

[153]Look upon all my misery and come be my hero to
rescue me,
for I will never forget what you've revealed to me.
[154]Take my side and defend me in these sufferings;
redeem me and revive me, just like you promised
you would.
[155]The wicked are so far from salvation,
for they could not care less about your message of
truth.
[156]Your tender mercies are what I need, O God;
give me back my life again
through the revelation of your judgments.
[157]I have so many enemies who persecute me,
yet I won't swerve from following your ways.

¹⁵⁸I grieve when I see how the faithless ones live,
for they just walk away from your promises.
¹⁵⁹Lord, see how much I truly love your instructions.
So in your tender kindness, breathe life into me
again.
¹⁶⁰The sum total of all your words adds up to absolute
truth,
and every one of your righteous decrees is
everlasting.

Devoted to God's Word

¹⁶¹The powerful elite have persecuted me without a
cause,
but my heart trembles in awe because of your
miracle-words.
¹⁶²Your promises are the source of my bubbling joy;
the revelation of your Word thrills me
like one who has discovered hidden treasure.
¹⁶³I despise every lie and hate every falsehood,
for I am passionate about keeping your
precepts.
¹⁶⁴I stop to praise you seven times a day,
all because your ways are perfect!
¹⁶⁵There is such a great peace and well-being that
comes
to the lovers of your Word, and they will never be
offended.
¹⁶⁶Lord, I'm longing for more of your salvation,
for I want to do what pleases you.
¹⁶⁷My love for your ways is indescribable;
in my innermost being I want to follow them
perfectly!
¹⁶⁸I will keep your instructions and follow your
counsel;
all my ways are an open book before you.

I Want to Follow You

¹⁶⁹Lord, listen to my prayer. It's like a sacrifice I bring
to you;
I must have more revelation of your Word!
¹⁷⁰Take my words to heart when I ask you, Lord;
rescue me, just like you promised!
¹⁷¹I offer you my joyous praise for all that you've taught
me.
¹⁷²Your wonderful words will become my song of
worship,
for everything you've commanded is perfect and true.
¹⁷³Place your hands of strength and favor upon me,
for I've made my choice to follow your ways.
¹⁷⁴I wait for your deliverance, O Lord,
for your words thrill me like nothing else!
¹⁷⁵Invigorate my life so that I can praise you even more,
and may your truth be my strength!
¹⁷⁶I'll never forget what you've taught me, Lord,
but when I wander off and lose my way,
come after me, for I am your beloved!

120 God Helped Me
A song of the stairway^a

¹I was desperate for you to help me in my struggles,
and you did!
²So come and deliver me now

---

a 120 Psalms 120–134 all begin with the words "A song to take you
higher" or "A song of ascent" or "A song of the stairway." It is likely
these fifteen songs were sung on the fifteen steps that would take
the worshiper into the temple. On each step they would stop to
worship and sing the corresponding psalm as they went up ever
higher into the temple to worship God. Others believe they were the
songs sung as David brought up the ark of glory to Jerusalem. They
are also known as "Songs of Degrees" or "Songs of Ascent." One
Hebrew manuscript titles them "Songs of the Homeward Marches."

from this treachery and false accusation.
³O lying deceivers, don't you know what is your fate?
⁴You will be pierced through with condemnation
and consumed with burning coals of fire!
⁵Why am I doomed to live as an alien,
scattered among these cruel savages?*a*
Am I destined to dwell in the darkened tents of
desert nomads?*b*
⁶For too long I've had to live among those who hate
peace.
⁷I speak words of peace while they speak words of war,
but they refuse to listen.

121 GOD PROTECTS US
A song of the stairway

¹⁻²I look up to the mountains and hills, longing for
God's help.
But then I realize that our true help and protection
is only from the Lord,
our Creator who made the heavens and the earth.
³He will guard and guide me, never letting me
stumble or fall.
God is my keeper; he will never forget nor ignore me.
⁴He will never slumber nor sleep;
he is the Guardian-God for his people, Israel.
⁵Yahweh himself will watch over you;
he's always at your side to shelter you safely in his
presence.

---

a 120:5 The Hebrew text includes the word *Meshech*, which is a foreign land. The meaning of the word *Meshech* is "to scatter" and may refer to ancient Persia.

b 120:5 The Hebrew text includes the word *Kedar*, who was one of Ishmael's sons, whose descendants became a wandering group of nomads. *Kedar* means "a dark place." See Song. 1:5.

⁶He's protecting you from all danger both day and
   night.
⁷He will keep you from every form of evil or calamity
   as he continuously watches over you.
⁸You will be guarded by God himself.
   You will be safe when you leave your home,
   and safely you will return.
   He will protect you now,
   and he'll protect you forevermore!

122 JERUSALEM
*A song of the stairway by King David*ᵃ

¹I was overjoyed when they said,
   "Let's go up to the house of the Lord."
²And now at last we stand here, inside the very gates
   of Jerusalem!
³O Jerusalem, you were built as a city of praise,
   where God and man mingle together.ᵇ
⁴This is where all the tribes of Yahweh are required
   to come and worship him.
⁵This is where the thrones of kings have been
   established
   to rule in righteousness;
   even King David ruled from here.
⁶Pray *and seek* for Jerusalem's peace,
   for all who love her will prosper!
⁷O Jerusalem, may there be peace for those
   who dwell inside your walls
   and prosperity in your every palace.

---

a 122 David wrote this song for the people to sing for the feasts. It was
   sung when the worshipers entered the gates of Jerusalem.
b 122:3 The Hebrew phrase "a city bound together" is taken from a
   root word that means "joined, united, coupled." By inference in the
   context, it is the city where God dwells and man worships.

⁸I intercede for the sake of my family and friends
  who dwell there, that they may all live in peace.
⁹For the sake of your house, Yahweh our God,
  I will seek the welfare and prosperity of Jerusalem.

123 A PRAYER FOR MERCY
A song of the stairway

¹O God-Enthroned in heaven, I lift my eyes toward you
  in worship.
²The way I love you
    is like the way a servant wants to please his
      master,
    the way a maid waits for the orders of her mistress.
    We look to you, our God, with passionate longing
    to please you and discover more of your mercy and
      grace.
³⁻⁴For we've had more than our fill of this scoffing and
  scorn—
    this mistreatment by the wealthy elite.
    Lord, show us your mercy!
    Lord, show us your grace!

124 VICTORY
A song of the stairway by King David

¹What if God had not been on our side? Let all Israel
  admit this!
²⁻³What if God had not been there for us?
    Our enemies, in their violent anger,
    would have swallowed us up alive!
⁴⁻⁵The nations, with their flood of rage, would have
  swept us away,
    and we would have drowned
    and perished beneath their torrent of terror!

⁶We can praise God over and over that he never left us!
  God wouldn't allow the terror of our enemies to
    defeat us.
⁷We are free from the hunter's trap;
  their snare is broken and we have escaped!
⁸For the same God who made everything,
  our Creator and our mighty maker,
  he himself is our helper and defender!

125 GOD'S SURROUNDING PRESENCE
A song of the stairway

¹Those who trust in the Lord are as unshakable,
  as unmovable as mighty Mount Zion!
²Just as the mountains surround Jerusalem,
  so the Lord's *wraparound* presence
  surrounds his people, protecting them now and
    forever.
³The wicked will not always rule over the godly,
  provoking them to do what is evil.
⁴God, let your goodness be given away to your good
    people,
  to all your righteous ones!
⁵But those who turn away from truth—
  them you will turn away from you, to follow their
    crooked ways.
  You will give them just what they deserve.
  May Israel experience peace and prosperity!

126 RESTORED
A song of the stairway

¹It was like a dream come true
  when you freed us from our bondage and brought
    us back to Zion!

²We laughed and laughed and overflowed with
    gladness.
    We were left shouting for joy and singing your
        praise.
    All the nations saw it and joined in, saying,
    "The Lord has done great miracles for them!"
³Yes, he did mighty miracles and we are overjoyed!
⁴Now, Lord, do it again! Restore us to our former glory!
    May streams of your refreshing flow over us
    until our dry hearts are drenched again.
⁵Those who sow their tears as seeds*ᵃ*
    will reap a harvest with joyful shouts of glee.
⁶They may weep as they go out carrying their seed to
    sow,
    but they will return with joyful laughter and shouting
        with gladness
    as they bring back armloads of blessing and a
        harvest overflowing!

127 GOD AND HIS GIFTS
A song of the stairway by King Solomon

¹If God's grace doesn't help the builders,
    they will labor in vain to build a house.
    If God's mercy doesn't protect the city,
    all the sentries will circle it in vain.
²It really is senseless to work so hard
    from early morning till late at night,
    toiling to make a living for fear of not having enough.
    God can provide for his devoted lovers even while
        they sleep!

---

a 126:5 Or "sow their seeds with tears." A sower weeps when he sows
his precious seed while his children are hungry. This is a picture of
sacrificing what little we have for the harvest to come.

³Children are God's love-gift; they are heaven's
   generous reward.
⁴Children born to a young couple will one day rise to
   protect
   and provide for their parents.ᵃ
⁵Happy will be the couple who has many of them!
   A household full of children will not bring shame on
      your name
   but victory when you face your enemies,
   for your offspring will have influence and honorᵇ
   to prevail on your behalf!

128 THE BLESSINGS OF THE LORD
A song of the stairway

¹How joyous are those who love the Lord and bow low
   before God,
   ready to obey him!
²Your reward will be prosperity, happiness, and
   well-being.
³Your wife will bless your heart and home.
   Your children will bring you joy as they gather
      around your table.
⁴Yes, this is God's generous reward for those who love
   him.
⁵May the Lord bless you out of his Zion-glory!
   May you see the prosperity of Jerusalem
   throughout your lifetime.

---

a 127:4 The Hebrew text refers to children as "arrows in the hands of
a warrior." Our children will be our future protection and provision.
So the more the merrier!

b 127:5 The Hebrew includes a reference to "speaking with your enemies at the gate." This is in the context of children being God's way
of blessing parents in their old age.

⁶And may you be surrounded by your grandchildren.
Happiness to you! And happiness to Israel!

129 PERSECUTED BUT NOT DEFEATED
A song of the stairway

¹Let all Israel admit it.
From our very beginning we have been persecuted
by the nations.
²And from our very beginning
we have faced never-ending discrimination.
Nevertheless, our enemies have not defeated us.
We're still here!
³They have hurt us more than can be expressed,
ripping us to shreds, cutting deeply into our souls.
⁴But no matter what, the Lord is good to us.
He is a righteous God who stood to defend us,
breaking the chains of the evil ones that bound us.
⁵May all who hate the Jews
fall back in disgrace to a shameful defeat!
⁶Let them be like grass planted in shallow soil
that soon withers with no sustenance.
⁷Let them be like weeds ignored by the reaper
and worthless to the harvester.
⁸Let no one who sees them say,
"May the blessings of Yahweh be upon your life.
May the Lord bless you."*ᵃ*

130 OUT OF THE DEPTHS
A song of the stairway

¹Lord, I cry out to you out of the depths *of my despair*!

---

a 129:8 In the Jewish culture, if you passed by one who was harvesting his crops, you would shout out, "The Lord bless you!"

²Hear my voice, O God!
　　Answer this prayer and hear my plea for mercy.
³Lord, if you measured us and marked us with our sins,
　　who would ever have their prayers answered?
⁴But your forgiving love is what makes you so
　　wonderful.
　　No wonder you are loved and worshiped!
⁵This is why I wait upon you, expecting your
　　breakthrough,
　　for your Word brings me hope.
⁶I long for you more than any watchman
　　would long for the morning light.
　　I will watch and wait for you, O God,
　　throughout the night.
⁷O Israel, keep hoping, keep trusting,
　　and keep waiting on the Lord,
　　for he is tenderhearted, kind, and forgiving.
　　He has a thousand ways to set you free!
⁸He himself will redeem you;
　　he will ransom you from the cruel slavery of your sins!

131 My Heart Is Meek
A song of the stairway by King David

¹Lord, my heart is meek before you.
　　I don't consider myself better than others.
　　I'm content to not pursue matters that are over my
　　　head—
　　such as your complex mysteries and wonders—
　　that I'm not yet ready to understand.
²I am humbled and quieted in your presence.
　　Like a contented child who rests on its mother's lap,ᵃ
　　I'm your resting child and my soul is content in you.

---

a 131:2 "Like a contented child" is literally "Like a weaned child."

[3]O people of God,[a] your time has come to quietly trust,
waiting upon the Lord now and forever.

132 DAVID'S DYNASTY
A song of the stairway

[1]Lord, please don't forget all the hardships
David had to pass through.
[2]And how he promised you, Jacob's mighty God, saying,
[3]"I will not cross the threshold of my own home
to sleep in my own bed.
[4]I will not sleep or slumber,
nor even take time to close my eyes in rest,
[5]until I find a place for you to dwell, O mighty God of
Jacob.
I devote myself to finding a resting place for you!"[b]
[6]First we heard that the ark was at Bethlehem.
Then we found it in the forest of Kiriath-Jearim.[c]
[7]Let's go into God's dwelling place
and bow down and worship before him.
[8]Arise, O Lord, and enter your resting place,
both you and the ark of your glorious strength!
[9]May your priests wear the robes of righteousness,
and let all your godly lovers sing for joy!
[10]Don't forsake your anointed king now,
but honor your servant David.

---

a 131:3 Or "O Israel."
b 132:5 Historically, this refers to David wanting to bring the ark of glory back to Jerusalem.
c 132:6 Although the Hebrew text does not have the word *ark* but simply *it*, this translation supplies the word *ark* from its reference in verse 8. For the sake of understanding the text, this translation substitutes "Bethlehem" for "Ephrathah" (Ephrathah was the ancient name for Bethlehem) and "Kiriath-Jearim" for "Jaar" ("the fields of Jaar" was a variant form of Kiriath-Jearim, which means "the city of forests").

¹¹For you gave your word and promised David
   in an unbreakable oath that one of his sons
   would be sitting on the throne to succeed him as
      king.
¹²You also promised that if David's sons
   would be faithful to keep their promise to follow
      you,
   obeying the words you spoke to them,
   then David's dynasty would never end.
¹³Lord, you have chosen Zion as your dwelling place,
   for your pleasure is fulfilled in making it your home.
¹⁴I hear you say, "I will make this place my eternal
   dwelling,
   for I have loved and desired it as my very own!
¹⁵I will make Zion prosper and
   satisfy her poor with my provision.
¹⁶I will cover my priests with salvation's power,
   and all my righteous ones will shout for joy!
¹⁷I will increase the anointing that was upon David,
   and my glistening *glory* will rest upon my anointed
      one.
¹⁸I will clothe his enemies with shame,
   but holiness will bloom on my anointed one."^{*a*}

133 UNITY
A song of the stairway by King David

¹How truly wonderful and delightful it is
   to see brothers and sisters living together in sweet
      unity!^{*b*}

---

a 132:18 As translated from the Septuagint. The Hebrew reads "his crown will sparkle and gleam."

b 133:1 This specifically speaks to the tribes of Israel that live in harmony, but it also applies to believers today. Nothing can be sweeter than the love of Christ we share with one another.

²It's as precious as the sacred scented oil
   flowing from the head of the high priest Aaron,
   dripping down upon his beard and running all the
      way down
   to the hem of his priestly robes.ᵃ
³This harmony can be compared to the dew
   dripping from Mount Hermon,
   which flows down upon the hills of Zion.
   Indeed, that is where Yahweh has decreed his
      blessings
   will be found, the promise of life forevermore!

134 THE NIGHT WATCH
A song of the stairway

¹All his loving priests who serve and sing,
   come and sing your song of blessing to God.
   Come and stand before him in the house of God
   throughout the night watch,
²lifting up your hands in holy worship; come and bless
   the Lord!
³May the Lord, whom you worship,
   the mighty maker of heaven and earth,
   bless you from Zion's glory!

135 HIS WONDERFUL WORKS
A song of the stairway

¹Shout hallelujah and praise the greatness of God!
   All his righteous ones, praise him!
²All you worshiping priests on duty in the temple,
³praise him, for he is beautiful!
   Sing loving praises to his lovely name.

---

a 133:2 Or "running down the collar of his robe."

⁴For Yahweh has chosen Jacob for his own purpose,
  and Israel is his special treasure.
⁵Next to every other god, the greatness of our God is
  unequaled.
  For our God is incomparable!
⁶He does what he pleases with unlimited power and
  authority,
    extending his greatness throughout the entire
      universe!
⁷He forms the misty clouds and creates thunder and
  lightning,
    bringing the wind and rain out of his heavenly
      storehouse.
⁸He struck down the eldest child in each Egyptian home;
  both man and beast perished that night.
⁹He did great miracles—mighty signs and wonders
  throughout the land
  before Pharaoh and all his subjects.
¹⁰He conquered many nations and killed their mighty
  kings,
¹¹like Sihon, king of the Amorites, and Og, king of
  Bashan,
  and kings from every kingdom in Canaan.
¹²He gave their land to Israel as an inheritance for his
  people.
¹³O Yahweh, your name endures forever!
  Your fame is known in every generation.
¹⁴For you will vindicate your persecuted people,
  showing your tender love to all your servants.
¹⁵The unbelieving nations worship what they make.
  They worship their wealth and their work.
  They idolize what they own and what they do.
¹⁶⁻¹⁸Their possessions will never satisfy.
  Their lifeless and futile works cannot bring life to
    them!

Their things can't talk to them or answer their
   prayers.
Blind men can only create blind things.
Those deaf to God can only make a deaf image.[a]
Dead men can only create dead idols.
And everyone who trusts in these powerless, dead
   things
will be just like what they worship—powerless and
   dead!
[19]Praise Lord Yahweh, all the families of Israel!
   Praise Lord Yahweh, you family of Aaron![b]
[20]Let all the priests[c] bless Lord Yahweh!
   Let all his lovers who bow low before him[d]
   praise the Lord Yahweh!
[21]So bless the Lord Yahweh who lives in Jerusalem
   and dwells in Zion's glory!
   Hallelujah and praise the Lord!

136 His Tender Love

[1]Let everyone thank God, for he is good, and he is
   easy to please!
   His tender love for us continues on forever!
[2]Give thanks to God, our King over all gods!
   His tender love for us continues on forever!
[3]Give thanks to the Lord over all lords!
   His tender love for us continues on forever!
[4]Give thanks to the only miracle-working God!
   His tender love for us continues on forever!

---

a 135:16–18 Referring to the idols, the Hebrew could be translated
   "with mouths, but they cannot speak; with eyes, but they cannot see;
   with ears, but they cannot hear."
b 135:19 The name Aaron means "light-bringer" or "light-bearer."
c 135:20 Or "all the family of Levi." Levi represents the holy priesthood.
d 135:20 Or "those who fear him."

⁵Give thanks to the Creator who made the heavens
  with wisdom!ᵃ
   His tender love for us continues on forever!
⁶To him who formed dry ground, raising it up from the
  sea!
   His tender love for us continues on forever!
⁷Praise the one who created every heavenly light!
   His tender love for us continues on forever!
⁸He set the sun in the sky to rule over day!
   His tender love for us continues on forever!
⁹Praise him who set in place the moon and stars to
  rule over the night!
   His tender love for us continues on forever!
¹⁰Give thanks to God, who struck down the firstborn in
  Egypt!
   His tender love for us continues on forever!
¹¹He brought his people out of Egypt with miracles!
   His tender love for us continues on forever!
¹²With his mighty power he brought them out!
   His tender love for us continues on forever!
¹³He split open the Red Sea for them!
   His tender love for us continues on forever!
¹⁴And led his people right through the middle!
   His tender love for us continues on forever!
¹⁵He vanquished Pharaoh's armies, drowning them all!
   His tender love for us continues on forever!
¹⁶He led his people through the wilderness!
   His tender love for us continues on forever!
¹⁷He's the one who smashed mighty kingdoms!
   His tender love for us continues on forever!
¹⁸He triumphed over powerful kings who stood in his
  way!
   His tender love for us continues on forever!

_a_ 136:5 See Ps. 104:24; Prov. 8:27–31.

¹⁹He conquered Sihon, king of the Amorites!
His tender love for us continues on forever!
²⁰He conquered the giant named Og, king of Bashan!ᵃ
His tender love for us continues on forever!
²¹Then he gave away their lands as an inheritance!
His tender love for us continues on forever!
²²For he handed it all over to Israel, his beloved!
His tender love for us continues on forever!
²³He's the God who chose us when we were nothing!
His tender love for us continues on forever!
²⁴He has rescued us from the power of our enemies!
His tender love for us continues on forever!
²⁵He provides food for hungry men and animals!
His tender love for us continues on forever!
²⁶Give thanks to the great God of the heavens!
His tender love for us continues on forever!

137 THE SONG OF OUR CAPTIVITY

¹Along the banks of Babylon's rivers
we sat as exiles, mourning our captivity,
and wept with great love for Zion.
²*Our music and mirth were no longer heard, only sadness.*
We hung up our harps on the willow trees.
³Our captors tormented us, saying, "Make music for us and
sing one of your happy Zion-songs!"
⁴But how could we sing the song of the Lord
in this foreign wilderness?
⁵May my hands never make music again
if I ever forget you, O Jerusalem.
⁶May I never be able to sing again if I fail to honor
Jerusalem supremely!

---

a 136:20 The name Og means "giant."

⁷And Lord, may you never forget
    what the sons of Edom did to us, saying,
        "Let's raze the city of Jerusalem and burn it to the
            ground!"ᵃ
⁸Listen, O Babylon, you evil destroyer!
    The one who destroys you will be rewarded above
        all others.
    You will be repaid for what you've done to us.
⁹Great honor will come to those who destroy you and
    your future,
        by smashing your infants against the rubble of your
            own destruction.

138 The Divine Presence
By King David

¹I thank you, Lord, and with all the passion of my
    heart
        I worship you in the presence of angels!ᵇ
    Heaven's mighty ones will hear my voice
        as I sing my loving praise to you.
²I bow down before your divine presence
    and bring you my deepest worship
        as I experience your tender love and your living
            truth.
    For your Word and the fame of your name
        have been magnified above all else!ᶜ
³At the very moment I called out to you, you answered
    me!
        You strengthened me deep within my soul
        and breathed fresh courage into me.

---

a 137:7 The Hebrew text reads "Strip her [Jerusalem] naked!"
b 138:1 Or "gods." The Hebrew *elohim* is literally "mighty ones" and
    can refer to either angels or the gods of the heathen.
c 138:2 Or "You have exalted your Word above all your name."

⁴One day all the kings of the earth
  will rise to give you thanks when they hear the
    living words
  that I have heard you speak.
⁵They too will sing of your wonderful ways,
  for your ineffable glory is great!
⁶For though you are lofty and exalted,
  you stoop to embrace the lowly.
  Yet you keep your distance from those filled with
    pride.
⁷By your mighty power I can walk through any
    devastation,
  and you will keep me alive, reviving me.
  Your power set me free from the hatred of my
    enemies.
⁸You keep every promise you've ever made to me!
  Since your love for me is constant and endless,
  I ask you, Lord, to finish every good thing that
    you've begun in me!

139 You Know All About Me
For the Pure and Shining One
King David's poetic song

¹Lord, you know everything there is to know about
    me.
²You perceive every movement of my heart and soul,
  and you understand my every thought before it
    even enters my mind.
³⁻⁴You are so intimately aware of me, Lord.
  You read my heart like an open book
  and you know all the words I'm about to speak
  before I even start a sentence!
  You know every step I will take before my journey
    even begins.

⁵You've gone into my future to prepare the way,
  and in kindness you follow behind me
  to spare me from the harm of my past.ᵃ
  You have laid your hand on me!
⁶This is just too wonderful, deep, and
  incomprehensible!
  Your understanding of me brings me wonder and
    strength.ᵇ
⁷Where could I go from your Spirit?
  Where could I run and hide from your face?
⁸If I go up to heaven, you're there!
  If I go down to the realm of the dead, you're there
    too!
⁹If I fly with wings into the shining dawn, you're there!
  If I fly into the radiant sunset,ᶜ you're there waiting!
¹⁰Wherever I go, your hand will guide me;
  your strength will empower me.
¹¹It's impossible to disappear from you
  or to ask the darkness to hide me,
  for your presence is everywhere, bringing light into
    my night.
¹²There is no such thing as darkness with you.
  The night, to you, is as bright as the day;
  there's no difference between the two.
¹³You formed my innermost being, shaping my delicate
  inside
  and my intricate outside,

ᵃ 139:5 Or "You hem me in [lit. "besiege me"] before and behind." The
  implication is that God protects the psalmist from what may come in
  the future and what has happened in the past.
ᵇ 139:6 As translated from the Septuagint. The Hebrew reads "too
  high to understand."
ᶜ 139:9 Implied in the Hebrew, which reads "the remote parts of the
  sea" or "beyond the horizon to the west." The sea is west of Israel.

and wove them all together in my mother's
   womb.*

¹⁴I thank you, God, for making me so mysteriously
   complex!
   Everything you do is marvelously breathtaking.
   It simply amazes me to think about it!
   How thoroughly you know me, Lord!
¹⁵You even formed every bone in my body
   when you created me in the secret place;*
   carefully, skillfully you shaped me* from nothing to
      something.
¹⁶You saw who you created me to be before I became
   me!*
   Before I'd ever seen the light of day,
   the number of days you planned for me
   were already recorded in your book.*
¹⁷⁻¹⁸Every single moment you are thinking of me!
   How precious and wonderful to consider
   that you cherish me constantly in your every
      thought!
   O God, your desires toward me are more
   than the grains of sand on every shore!
   When I awake each morning, you're still with me.
¹⁹O God, come and slay these bloodthirsty, murderous
   men!
   For I cry out, "Depart from me, you wicked ones!"

---

a 139:13 The Hebrew word for "knit" or "wove" can also be translated
   "covered" or "defended." God places an eternal spirit inside the conceived child within the womb of a mother and covers that life, sends
   the child a guardian angel, and watches over him or her.
b 139:15 The Hebrew text is literally "the depths of the earth."
c 139:15 Or "embroidered me."
d 139:16 The Hebrew could be translated "as an embryo."
e 139:16 See Ps. 69:28.

²⁰See how they blaspheme your sacred name
   and lift up themselves against you, but all in vain!
²¹Lord, can't you see how I despise those who despise
   you?
   For I grieve when I see them rise up against you.
²²I have nothing but complete hatred and disgust for
   them.
   Your enemies shall be my enemies!
²³God, I invite your searching gaze into my heart.
   Examine me through and through;
      find out everything that may be hidden within me.
   Put me to the test and sift through all my anxious
      cares.
²⁴See if there is any path of pain I'm walking on,
   and lead me back to your glorious, everlasting way—
   the path that brings me back to you.

140 A Prayer for Protection
For the Pure and Shining One
King David's poetic song

¹Lord, protect me from this evil one!
   Rescue me from these violent schemes!
²He concocts his secret strategy to divide and harm
   others,
   stirring up trouble one against another.
³They are known for their sharp rhetoric
   of poisonous, hateful words.
                              Pause in his presence

⁴Keep me safe, Lord, out of reach from these wicked
   and violent men,
   and guard me, God, for they have plotted an evil
      scheme
   to ruin me and bring me down.

⁵They are proud and insolent; they've set an ambush
  for me in secret.
  They are determined to snare me in their net like
    captured prey.

Pause in his presence

⁶⁻⁷O Lord, you are my God and my saving strength!
  My Hero-God, you wrap yourself around me to
    protect me.
  For I'm surrounded by your presence in my day of
    battle.
  Lord Yahweh, hear my cry.
  May my voice move your heart to show me mercy.
⁸Don't let the wicked triumph over me,
  but bring down their every strategy to subdue me
  or they will become even more arrogant!

Pause in his presence

⁹Those who surround me are nothing but proud
  troublemakers.
  May they drink the poison of their own poisonous
    words.
¹⁰⁻¹¹May their slanderous lives never prosper!
  Let evil itself hunt them down and pursue them
    relentlessly
  until they are thrown into fiery pits
  from which they will never get out!
  Let burning coals of hellfire fall upon their heads!
¹²For I know, Lord, that you will be the hero
  of all those they persecute,
  and you will secure justice for the poor.
¹³Your godly ones will thank you no matter what
  happens.
  For they choose and cherish your presence
  above everything else!

141 An Evening Prayer
King David's poetic song

¹Please, Lord, come close and come quickly to help me!
Listen to my prayer as I call out to you.
²Let my prayer be as the evening sacrifice
that burns like fragrant incense, rising as my offering to you
as I lift up my hands in surrendered worship!
³God, give me grace to guard my lips*a*
from speaking what is wrong.
⁴Guide me away from temptation and doing evil.
Save me from sinful habits and from keeping company
with those who are experts in evil.
Help me not to share in their sin in any way!
⁵When one of your godly ones corrects me
or one of your faithful ones rebukes me,
I will accept it like an honor I cannot refuse.
It will be as healing medicine that I swallow
without an offended heart.
Even if they are mistaken, I will continue to pray.*b*
⁶When the leaders and judges are condemned,
falling upon the rocks of justice,*c*
then they'll know my words to them were true!
⁷Like an earthquake splits open the earth,
so the world of hell will open its mouth
to swallow their scattered bones.

---

a 141:3 The Septuagint reads "Set a fortress door before my lips."
b 141:5 This is one of most difficult verses to translate, with scholars divided over the meaning of the Hebrew text. Another translation could be "Don't let the oil of the wicked anoint my head, for I pray continually against their wickedness."
c 141:6 See 2 Chron. 25:12.

[8]But you are my Lord and my God; I only have eyes for
  you!
  I hide myself in you, so don't leave me defenseless.
[9]Protect me! Keep me from the traps of wickedness
  they set for me.
[10]Let them all stumble into their own traps
  while I escape without a scratch!

142 My Only Hope

King David's poetic song of instruction
A prayer when he was confined in a cave

[1]God, I'm crying out to you!
  I lift up my voice boldly to beg for your mercy.
[2]I spill out my heart to you and tell you all my
  troubles.
[3]For when I was desperate, overwhelmed, and about
  to give up,
  you were the only one there to help.
  You gave me a way of escape
  from the hidden traps of my enemies.
[4]I look to my left and right to see if there is anyone
  who will help,
  but there's no one who takes notice of me.
  I have no hope of escape, and no one cares whether
    I live or die.
[5]So I cried out to you, Lord, my only hiding place.
  You're all I have, my only hope in this life,
  my last chance for help.
[6]Please listen to my heart's cry,
  for I am low and in desperate need of you!
  Rescue me from all those who persecute me,
  for I am no match for them.
[7]Bring me out of this dungeon so I can declare your
  praise!

And all the righteous will celebrate
all the wonderful things you've done for me!

143 MY HUMBLE PRAYER

*King David's poetic song when he was chased by
Absalom[a]*

¹Lord, you must hear my prayer,
   for you are faithful to your promises.
   Answer my cry, O righteous God!
²Don't bring me into your courtroom for judgment,
   for there is no one who is righteous before you.
³My enemies have chased and caught me
   and crushed my life into dust.
   Now I'm living in the darkness of death's shadow.
⁴My inner being is in depression
   and my heart is heavy, dazed with despair.
⁵I remember the glorious miracles of days gone by,
   and I often think of all the wonders of old.
⁶Now I'm reaching out to you, thirsting for you
   like the dry, cracked ground thirsts for rain.
                              Pause in his presence

⁷Lord, come quickly and answer me,
   for my depression deepens and I'm about to
      give up.
   Don't leave me now or I'll die!
⁸Let the dawning day bring me revelation
   of your tender, unfailing love.
   Give me light for my path and teach me, for I trust in
      you.
⁹Save me from all my enemies, for I hide myself in
   you.

---

a 143 As translated from the Septuagint.

¹⁰I just want to obey all you ask of me.
So teach me, Lord, for you are my God.
Your gracious Spirit is all I need, so lead me on
good paths
that are pleasing to you, my one and only God!
¹¹Lord, if you rescue me, it will bring you more
glory,
for you are true to your promises.
Bring me out of these troubles!
¹²Since I am your loving servant, destroy all those
who are trying to harm me.
And because you are so loving and kind to me,
silence all of my enemies!

144 RESCUE ME
King David's poetic song as he stood before Goliath[a]

¹There is only one strong, safe, and secure place for
me;
it's in God alone who gives me strength for the
battle.
²He's my shelter of love and my fortress of faith,
who wraps himself around me as a secure shield.
I hide myself in this one who subdues enemies
before me.
³Lord, what is it about us that you would even notice
us?
Why do you even bother with us?
⁴For man is nothing but a faint whisper, a mere
breath.
We spend our days like nothing more than a
passing shadow.

---

a 144 As translated from the Septuagint. Put yourself in David's place
as he faced a giant named Goliath. Imagine how he felt as you read
through this psalm.

⁵Step down from heaven, Lord, and come down!
   Make the mountains melt at your touch.
⁶Loose your fiery lightning flashes and scatter your
   enemies.
   Overthrow them with your terrifying judgments.
⁷Reach down from your heavens
   and rescue me from this hell
   and deliver me from these dark powers.
⁸They speak nothing but lies; their words are pure
   deceit.
   Nothing they say can ever be trusted.
⁹My God, I will sing you a brand-new song!
   The harp inside my heart will make music to you!
¹⁰I will sing of you, the one who gives victory to
   kings—
   the one who rescues David, your loving servant,
   from the fatal sword.
¹¹Deliver me and save me from these dark powers
   who speak nothing but lies.
   Their words are pure deceit,
   and you can't trust anything they say.
¹²Deliver us! Then our homes will be happy.
   Our sons will grow up as strong, sturdy men
   and our daughters with graceful beauty,
   royally fashioned as for a palace.
¹³⁻¹⁴Our barns will be filled to the brim,
   overflowing with the fruits of our harvest.
   Our fields will be full of sheep and cattle,
   too many to count,
   and our livestock will not miscarry their young.
   Our enemies will not invade our land,
   and there'll be no breach in our walls.
¹⁵What bliss we experience when these blessings fall!
   The people who love and serve our God will be
      happy indeed!

145 GOD'S GREATNESS
King David's poetic song of praise

¹My heart explodes with praise to you!
  Now and forever my heart bows in worship to you,
  my King and my God!
²Every day I will lift up my praise to your name
  with praises that will last throughout eternity.
³Lord, you are great and worthy of the highest
  praise!
  For there is no end to the discovery
  of the greatness that surrounds you.
⁴Generation after generation will declare more of your
  greatness
  and declare more of your glory.
⁵Your magnificent splendor and the miracles of your
  majesty
  are my constant meditation.
⁶Your awe-inspiring acts of power have everyone
  talking!
  I'm telling people everywhere about your excellent
    greatness!
⁷Our hearts bubble over as we celebrate the fame
  of your marvelous beauty, *bringing bliss to our
    hearts.*
  We shout with ecstatic joy over your breakthrough
    for us.
⁸You're kind and tenderhearted to those who don't
  deserve it
  and very patient with people who fail you.
  Your love is like a flooding river overflowing its
    banks with kindness.
⁹God, everyone sees your goodness,
  for your tender love is blended into everything you
    do.

[10]Everything you have made will praise you, fulfilling
  its purpose.
  And all your godly ones will be found bowing before
    you.
[11]They will tell the world of the lavish splendor of your
  kingdom
  and preach about your limitless power.
[12]They will demonstrate for all to see your miracles of
  might
  and reveal the glorious majesty of your kingdom.
[13]You are the Lord who reigns over your never-ending
  kingdom through all the ages of time and eternity!
  You are faithful to fulfill every promise you've made.
  You manifest yourself as kindness in all you do.[a]
[14]Weak and feeble ones you will sustain.
  Those bent over with burdens of shame you will lift
    up.
[15]You have captured our attention
  and the eyes of all look to you.
  You give what they hunger for at just the right time.
[16]When you open your generous hand, it's full of
  blessings,
  satisfying the longings of every living thing.
[17]You are fair and righteous in everything you do,
  and your love is wrapped into all your works.
[18]You draw near to those who call out to you,
  listening closely, especially when their hearts are
    true.
[19]Every godly one receives
  even more than what they ask for.
  For you hear what their hearts really long for,
  and you bring them your saving strength.

---

a 145:13 The last two lines of this verse are only found in one reliable
Hebrew manuscript and in the Septuagint. It could also be translated "All your works are very holy."

²⁰God, you watch carefully over all your devoted lovers
like a bodyguard,
but you will destroy the ungodly.
²¹I will praise you, Lord!
Let everyone everywhere join me in praising
the beautiful Lord of holiness from now through
eternity!

146 OUR TRUE HELP
A poetic psalm by Haggai and Zechariah[a]

¹Hallelujah! Praise the Lord!
My innermost being will praise you, Lord!
²I will spend my life praising you and
singing high praises to you, my God, every day of
my life!
³⁻⁴We can never look to men for help;
no matter who they are, they can't save us,
for even our great leaders fail and fall.
They too are just mortals who will one day die.
At death the spirits of all depart and their bodies
return to dust.
In the day of their death all their projects and plans
are over.
⁵But those who hope in the Lord will be happy and
pleased!
Our help comes from the God of Jacob!
⁶You keep all your promises.
You are the Creator of heaven's glory,
earth's grandeur, and the ocean's greatness.

---

a 146 As translated from the Septuagint. Pss. 146–150 are called "Hallelujah Psalms" because they all begin in Hebrew with the words
"Hallelujah, praise the Lord."

[7]The oppressed get justice with you.
The hungry are satisfied with you.
Prisoners find their freedom with you.
[8]You open the eyes of the blind,
and you fully restore those bent over with shame.
You love those who love and honor you.
[9]You watch over strangers and immigrants
and support the fatherless and widows.
But you subvert the plans of the ungodly.
[10]Lord, you will reign forever!
Zion's God will rule throughout time and eternity!
Hallelujah! Praise the Lord!

147 OUR AMAZING GOD

[1]Hallelujah! Praise the Lord!
How beautiful it is when we sing our praises to the
beautiful God,
for praise makes you lovely before him
and brings him great delight!
[2]Yahweh builds up Jerusalem;
he gathers up the outcasts and brings them home.
[3]He heals the wounds of every shattered heart.
[4]He sets his stars in place, calling them all by their
names.[a]
[5]How great is our God!
There's absolutely nothing his power cannot
accomplish,
and he has infinite understanding of everything.
[6]Yahweh supports and strengthens the humble,
but the ungodly will be brought down to the dust.
[7]Sing out with songs of thanksgiving to the Lord!
Let's sing our praises with melodies overflowing!

---

a 147:4 See Job 9:9; 38:31–33; Isa. 40:26; Amos 5:8.

⁸He fills the sky with clouds, sending showers to water the earth
  so that the grass springs up on the mountain fields
  and the earth produces food for man.ᵃ
⁹All the birds and beasts who cry with hunger to him
  are fed from his hands.
¹⁰His people don't find security in strong horses,
  for horsepower is nothing to him.
  Manpower is even less impressive!
¹¹Yahweh shows favor toᵇ those who fear him,
  those who wait for his tender embrace.ᶜ
¹²Jerusalem, praise the Lord! Zion, worship your God!
¹³For he has strengthened the authority of your gates.
  He even blesses you with more children.
¹⁴He's the one who brings peace to your borders,ᵈ
  feeding you the most excellent of fare.
¹⁵He sends out his orders throughout the world;
  his words run as swift messengers, bringing them to pass.
¹⁶He blankets the earth with glistening snow,
  painting the landscape with frost.
¹⁷Sleet and hail fall from the sky,
  causing waters to freeze before winter's icy blast.
¹⁸Then he speaks his word and it all melts away;
  as the warm spring winds blow, the streams begin to flow.
¹⁹In the same way, he speaks his word to Jacob,
  and to Israel he brings his life-giving instruction.
²⁰He has dealt with Israel differently than with any other people,

---

a 147:8 As translated from the Septuagint.
b 147:11 Or "takes pleasure in," "delights in," "sets his affection on," "enjoys," "finds pleasing," "is satisfied with."
c 147:11 Or "who wait for his loyal, unfailing love."
d 147:14 The Septuagint reads "He makes peace your borders."

for they have received his laws.
Hallelujah! Praise the Lord!

148 THE COSMIC CHORUS OF PRAISE

¹Hallelujah! Praise the Lord! Let the skies be filled with
praise
and the highest heavens with the shouts of glory!
²Go ahead—praise him, all you his messengers!
Praise him some more, all you heavenly hosts!
³Keep it up, sun and moon!
Don't stop now, all you twinkling stars of light!
⁴Take it up even higher—up to the highest heavens,
until the cosmic chorus thunders his praise!ᵃ
⁵Let the entire universe erupt with praise to God.
He spoke and created it all—from nothing to
something.
⁶He established the cosmos to last forever,
and he stands behind his commands
so his orders will never be revoked.
⁷Let the earth join in with this parade of praise!
You mighty creatures of the ocean's depths,
echo in exaltation!
⁸Lightning, hail, snow, clouds,
and the stormy winds that fulfill his word—
⁹bring your melody, O mountains and hills;
trees of the forest and field, harmonize your praise!
¹⁰⁻¹²Praise him, all beasts and birds, mice and men,
kings, queens, princes, and princesses,
young men and maidens, children and babes,
old and young alike, everyone everywhere!

---

a 148:4 Poetic implication in the text. The literal Hebrew reads "[Praise
him] you waters above the sky."

¹³Let them all join in with this orchestra of praise.
   For the name of the Lord is the only name we raise!
   His stunning splendor ascends higher than the
      heavens.
¹⁴He anoints his people with strength and authority,
   showing his great favor to all his godly lovers,
   even to his princely people, Israel,
   who are so close to his heart.
   Hallelujah! Praise the Lord!

149 TRIUMPHANT PRAISE

¹Hallelujah! Praise the Lord!
   It's time to sing to God a brand-new song*a*
   so that all his holy people will hear how wonderful
      he is!
²May Israel be enthused with joy because of him,
   and may the sons of Zion pour out
   their joyful praises to their King.
³Break forth with dancing!
   Make music and sing God's praises with the rhythm
      of drums!
⁴For he enjoys his faithful lovers.
   He adorns the humble with his beauty,
   and he loves to give them victory.
⁵His godly lovers triumph in the glory of God,
   and their joyful praises will rise even while others
      sleep.
⁶God's high and holy praises fill their mouths,
   for their shouted praises are their weapons of
      war!
⁷These warring weapons will bring vengeance
   on the nations and every resistant power—

---

a 149:1 Or "a spontaneous song."

[8]to bind kings with chains and rulers with iron
shackles.
[9]Praise-filled warriors will enforce
the judgment decreed against their enemies.
This is the honor he gives to all his godly lovers.
Hallelujah! Praise the Lord!

150 THE HALLELUJAH CHORUS

[1]Hallelujah! Praise the Lord! Praise God in his holy
sanctuary!
Praise him in his stronghold in the sky!
[2]Praise him for his mighty miracles!
Praise him for his magnificent greatness!
[3]Praise him with trumpets blasting!
Praise him with piano and guitar!
[4-5]Praise him with drums[a] and dancing!
Praise him with loud clashing of cymbals!
Praise him upon the high-sounding cymbals!
[6]Let everyone everywhere join in the crescendo
of ecstatic praise to Yahweh!
Hallelujah! Praise the Lord!

---

a 150:4–5 Or "tambourines."

YOUR PERSONAL INVITATION

TO FOLLOW JESUS

We can all find ourselves in dark places needing some light—light that brings direction, healing, vision, warmth, and hope. Jesus said, "I am light to the world, and those who embrace me will experience life-giving light, and they will never walk in darkness" (John 8:12). Without the light and love of Jesus, this world is truly a dark place and we are lost forever.

Love unlocks mysteries. As we love Jesus, our hearts are unlocked to see more of his beauty and glory. When we stop defining ourselves by our failures, but rather as the ones whom Jesus loves, our hearts begin to open to the breathtaking discovery of the wonder of Jesus Christ.

All that is recorded in the Scriptures is there so that you will fully believe that Jesus is the Son of God, and that through your faith in him you will experience eternal life by the power of his name (see John 20:31).

If you want this light and love in your life, say a prayer like this—whether for the first time or to express again your passionate desire to follow Jesus:

Jesus, you are the light of the world. I want to follow you, passionately and wholeheartedly. But my sins have separated me from you. Thank you for your love for me. Thank you for paying the price for my sins. I trust your finished work on the cross for my rescue. I turn away from the thoughts and deeds that have separated me from you. Forgive me and

awaken me to love you with all my heart, mind,
soul, and strength. I believe God raised you from the
dead, and I want that new life to flow through me
each day and for eternity. God, I give you my life.
Fill me with your Spirit so that my life will honor you
and I can fulfill your purpose for me. Amen.

You can be assured that what Jesus said about those
who choose to follow him is true: "If you embrace my
message and believe in the One who sent me, you will
never face condemnation, for in me, you have already
passed from the realm of death into the realm of eternal life!" (John 5:24). But there's more! Not only are you
declared "not guilty" by God because of Jesus, you are
also considered his most intimate friend (John 15:15).

As you grow in your relationship with Jesus, continue
to read the Bible, communicate with God through prayer,
spend time with others who follow Jesus, and live out
your faith daily and passionately. God bless you!

ABOUT THE TRANSLATOR

Brian Simmons is known as a passionate lover of God. After a dramatic conversion to Christ, Brian knew that God was calling him to go to the unreached people of the world and present the gospel of God's grace to all who would listen. With his wife, Candice, and their three children, he spent nearly eight years in the tropical rain forest of the Darien Province of Panama as a church planter, translator, and consultant. Having been trained in linguistics and Bible translation principles, Brian assisted in the Paya-Kuna New Testament translation project, and after their ministry in the jungle, Brian was instrumental in planting a thriving church in New England (U.S.). He is the lead translator for The Passion Translation Project and travels full time as a speaker and Bible teacher. He has been happily married to Candice since 1971 and boasts regularly of his three children and eight grandchildren.

Follow The Passion Translation at:

Facebook.com/passiontranslation
Twitter.com/tPtBible
Instagram.com/passiontranslation

For more information about the translation project please visit:

ThePassionTranslation.com

NOTES

ThePassionTranslation.com